PROFESSIONAL MANAGEMENT:
New Concepts and Proven Practices

Professional Management:

New Concepts and Proven Practices

by Louis A. Allen
President, Louis A. Allen Associates, Inc.

McGRAW-HILL BOOK COMPANY

New York   St. Louis   San Francisco   Dusseldorf
Johannesburg   Kuala Lumpur   London   Mexico
Montreal   New Delhi   Panama   Toronto
Rio de Janeiro   Singapore   Sydney

Library of Congress Cataloging in Publication Data

Allen, Louis A
  Professional management.

  (McGraw-Hill European series in management)
  Includes bibliographical references.
  1. Management.   I. Title.
HD31.A415   1973b   658.4   73-10109
ISBN 0-07-001110-9

First published in 1973 by the McGraw-Hill Book Company
(UK) Limited, Maidenhead, Berkshire, England.

678910   VBVB   09876543

CONTENTS

Chapter

Chapter

PREFACE

You probably have several questions in mind as you open this book. First, 'What has the book been designed to accomplish?' The objective of this volume is to assist you, as a manager, to perform more effectively on your job. To help you, the book presents a unified statement of the essentials of management practice, including the most effective concepts, principles, and techniques in current use.

Your second question might be, 'How will this book, more than others of its type, benefit me?' There are several answers. Most important, it brings you up to date. And it does so, not from the viewpoint of any one specialist—behavioural scientist, operations researcher, or computer expert; rather, it integrates pertinent findings from the relevant fields of biology and genetics, economics and history, and the behavioural and managerial sciences.

A further benefit is that the book provides a logical classification of management work. In all disciplines, before knowledge could advance, it has been necessary to develop a system of classification and nomenclature which could be commonly understood and applied. This has been equally true for professional management, where precise definition and distinction of terms and the development of principles are necessary precedents to study of concepts and application of techniques. You will find in the book a system developed to meet this need, a taxonomy of management work, which will enable you to relate the technical vocabularies with which you are familiar to logical and precisely defined management terms.

You will also find that the book outlines specific techniques which will enable you to put what you learn to work on your own job. These techniques are supported by step by step approaches which will help you strengthen your relationships not only with your subordinates, but with your superior and peers as well.

By now, a third question may enter your mind, 'What qualifies this author to tell me how to be a better manager?' You may find an acceptable qualification in twenty-eight years as a practising manager, consultant, and educator, much of it spent in observing and analysing management in the United States, Britain, Japan, Australia, and Africa. This has been reinforced by a careful review of current writing and research in the disciplines pertinent to management.

The techniques and principles offered here have been used by practising managers throughout the world, both as individuals and in project teams, to analyse and solve their own management problems. You may find this tested guidance the answer to the final question, 'Why should I read another book on management?'

ACKNOWLEDGEMENTS

A great many managers from business and industry, government, hospitals, associations, and other groups have contributed to the information outlined here. I owe them my continuing gratitude for their understanding, assistance, and patience. I wish to thank Malcolm Levin of Stanford University for checking the factual accuracy of chapter 1 and Michael Lawson of Stanford University for his assistance in library research.

Members of my own firm have provided most valuable inputs from their consulting and educational assignments in all parts of the world. Here I am most appreciative of the contributions of Richard Allen Stull, Grant B. Powell, W. Kyle Coltman, Charles B. Alvord, Ralph B. Bettman, Dudley P. Biggs, B. Ernest Bryans, Frank G. Edwards, Beverly T. Galloway, Dale M. Johnson, T. Harry Makepeace, Paul B. McNicol, William H. Peretti, Anacleto Del Rosario, Henry W. Seeley, Fred C. Stanford, and Keith L. Walter. The editorial assistance provided by Eileen E. Parsons and Linda Hall was most valuable in preparing the final manuscript. Finally, I wish to extend both my admiration and appreciation to Kay Vandewall for her dedication and splendid support in every stage of preparation. For interpretation and presentation of the final material, the author, of course, remains accountable.

Louis A. Allen

For Ruth

PROFESSIONAL MANAGEMENT:
New Concepts and Proven Practices

1.   MANAGEMENT BEGINS WITH MAN

Management today is in the throes of massive change, which has extended not only to the methods of practice, but also to the philosophy and theory which shape them. Assumptions about people are being modified as fast as those concerning technology. Techniques based on theories developed only ten years ago are now discredited by new data and replaced by more realistic and effective approaches. This pattern of dynamic change is salutary, but it makes new demands on managers long entrapped in the pressures and problems of daily activity. More than ever, mangement demands not only a readiness to change but a willingness to invest the time and effort necessary to evaluate the fads and panaceas which claim attention and to adopt only those measures which will truly enhance operating effectiveness.

To see this developing pattern in perspective requires more than occasional reading; it demands a careful survey of the factors which govern effective management, and understanding of the trends now developing. To secure this perspective, we shall first look at people and their beginnings and, because management is uniquely concerned with the work of people, the forces that shape our behaviour. The behavioural and biological sciences make useful contributions to this understanding.

Scientists have established that our earliest ancestors became numerous on the earth more than a million years ago. These first humans struggled to survive and reproduce. Environmental challenges weeded out the weak and incompetent and ensured that the strongest and most alert would beget the most children.

In the screening of a thousand and more generations, the genetic combinations which enabled man to cope with the environment have been preserved. Changes in the genes occurred through mutations, which are unexpected and haphazard variations. Favourable mutations survived; the others were eliminated by the environmental challenge. Adaptation of both physiological and behavioural characteristics occurred. Physical qualities such as warm blood, non-opposed fifth toe, and large brain enabled early man to cope with changing climate, to pursue elusive game, and to think and act quickly. But the physical organism had to be motivated. Those individuals who were driven to find food, to protect themselves, and to reproduce used their physical attributes most effectively and passed on their successful genes to their more numerous progeny.

We have become what we are through two influences: our genetic inheritance and the forces of the environment. From each parent we inherit half our chromosomes; within the chromosomes, the genes emit energy which commands bodily growth and action, and in the process, determines our basic physical and mental characteristics.

We can inherit only those genes which our parents already possess, but because the halved mix they transmit to us is randomly different, we also differ as individuals. Every normal person has one head and two hands because his parents did, but the shape of the head and its contents will vary considerably. This genetic linkage through the past indicates why, biologically, we are very much like our most remote ancestors, yet distinctly different in some respects from our own parents and from one another.

The genes are the infinitely small generators which power our basic behaviour. Their energy output actuates the genetic drives, which constantly impel us to action, creating tension which is relieved only by satisfaction. When the need and its satisfaction are accomplished directly, the cycle repeats and nature has taken its course without problem. However, one consequence of human evolution is that the genetic drives are often blocked or diverted by the impact of environment and culture. Environment is the complex of factors related to the earth, climate, and living things which influences our development and existence. Culture is part of environment, in that it refers to the traditions, laws, rules, conventions, and beliefs which we must learn and apply in order to be accepted by the groups to which we belong.

Culture has two characteristics pertinent to our study of management. One is that culture must be learned; it is not inherited through the genes. Because of this characteristic, culture can change quickly, even within a few years, whereas genetic changes require hundreds if not thousands of generations.

Another important characteristic of culture is that, since it is learned by each generation, it must be sufficiently formalized to be communicated. Cultural forms change and evolve much as do biological forms, but much faster. Throughout history, most cultural evolution has been by natural selection. Those cultural forms which best met environmental needs survived; those which were inadequate died out.

At some point in his early history, man acquired two cultural characteristics which differentiated him from all other creatures. The use of language was a means of transmitting ideas apart from the *things* they represented. Because words were symbols for things, man, unique among animals, was able to think, to communicate, and to act in terms of symbols. As a result, he developed a mental and emotional life derived from, but also different from, his genetic life. The use of tools also separates humans from other living creatures. Man becomes as strong and capable as the tools which he has devised, and which are extensions of himself. As anthropologist Sherwood L. Washburn noted, 'Tools changed the whole pattern of life, bringing in hunting, cooperation, and the necessity for communication and language. Memory, foresight and originality were favoured as never before, and the complex social system made possible by tools could only be realized by domesticated individuals.'[1]

Man, in common with other animals, is still largely a biological creature. However, he is unique in his ability to reason and convey understanding to other humans by using symbols to represent what he means. Other animals teach their young distinctive habits of behaviour, but only humans have cultural traits which deal with ideas and not physical things. Most significantly, this complex and diverse culture he has developed can be taught to succeeding generations so that each new human not only has opportunity to learn and profit from the experience of the entire race, but also to suffer from the mistakes the culture perpetuates.

THE HUMAN DRIVES

There has been great and continuing debate about the nature and operation of the genetic drives. While this is of absorbing interest to scholars, the manager's concern is a working hypothesis which will help

3

him to understand the people he must lead. Since each discipline has its own territory to defend, in analysing human drives we have proceeded on the assumption that there would be advantages in not being committed to any one point of view, but rather to act as a neutral analyst of the available data. We have summarized this analysis in the process concept of human drives.

THE PROCESS CONCEPT OF HUMAN DRIVES

The process[2] concept is based on the idea that human behaviour[3] is the result of a progressive series of energy outputs which originate in the cells of the body and give rise to impulsions to action. The drives are instinctive, in that they are genetic and inherited, but a large part of human behaviour is also influenced and shaped by culture and environment. This concept emphasizes that the drives are not theoretical abstractions, but rather, types of energy applications created by gene action which actuate specific types of behaviour. The drives thus are identifiable kinds of work.[4]

Key points in the process concept of human drives are as follows:

(a) *Definition.* A drive is genetic energy which is developed and applied by the organism to enable it to accomplish its objective.

(b) *Objective.* The objective of the human organism is to survive and utilize its resources most effectively.

(c) *Source.* Human drives arise as a result of energy developed and applied through the genes. In nature and functioning, the drives are similar to other bodily processes, such as metabolism, breathing, or the work of nerves or brain.

(d) *Mode.* Drives operate instinctively, at the command of the subconscious. By conscious thought, we can govern the functioning of the drives to about the same degree as that of other bodily processes. Just as we cannot change how our brains work to any great extent, but can modify the work they do, we cannot change the basic nature of the drives, but can modify the physical and mental effort they activate.

(e) *Conversion.* In terms of the principle of conservation of energy in a system, energy can never be lost or destroyed, but rather, is converted from one state to another. If a genetic drive is blocked from accomplishing its objective, its energy is not lost, but is converted either into another drive or into a derivative form evolved by the culture—which we call a cultural urge.

(f) *Cultural Urges.* A cultural urge is work in the sense that it involves

4

application of part or all of the energy of the basic drive; however, it differs in its manifestation. We define a cultural urge as energy displaced from a genetic drive applied by the organism in a form different from the drive to enable it to accomplish its objectives. Successive cultural urges may be activated in the attempt to satisfy a basic need. Cultural urges are often expressed through language, and many activities which appear as motor acts in lower species appear linguistically, as cultural urges, in man.

Cultural urges modify or divert the impact of the basic drives and ameliorate troublesome behaviour. Their role is often overlooked due to their silent success in alleviating potential hostility and tension, while still achieving intended objectives. Since, usually, cultural urges are less satisfying than the genetic drives from which they are derived, every culture tends to build up in its members a pool of undischarged tension which results from energy attempting to find an appropriate cultural outlet. This idea of tension build-up and catharsis has received much research attention. Investigations by Schafer, Berkowitz, Holt, Hartmann, and others, lead us to conclude that the more the culture restricts free expression of the genetic drives, the greater the need for satisfaction in the form of appropriate cultural urges.

This concept enables us to carry forward the hierarchy of needs developed by Abraham Maslow. All action is motivated by the body's attempt to satisfy a graded succession of needs, Maslow believed, ranging from basic physiological needs—which must be satisfied before others become operative—to safety, love, esteem, and finally, the highest, self-actualization needs. This gradation of needs is now open to question, for it appears that the genetic drives are continuously operative, acting either directly or through culture. As the renowned geneticist Theodosius Dobzhansky points out, biological and cultural evolution 'go together, interacting and usually mutually reinforcing each other. There is feed-back between genetics and culture'. Social needs are not separate and disparate, as Maslow thought, but cultural urges which originate from and interact continuously with the gentic drives. This understanding is important to the manager, for it makes clear that the drive to secure food, and the urge to acquire money and to be loved, are continuously interactive. Depending on the person and the situation, to some, money is equivalent to and interchangeable with both food and love, while to others, love can displace both food and money. To give each sequential primacy in terms of an arbitrary hierarchy does not seem in accord with the facts we know today.

While there is little agreement on the specific number or nature of the biological drives, there is fairly general consensus on certain key drives, notably, hunger, sex, and safety. These are discussed below, together with the teleological drive, which is also amply substantiated by available evidence.

THE TELEOLOGICAL DRIVE

As we analyse human drives and urges, our first conclusion is a predictive one: it assumes a logical need for certain types of drive functions if the organism is to accomplish its objective of surviving successfully. The first kind of mental and physical effort the drives must energize is that necessary to give direction to behaviour. The alternative is unceasing random action resulting in extinction.

We define the teleological drive as the application of genetic energy to fix the ends to be achieved. The objective of the teleological drive function is to provide direction for action. This is accomplished by performing two kinds of work: identifying the need and forming the objective.

TELEOLOGICAL CULTURAL URGES

As we grow and develop from infancy and come into contact with our environment and culture, we find that many ends we instinctively seek are blocked, so we convert the genetic drive into cultural urges which yield satisfaction and pleasure. Because our culture is rich and diversified and we can develop teleological images in terms of abstract symbols as well as concrete things, the cultural derivatives are so varied that we often find it difficult to identify their source.

The vital point is that we are driven to find purpose in what we do. We can change our cultural objectives either spontaneously or by conscious intention. Only man can use his teleological drive to change from instinctive to rational purposes and, in the process, change himself beyond the confines of both his biology and culture. Thus, only man has the potential to escape the bonds of his past and command his environment as well as himself.

THE PLANNING URGE

Perhaps the most significant cultural derivative of the teleological drive is the acquired cultural trait of planning. This involves not only establishing purpose, but also predetermining the steps to be taken, the time required, and the resources needed to accomplish that purpose. The teleological drive is spontaneous and most often involves subconscious determination of the purpose that will guide action; the planning urge, however, is rational and conscious, and thus, is more difficult to carry out. This is the reason we often carefully think through a plan, then spontaneously embark on a contrary course of action.

THE HUNGER DRIVE

The drive to satisfy hunger is part of the genetic mechanism of every person. The objective of the hunger drive is to secure food adequate for survival and health. During the millions of years in which this genetic combination was selectively established, the finding of food always led to its consumption. The genetic drive, then, is satisfied by the work of finding and consuming food.

THE ACQUISITIVE CULTURAL URGE

The hunger drive converts into a great many cultural urges, one of which is the acquisitive urge. People learned to convert the energy needed to satisfy hunger to include other physical things of value, such as weapons, tools, articles of adornment, and implements which could be used to gather and prepare food. The process of finding and consuming food is biologically determined; the acquisitive urge to find, consume, and store material objects is a cultural urge which is relearned by each generation. Because it is learned, it can be changed by indoctrination, education, and example. We are driven to find and consume, but *what* and *how*, we learn from our culture.

If the acquisition of wealth or material goods, for example, is the cultural urge, this will provide the spontaneous satisfaction which people seek in a culturally sanctioned form. Since cultural urges can be modified by communication and education, the society that wishes to do so can provide other satisfactions for the acquisitive urge.

On the job, people satisfy their acquisitive urge largely in terms of the money they make. Money is a symbol which can be translated into material goods that mean comfort, status, enjoyment, and relaxation. Therefore, it becomes a most pervasive cultural motivator. The body has automatic controls for hunger; it is difficult to eat much beyond satiation at any one time. However, we have few cultural controls for the acquisitive urge; therefore, we frequently pursue this well beyond the limits of what we need for our well-being. Since all humans are actuated by the same drives, it is clear that the culture that wishes to survive must evolve controls for such urges as the acquisitive, and that this can be done most effectively by displacement into other, equally compelling urges.

THE REPRODUCTIVE DRIVE

If people are to pass on their genes, they must possess a reproductive drive. The objective of the reproductive drive is to produce and rear offspring. This genetic drive is satisfied by attracting a mate, consummating sexual union, and rearing the young. While the other drives can be satisfied, at least in part, by one person without cooperation from other humans, the reproductive drive requires successful cooperation of two individuals for consummation, and of three to rear the young. Therefore, the reproductive drive is uniquely social in effect.

REPRODUCTIVE CULTURAL URGES

Cultural urges arising from the reproductive drive are numerous, ranging from artistic expression to cooperative group action. Successful rearing of human young requires continued presence of both parents, thus evolution has shown selective preference for genes which motivate sustained cooperation.

The need to attract a mate gives rise to personal adornment and to behaviour traits which attract the opposite sex. Cultural urges thus encourage those types of accomplishment which evoke favourable attention, whether it be winning a sales contest or earning a promotion to department head. The need to rear young reinforces the cultural urge to educate and train, which is deeply imbedded in the habits and laws of all societies. This cultural urge is rapidly changing today to encourage formalized education as a continuing process, to be engaged in throughout the whole of a person's life. Hopefully, it will also encompass conscious change of undesirable cultural urges such as uncontrolled acquisitiveness, destructive aggression, and war.

THE SECURITY DRIVE

From the beginning, people have been beset by constant danger. Those that had genes which triggered quick outpouring of adrenalin, and requisite action, survived. Today, we inherit the same genetic equipment that preserved our distant ancestors. We define the security drive as the application of genetic energy to safeguard the organism. The objective of the security drive is to protect from danger. The drive is satisfied through fear, flight, and fight. We cannot be secure unless our genes make us apprehensive for our safety and then motivate us either to combat the danger or run away. If we sense danger, we instinctively evaluate the threat to life or safety, adrenalin pours out and we fight or flee. Stimuli such as pain and sudden noises activate the security mechanism.

PROTECTIVE CULTURAL URGES

Under the impact of culture, our fears have expanded enormously and converted into a great variety of cultural urges. Prompted by fear, our culture may urge us to work harder or to stop working. Instead of fighting or fleeing, we may lie, cheat, or steal. To protect ourselves, we join forces with others and, through continued association, develop relatively fixed cultural patterns that pervade much of our daily life, although by now, relatively independent of the original incitement of fear. Threats to security, today, are more often economic and emotional; however, the same adrenalin pours out and prompts a similar physical response as in our primitive beginnings. The response may be translated into anger, argument, or ulcers. Since the cultural urges are learned and can be changed, both our fears and methods of handling them can be modified and mastered by conscious action.

THE VITAL CULTURAL URGES

The various drives described above usually act in combination to actuate the complex behaviour characteristic of humans. The cultural urges resulting from action of several, or all, the drives are varied and complex. Three patterns are so consistent that we can identify them as universals— the aggressive, territorial, and cooperative cultural urges.

THE AGGRESSIVE URGE

If people cannot satisfy their drives, tension increases and they are impelled to put forth additional energy to secure satisfaction. This gives rise to the aggressive cultural urge, which we define as the application of drive-displaced energy into forceful, assertive behaviour necessary to overcome obstacles to satisfaction.[5] This aggressiveness translates into other forms of behaviour, particularly when it relates to the acquisitive urge, so that we find humans becoming quarrelsome and aggressive, not only over food and sex, but also such things as property, political forms, and religious beliefs. Cultural urges, developed either spontaneously or rationally, can emphasize and perpetuate this aggressiveness or neutralize and minimize it. Aggressiveness is a derivative cultural urge of all the drives and is, thus, one of the most pervasive factors in human behaviour.

THE TERRITORIAL URGE

People need personal space around their immediate persons to feed, reproduce, and move; they need territorial space of varying dimensions to find food, erect shelter, and rear young. The territorial urge is defined as the application of drive-displaced energy to provide adequate living space.[6] There can be little doubt that this is a significant cultural urge with far-reaching implications. As managers, we can better understand people if we keep basic territorial factors in mind. We need a piece of territory we can call our own. Culturally, this may be the habitual place at which we sit at meals, the responsibilities and authorities assigned to us on the job, or the space our car occupies on the road. In each case, we identify in our minds what we consider to be our personal territory and react strongly to anything that threatens it, whether the danger be real or imagined. If we are never sure what our work is, if we are shuttled from one responsibility to another, we cannot satisfy our territorial urge, and tension builds.

THE COOPERATIVE URGE

Man has been able to survive in his adaptation to the environment only by working effectively with others of his species. We define the cooperative urge as the transfer of drive-displaced energy into mutually helpful and beneficial action. The form which this cooperative action takes is culturally defined. We cooperate against threat by becoming collectively aggressive; cooperation for reproductive purposes results in tender regard; cooperation to satisfy the hunger drive and its derivative cultural urges requires sharing.

DIFFERENCES OF OPINION ABOUT AGGRESSION AND TERRITORIALITY

There is sharply divided opinion as to whether territoriality and aggression are biological drives or cultural displacements.[7] This argument is not important for management purposes, for there can be no question that people are deeply impelled to seek and hold their own living space and territory and that they do, in fact, act in a distinctively aggressive manner under certain conditions. Current consensus would seem to agree that there is at least a cultural urge for personal living space, but there is no evidence to support the idea of aggression as a drive to kill other members of the same species. Animals kill those of other species to satisfy hunger; man appears to be the only animal which has developed a cultural urge to kill its own kind. Thus, we have concluded that territoriality and aggression are strong, and probably universal, cultural urges and will so refer to them in the following chapters.

DRIVES AND CULTURAL URGES

The drives and cultural urges are shown schematically in Fig. 1.1. This

Genetic drive	Significant cultural urge derived from this drive	Universal cultural urges derived by inputs from all drives
Teleological	Planning	Aggressive
Hunger	Acquisitive	Territorial
Reproductive	Creative	
Security	Protective	Cooperative

Fig. 1.1 *Drives and urges. Primary cultural urges derived from each drive are shown, together with three cultural urges which result from varying energy inputs from all the drives.*

identifies the four universal genetic drives—teleological, hunger, reproductive, and security—found in all human beings. The nature of the cultural urges derived from the drives depends on the society and environment in which the individual lives and, also, on his particular experiences, education, and relationships with others. In other words, the general culture of the society strongly influences the personal culture of the individual. The cultural urges derived from single genetic drives—planning, acquisitive, creative, and protective—are especially significant in industrialized societies. The three cultural urges which are formed by combined inputs from all the drives—aggressive, territorial, and cooperative—are universals, although their specific action tends to vary with the individual and his environment.

11

SUMMARY

(a) From his ancient predecessors, modern man has inherited genetic codes which generate basic biological drives. These genetic drives are strongly influenced by culture, which is the complex pattern of habits, skills, and attitudes learned from one generation to the next.

(b) An examination of the basic genetic drives gives a better understanding of the actions of other people. The process concept of human drives explains the operation of the drives. Generalizations as to definition, objective, source, mode, conversion, and cultural urges apply to all the drives. A two-step logic is used to develop the process concept. (i) State the drive and its objectives. (ii) Establish the categories of work necessary to accomplish the objective.

(c) The teleological drive provides direction by identifying the need and forming the objective of action. The teleological drive provides energy for developing mental images or objectives. This drive often appears as the derivative cultural planning urge. By conscious development of objectives and action to implement them, man, unique among living creatures, has the potential for commanding his environment instead of being commanded by it.

(d) The hunger drive prompts the individual to secure food and water adequate for survival, by finding, consuming, and storing food. The drive is often expressed as the derivative cultural acquisitive urge.

(e) The reproductive drive prompts the individual to produce and raise young by attracting a mate, consummating sexual union, and rearing the young. The derivative cultural urges include artistic expression, attracting favourable attention, and education and training.

(f) The security drive prompts the individual to protect himself from danger through fear, flight, and fight. The derivative cultural urges are often economic and emotional in nature.

(g) Three urges—the aggressive, territorial, and cooperative—result from the operation of all the drives and are universals. The aggressive urge impels forceful, assertive action when drive satisfaction is blocked. The territorial urge leads to provision of adequate living space. The cooperative urge motivates the mutually helpful behaviour necessary for successful group action.

2. THE MODES OF ACTION

As we have seen, all living creatures have evolved in response to the pressures of their environment. This evolution occurs through selective dominance of successful genetic patterns and through mutations in the genes. Virtually the whole of this pattern of change has been without conscious direction, for natural selection is opportunistic. Living things, then, have become what their genes and environment made of them. Man can become the only exception, for humans have the potential to make conscious changes in their culture. Many theories and principles have been developed to explain the predictable pattern of human evolution. First is Darwin's theory of natural selection which evolutionary biologists generally consider basic and amply verified. From Darwin's ideas have arisen related concepts of cultural evolution which anticipate adaptive changes in learned behaviour.

These separate developments are of importance to the manager concerned with working effectively through and with other people. Unfortunately, integration of this knowledge in terms useful to the practising manager has not yet been undertaken. To fill this gap, we have attempted to isolate the broad patterns of human action and to provide a conceptual framework within which they can be seen as part of the total management process. This has led to the identification of four modes of human action—the spontaneous, rational, centric, and radic. Conscious of the dangers of introducing 'jargon', that is, a predilection to label incompletely or imperfectly understood management phenomena with

13

an imposing term, implying that the word clearly explains the phenomena, we have introduced the 'modes' and the terminology relating to them only because the terms in use are inadequate to the need.

THE SPONTANEOUS MODE

The spontaneous mode is intuitive action taken to accomplish intuitive objectives. Using this mode, we do what comes naturally, largely in terms of our genetic drives or the cultural urges which happen to be influential at the time. Virtually the whole of biological evolution has been spontaneous; since our behaviour has been governed largely by spontaneous operation of the genetic drives and their derivative cultural urges, most of our culture is also spontaneous. Technology, developed largely during the past century, has been logical and disciplined; however, our use of technology is spontaneous and undisciplined. We can see the implications of this if we examine the advantages and disadvantages of the spontaneous mode.

Arising from the subconscious, the spontaneous mode is based on past memories and experience and is characterized by trial and error. However, if it is successful, it is immediately rewarding. This satisfaction conditions our response so the spontaneous approach becomes habitual. Since the spontaneous mode does not demand the effort and discipline necessary to arrive consciously at decisions or to follow a predetermined course of action, it requires least effort.

When we act spontaneously, our reaction is to the immediate problem. We become so involved in it that we rarely search for the cause of the problem or anticipate its long-term consequences. After developing an instinctive solution, we repeat the successful pattern to solve other problems, even though it is no longer appropriate. Thus, spontaneous action tends to become obsolete without our recognizing it.

THE RATIONAL MODE

The rational mode is purposeful action taken to accomplish predetermined objectives. This requires time and effort: we develop an objective and think through the steps necessary to accomplish it.

Use of the rational mode demands some skill and a good deal of self-discipline, for, in essence, it requires that we develop new cultural urges to displace existing ones and the basic drives. Spontaneous drives such as hunger and reproduction survived because they were successful. This success reinforced the mechanism underlying the drive so that it became, in effect, a fixed and genetically transmitted 'habit'. To establish the rational mode, we must take conscious action to make our first use of the substitute cultural urge successful, so that the necessary reinforcement will occur and rational action will also become habitual.

The rational mode can be frustrating. When we are confronted by an emergency, the security drive is activated, our genes stimulate the adrenal glands to pour out adrenalin with its accompanying urge to flee or fight. If we force ourselves to think instead of act, tension builds unless we know how to redirect our energies. The rational mode tends to be long term; the immediate steps are often relatively unrewarding and may not be successful immediately. However, since it anticipates long-term consequences and consciously provides for them, the rational mode has the greatest probability of continuing success. A well-founded objective is relatively constant compared with spontaneous action; thus trial and error efforts, with their attendant waste, are minimized. The rational mode, costing more time and effort initially, is most economical over the long term.

THE CENTRIC MODE

The centric mode is action taken by an individual to give priority to his needs and objectives and secondary concern to the needs and objectives of the group as a whole and the others with whom he works. The centric mode is a direct expression of our genetic drives. If we are hungry, instinctively we try to satisfy our own hunger; it requires a distinct act of will to concern ourselves at the same time with the hunger of others. When we believe that others have encroached on our territory, intuitively we try to protect what we believe to be ours; rarely do we attempt to make a balanced assessment of the other person's claims. Giving ourselves first preference satisfies our own needs most quickly and directly; this success reinforces the tendency, so that it becomes deeply imbedded in our make-up. Acting in the centric mode is easy, for it is directed to our own gratification; if we try to give consideration to the needs of others, their understanding is often at variance with our intention and the effort may fail. Even greater effort and discipline are then needed to try again.

Acting in the centric mode is the natural and characteristic way in which to act. We must develop a firm basis of self-confidence and personal success before we can have the strength and assurance to shift from the centric mode of action. This is why this mode is desirable for

15

the young and inexperienced, for new and untried situations, and in times of emergency or change. Since it is the natural mode, we can always renourish our ego by coming back to it. During most of human existence, the centric mode has been the dynamic of survival. The centric mode, however, does become self-defeating. The more we act in the centric mode, the more we prompt other people to act in the same mode and, thus, to give increasing concern to their own interests. To satisfy ourselves, the centric mode is quickest and most rewarding; to secure our satisfaction and rewards through and with others, the centric mode becomes an obstacle to the very end we are trying to achieve.

THE RADIC MODE

The radic mode is purposeful action taken by an individual to balance concern for his needs and objectives with concern for the needs and objectives of others. The radic mode runs contrary to the thrust of our genetic drives and to many of our cultural urges. Acting in this mode is not intuitive; it must be learned. Like other personal skills, it requires self-discipline.

When we act in the radic mode, we show genuine concern for the needs and objectives of others. This does not mean that we overlook our own needs or minimize them. Rather, we proceed in the conscious knowledge that if we give first attention to others, we motivate other people to want to do things for us because we are already acting in their interests. This may mean we forego some immediate benefits for ourselves, but we do so in the knowledge that we will thus achieve much more in the long run.

To act in the radic mode, we must first find out what others need and want. We must balance our own insistent personal drives and urges while we give considered attention to the needs and objectives of others with whom we deal. We will then generate increasing concern from others towards our needs and objectives.

When we deal with other people, they reciprocate our intentions as they understand them; thus, their intuitive approach to us is centric. This mode on both sides requires least energy to maintain. Radic action, on the other hand, requires that we neutralize and reverse both our own instinctive centric tendency and that of others. This does not occur naturally; it requires both conscious effort and skill. However, once radic action is established, it reinforces itself, because the more we continue radic action, the greater the radic response we secure.

16

When working with or through other people, we either fall spontaneously into the centric or radic mode or purposefully change from one to the other to suit the needs of the situation. When we act in the centric mode, we satisfy our personal, short-term objectives most quickly. Over a period of time, however, this approach is self-defeating. The more we continue centric action, the more we prompt other people to give increasing concern to their own interests. When we show genuine concern for the needs of others, we set in motion a reciprocity which increasingly prompts others to act with concern for what we want.

THE PRINCIPLE OF HUMAN REACTION

Spontaneous and intuitive action means that we are mastered by our environment; rational and purposeful action enables us to master our environment. To use the centric and radic modes most effectively, we attempted to develop a fundamental truth or principle that would identify cause and effect relationships and would apply in new situations much as it had in those already observed. We began by analysing human actions and emotions. For example, if we express hate to another, he will be prompted to hate, not love us. If we do good to another, he will do good, not evil, to us in return.

Human action tends to feed on itself and generate its own energy when influenced by the action of another; for example, a mild reproof tends to generate antagonism greater than the words or intention warrant; hate inevitably generates even greater hate. Radic action has an equally predictable radic response, but here, there is a time lag until the other person is convinced that the mode of action is sincere and intended as he understands it. Because the underlying, spontaneous centric drive is always present while the radic mode is a cultural overlay, continued effort is needed to maintain a radic response. As soon as the effort is relaxed, the response returns to the spontaneous centric. The following principle summarizes these human tendencies.

PRINCIPLE OF HUMAN REACTION	*Every action directed at another person evokes a similar and increasing reaction in the terms in which it is understood*

If centric action is interpreted as centric action, then it produces increasing and self-generating centric response. If radic action is interpreted as radic action, then it produces increasing and effort maintained radic response. If radic action is misinterpreted as centric action, then it produces increasing and self-generating centric response.

As we worked out this principle, we found it interesting to relate it to some of the enduring precepts imbedded in human culture. In primitive times, 'an eye for an eye' expressed the need to meet force with force or be overcome. This adage is expressed in many cultures. As civilization advanced, it became clear to some that this spontaneous mode, while necessary to establish common ground in the short term, was, in time, self-defeating. For this reason, in all the great religions of the world, a precept is found which approximates, 'Do unto others as you would have others do unto you'.

USE OF THE MODES

If we want to change another person's mode, we should adopt the opposite mode at the level we perceive the other person to be. For example, to make a friend of an enemy, we must first find the common ground. We act towards him at first in as neutral a manner as possible. We make him understand we are purposefully not reacting to his mode, but that we want to become friendly. We make this intention operative by taking some concrete action, however small, to demonstrate a desire to be friendly. We continue this pattern of response until we secure the reaction we are consciously seeking. Why must we find the common ground, either centric or radic? If our action is too far removed from that which the person we want to influence would spontaneously expect, he will become suspicious and distrustful. This will reinforce his mode, rather than help to change it.

It is clear that the spontaneous mode intensifies any mode it encounters; it heightens friendliness or enmity, but does not change them. To change the mode of another requires conscious action which must encompass identification of the desired objective and knowledge and skill in carrying out the action necessary to achieve it.

This becomes of greatest importance if we want to influence and guide others, for we must act in such a way as to prompt other people to do what we want them to do. We get from others only what they are willing to give.

This is true whether our action is spontaneous or rational. However, if we exhibit spontaneous action towards another person who acts in a similar mode, the action intensifies in the direction in which it is expressed; that is, intuitive friendliness generates increasing intuitive friendliness, while intuitive enmity generates the same feeling increasingly in the terms in which it is understood.

What happens if we adopt the conscious mode in dealing with others? If we know another person is being consciously centric, spontaneously we will become more so, but consciously we will think through the result we want to achieve and act in either the centric or radic mode, as best fits our purpose.

CENTRIC BEFORE RADIC

Although radic action has potential superiority in the long term, it is not always indicated, nor the best way to act. Because the centric mode has its basis in genetic drives, it must be satisfied just as much as the hunger, reproductive, and other drives.

In any situation, we should first take centric action, for this helps us to establish our objectives, to find a common meeting ground and to meet the other person's action. It also sets up the emotional supports that confident, positive action in the radic mode requires. We must know our own needs and objectives before we can be properly concerned with those of others. To pretend otherwise is unrealistic.

When we deal with others, we should always anticipate an initial centric response, for the other person cannot adopt the radic mode unless he has the necessary emotional assurance. Thus, most human action is initially centric on both sides.

We often have great success when we act in the centric mode. However, if we persist in this mode when others are involved, success tends to be episodic. Almost literally, it wears out and we have to begin again. In contrast, timely change to the radic mode builds enduring success which regenerates itself as long as we can maintain the mode. Action in the radic mode continues to generate reaction in that same mode.

THE COMPOUND MODES

Human action is a combination of spontaneous or rational and centric or radic action. We call these combinations compound modes. They are shown in Fig. 2.1.

THE SPONTANEOUS CENTRIC MODE

This is the normal compound mode which governs most human action. Easiest and immediately rewarding, it generates a similar reaction which is self-defeating. In emergency or danger, the teleological and security drives force us to this compound mode. When the prevalent mode for all members of a group is spontaneous centric, the typical pattern is authoritarian leadership, sustained competition among members, early success and reward, or prompt failure and dissolution of the group.

	Centric	Radic
Spontaneous	Short-term rewards ; long-term self-defeating.	Rare; occurs in specific relationships-mother/child.
Rational	Used to shift to neutral.	Best basis for sustained mutual benefits.

Fig. 2.1 The compound modes. The spontaneous and rational modes always occur in some combination with the centric and radic. The characteristics of the combined modes are summarized above.

THE RATIONAL CENTRIC MODE

This compound mode requires conscious placing of personal objectives and needs before those of others. It is a means of re-establishing self-confidence and assurance when objectives become clouded or uncertain. If danger or emergency threatens, the shift to the rational centric mode by the manager results in the focusing of divergent viewpoints and efforts, and forceful direction to regain momentum.

When first establishing relationships, or when dealing with strangers, adoption of the rational centric mode is necessary to overcome suspicion and to establish a neutral base for movement to the rational radic mode. Thus, the rational centric mode is a means of recovery and a threshold for entry into the rational radic mode.

THE SPONTANEOUS RADIC MODE

Giving intuitive priority to others' needs and objectives is most commonly found in the relationship of a parent towards a child. It is also found when an organization wishes to become radic, but does not know how, and stumbles from one to another trial and error alternative. If the response is spontaneous centric, as is often the case, the radic action diminishes and becomes increasingly centric. Since maintenance of the radic mode requires effort, the spontaneous radic is difficult to maintain. It provides meagre returns to the initiator, so great motivation is

20

necessary to continue it. To be sustained, it must be shifted to the rational radic mode.

THE RATIONAL RADIC MODE

Most rewarding and yet most difficult, this compound mode results in optimum long-term returns and satisfaction for all involved. However, because it requires thought and effort to be sustained if it is one-sided, it is most difficult to master. Thus, rational radic action is completely successful only when all involved act in this mode. This results in mutual assessment of needs and objectives for the common good, cooperative effort, and reciprocal support.

Effective use of the rational radic mode was demonstrated in one plant of a food processing company. An early leader in professional management, the company had developed successful mechanisms for securing participation and involvement of managers and employees as part of their routine responsibilities. Development of new dehydrating equipment made it possible for the company to consolidate three production departments, with potential savings of $360,000 monthly, but also entailed the need to dismiss more than a hundred employees and managers. Rather than announcing the decision and making the cuts unilaterally, the plant manager outlined the new development at his regular monthly staff meeting and suggested that a task force of five managers and employees draw up a recommended plan for instituting the changes. His managers agreed, the task force was appointed, and its membership and purpose were communicated at each departmental staff meeting. Within a month the plan was completed, approved, and put into effect. It included a 12 per cent reduction in labour force. As one of the production line foremen who was laid off said, 'We all knew it was important both to the company and to employees to install the new equipment. No one was happy, but the choices were fair and almost everybody had a say in the changes, so there were few complaints. In addition, the personnel department is helping me get relocated, so I carry nothing but goodwill.'

SHIFTING THE MODES

Shifting from one mode to another can be spontaneous or rational. If spontaneous, the shift will resolve into spontaneous centric action on both sides. If a manager understands the modes, and the human behaviour they reflect, he can shift consciously to the mode that best fits the needs of any situation.

The rational centric mode is the neutral mode. When we want to change, we move for the necessary time into this mode, then into the action pattern we want to establish. See Fig. 2.2.

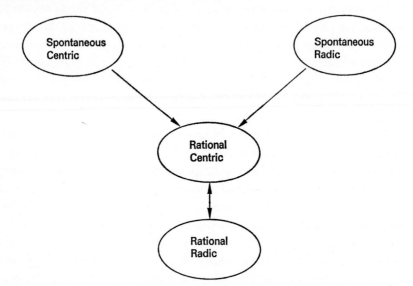

Fig. 2.2 Shift diagram for the modes of action. It is always necessary to shift through the rational centric to go from either spontaneous mode to the rational radic.

This conscious shift through rational centric enables us to establish our own objectives, gain assurance, and minimize suspicion. We can shift, as needed, from rational centric to rational radic.

THE OMNIMODE

There is no one preferred way of acting. Despite our own wishes, the way others act inevitably influences our mode. The professional manager is familiar with all the modes and has the skill necessary to work with each. He knows how to shift from the spontaneous mode, if he finds himself in it, to rational centric and rational radic. He concentrates his own actions in the rational modes when he wants to move or change other people; however, he acts in the spontaneous modes for a large part of the time. This does not worry him, for he knows that he cannot expect to maintain the peak of physical and mental effort necessary to act continually in the rational modes. As time goes on, however, he notes that he does begin to fall habitually into the rational centric or radic modes to meet the needs of different people and situations. He recognizes that this ability to harness and channel his primitive drives is the source of greatest satisfaction and reward.

In the omnimode, a person has the ability to act in all modes to meet differing situations. For the reasons we have noted, it includes both the spontaneous and rational modes. A professional in management understands and uses the omnimode by preference.

THE EVOLUTION OF INDIVIDUALS, GROUPS, AND LEADERS

As individuals, we change predictably in the way we act to fulfil ourselves. Centric action precedes radic. The intuitive and natural mode is centric because we do those things that most completely satisfy us without equivalent regard for the needs and objectives of others. Because we need the cooperation, association, and liking of others, we can never be completely fulfilled in the centric mode, for this always entails our satisfaction at the expense of others.

Just as we need certain basic satisfactions of our physical hungers before we can give proper attention to our psychological hungers, so also, we need certain basic centric satisfactions before we can evolve to radic fulfilment. After we have had enough success in fulfilling our needs to achieve the necessary level of confidence, we will then be motivated to take the next step; that is, satisfaction of ourselves through the satisfaction of others.

Groups change just as individuals do. This is important to our study of leadership because the leader will remain successful only if he changes to satisfy the needs of the group he leads. It is easy to see the difference between a newly organized orchestra and a seasoned, experienced one, or between a football team at the beginning of the season when everybody is new and at the end of the season when effective teamwork has developed. Changes occur because the individuals in the group learn that they can gain more by putting the interests and objectives of the group first. This is a learned process; it does not occur intuitively. Change occurs because the individuals in the group attempt to use the facilities and resources of the group to fulfil themselves; that is, to use their aptitudes and abilities to the full in the group's interest, so that they will achieve more for themselves.

Leaders also predictably change from a centric to a radic orientation, while they lead. At first, they will secure results and satisfaction through the centric mode by using their leadership position as a means of satisfying their personal needs. Eventually, if the leader matures and remains successful, he will adopt the radic mode in his leadership. He will give equivalent attention to the needs and satisfactions of his followers and, thus, will enhance his own status and fulfilment by helping them to achieve what they want. If the leader cannot satisfy his needs, he will become frustrated. However, since he is in command, his frustration is not only rarer, but also more easily resolved.

In modern societies, most work is done by people in groups. A large share of our problems occurs because people are spontaneously centric; as a result, they are not able to work harmoniously and effectively together. This is why we need professional managers who know how to work with groups so that each individual gains most personally from the accomplishments of the group.

In practising management, we can use whatever intuitive abilities we may have, or we can systematically study and master logical and proven methods. As every professional knows, this latter course is most effective and eventually most enjoyable, even though it requires more effort and self-discipline. If we master the rational mode in our approach to management, we learn how to get others to work more quickly and efficiently to accomplish the results we want. We know how to get the support and enthusiastic cooperation of other people. If we are rational, we know how to develop satisfying objectives and to help other people work towards them so that they receive greatest personal rewards for their time and effort.

SUMMARY

(a) The modes of action are typical patterns of human behaviour. (i) In the spontaneous mode, intuitive action is taken to accomplish intuitive objectives. (ii) In the rational mode, purposeful action is taken to accomplish a predetermined objective. (iii) In the centric mode, action is taken by an individual to give priority to his needs and objectives and secondary concern to the needs and objectives of the group as a whole and the others with whom he works. (iv) In the radic mode, purposeful action is taken by an individual to balance concern for his needs and objectives with concern for the needs and objectives of others.

(b) Every action directed at another person evokes a similar and increasing reaction in the terms in which it is understood. To change another person's mode, adopt the mode of the other person and then gradually move to the desired mode. In any situation, first take rational centric action to establish objectives, to find a common ground, and to neutralize the actions of the other person.

(c) All human action is a combination of the four modes. This results in four compound modes: spontaneous centric, rational centric, spontaneous radic, and rational radic.

(d) Shifting from one mode to another is either spontaneous or rational. It necessitates adoption of the neutral mode of action, the rational centric, before beginning action in a new mode.

(e) Because no two persons or situations are ever alike, the best mode of action is the omnimode, the ability to act in all modes to meet differing situations.

(f) Individuals, groups, and leaders change predictably in the way they act to fulfil themselves, from spontaneous to rational and from centric to radic.

3. THE LEADER AS A MANAGER

Management is a unique skill. It is the ability to get other people to work with you and for you to accomplish common objectives. A manager, then, is an expert in performing the work necessary to secure results through and with other people.

The ability to lead people was once thought to be largely a matter of personality. Good managers, however, have personalities as varied as doctors or lawyers. They are brilliant or plodding, cautious or bold, friendly or reserved; their education ranges from liberal arts to nuclear physics, from accounting to business administration. The one common characteristic of the many kinds of people who are professional managers is that they are all doing a particular kind of work and doing it in a particular way.

There is much misunderstanding about leaders, what they are, what they do and how they can be most effective. For leaders to achieve and maintain success over a period of time, their actions must evolve from the spontaneous centric mode to the omnimode. Because pressures are multiplied by the predictable changes which take place in the group, leaders who do *not* change are forced into a corridor of crisis. This is the transition stage between the centric and radic modes, hence we term it the cenrad transition. At this transition point, the leaders either fail or develop and use more effective action modes. We will now investigate the sequential management stages: the spontaneous centric or natural leadership stage, the cenrad transition, the rational radic or management leadership stage, and the omnimode.

THE NATURAL LEADERSHIP STAGE

When first assuming a leadership position, a person who has not been trained in professional management will act in the spontaneous centric mode. He will use his innate aptitudes and personality characteristics as he guides and directs the people he leads. This natural leader can be compared to a natural golfer, a natural musician, or a natural engineer. In each case, the individual has strong aptitudes and obtains results by using his intuitive skills.

In the same way that we can tell whether a golfer is a 'natural' or a 'pro' by the way he plays, or whether an engineer is 'self-taught' or 'professional' by the way he goes about his work, so we can tell whether a person in a leadership position is a 'natural' leader who relies almost completely on the spontaneous centric mode of action, or whether he is a 'professional' who has mastered the omnimode. The natural leader in the spontaneous centric stage exhibits some, or all, of the following characteristics.

PROMOTION OF PERSONAL INTERESTS

Intuitively, every action we take is aimed primarily at satisfaction of our own needs, not those of others. When a person acts in the role of leader of a group, his intuitive tendency is to put his own personal interests above those of the group. He gives first attention to his own rewards, whether financial or psychological, and is most concerned with accomplishing the objectives that he deems important.

This has advantages and disadvantages. In a new, young group or one that is uncohesive or poorly organized, there is unlikely to be commitment to a guiding objective that will yield optimum benefits to all. Since the leader is the link between his group and upper levels of organization, his personal interests and objectives most closely approximate the overall objectives of the organization as a whole. His decisions and actions thus establish uniformity of action and hold his followers in line. At first, this is effective, for it gives clear direction, reduces interpersonal friction, and consolidates divergent effort in the most productive manner.

During the early, immature stages of organizational growth, both the leader and his followers want material rewards. They are most concerned with their own objectives and will aggressively seek to satisfy them. Although, at later stages, these centric attitudes may seem undesirable, during this early phase they are to be expected and, in fact, motivate intense effort.

TECHNICAL EMPHASIS

Our territorial urge prompts us to concentrate on our own work and to organize it to fit our personal needs. We want our own responsibility, work which is ours alone, and in which our proprietary right is recognized. Every leader also has these needs. If he is a natural leader acting in the spontaneous centric mode, he will not have specialized in management work and will not know enough about it to find satisfaction in it. His only recourse is to specialize in work he is familiar with—technical work. As a result, he spends most of his time and effort doing work that is much the same as that done by those he supervises.

When he is involved in his area of previous technical experience, he is familiar and expert and assured. This is highly advantageous at first, because the critical need is technical excellence. Unless functions such as sales, manufacturing, and engineering are performed efficiently, the enterprise cannot succeed. While good management might expedite the technical development, it is also true that the basic technology must be perfected before it can be taught. If managers are technically expert and do much of the more complex technical work themselves, a sound foundation will be laid for effective management. After all, management can exist only to the extent that there is technical work to be managed.

If the leader continues too long in the spontaneous centric mode, however, he will not train his subordinates to assume the more difficult technical work. This not only impoverishes their jobs, but also burdens him so that he cannot concentrate on management work. Job enrichment, as a device for building more planning and controlling work into the lowest-level jobs, often fails at this stage because it does not emphasize delegation of the technical work to operating people.

CENTRALIZED DECISION MAKING

Our genetic drives impel us to work aggressively to accomplish our own objectives. The natural leader expresses these drives in many cultural derivations, most typical of which is authoritarianism. He needs to command others, so he centralizes decision making and makes most of the decisions for his group. He makes not only the decisions he should, but also many that could be made more soundly by others. This is effective during the early stages of group development and so long as the organization does not integrate its objectives and unify its effort. Two conditions must exist if decision making is to be decentralized to the people who do the work. First, there must be effective controls, otherwise each person goes his own way and chaos results. Second, controls cannot exist unless sound plans are first developed on which to base them. We cannot control results unless we first determine what results we want. These conditions cannot exist until the group has had enough experience to know what objectives it does want. Thus, *an initial period of centralized decision making is mandatory and is characteristic of every successful organization.*

The leader becomes conditioned to centralization. It gives him a sense of power and is much easier than trying to decentralize. Most often, he does not know how to set in motion the sequence of planning, controlling, and delegating necessary to decentralization.

As his followers show capacity for exercising more authority, he reacts spontaneously. Typically, if members of his group make decisions for themselves, he questions what they have done, infers there is a better way, known only to him, and frequently, reverses the decision or disparages it. If people show too much independent action, the leader generally hauls them smartly back to heel, or sees to it that they leave his group.

INTUITIVE ACTION

The entire thrust of evolution is spontaneous. Only humans have developed the ability to think and act rationally. The natural leader intuitively takes the easy way; he takes action first, thinks about it later. This is typified by his tendency to assess the superficial aspects of a problem and to plunge at once into the first course of action that appears.

The successful natural leader is sharp, alert, and dynamic; his instincts must be good if he is to survive. For him, intuitive action gives quick and effective results. Most often, he has a clear picture in his mind of what he is trying to accomplish and how he expects to go about it. He is fixed in this idea and persistent in his actions. His subconscious is stored with memories of past successes and mistakes, and it is on this reservoir that he draws in taking his intuitive actions. In this respect, he is much like a football player trying to make a run through the opposing team. If he hesitates to figure out what to do next, he is lost. Given outstanding ability and quick enough reflexes, he may singlehandedly win the game, with no requirement but that the other members of his team give him what support they can.

However, like the football team that depends on one star, the group under a natural leader who does not change, eventually loses out.

Intuitive action is effective only so long as it is monolithic. Given centralized authority and technical expertise by the top man, it remains monolithic for a time. But only a limited number of people can follow his intuitive and, therefore, unplanned moves. Like the football team, a successful group must build strength in depth and not only at the top. The strategy and plays must be thought through so that all can make a maximum contribution, and individual genius must be supported by disciplined contributions from all pooling their strongest efforts.

PERSONALIZED ORGANIZATION

As head of his organization, the leader must assign work to others; this calls for him to share his work and territory through use of a cultural device, delegation. The natural leader, acting in the spontaneous centric mode, does this intuitively. Instead of thinking through a logical way of dividing the work, he builds his organization around personalities by selecting key individuals and allocating them the important work to be done. His primary concern is whether the individual can do the work satisfactorily, not whether, logically, he should be doing the work at all. At first, this is good, for it enables followers to use the best of their abilities, no matter how varied they may be. Initially, there is much more work to be done than there are people, so, like settlers newly arrived in a virgin wilderness, each person can stake out his personal territory with little danger of encroaching on others. Personalized organization encourages people to contribute wherever they can. Unfettered by limiting job descriptions or organization charts, these first followers secure immediate gratification of some of their basic genetic needs. With increasing size and new people, however, this undisciplined but highly effective growth gives rise to problems. Sooner or later, strong individuals accumulate diverse and unrelated responsibilities. Most likely, their successors will not have the unique combination of talents or the experience necessary to perform all the varied tasks satisfactorily. As a result, each new individual entering the group tends to trigger a reorganization. Overlap, duplication, and personal frustration result.

ONE-WAY COMMUNICATION

The communication urge impels each person to give priority to his own ideas without much concern for those of others; therefore, our natural tendency is to communicate what we want. This priority is necessary, for if we did not satisfy our own needs sufficiently to ensure our survival, there would be no ideas to communicate. Our culture properly recognizes this basic need. Children are taught to express their own wants, feelings, ideas, and it must be so if they are to secure the satisfaction and confidence that will make it possible for them to give attention to what others want. The fact that radic communication is infrequent and sporadic simply attests to the early stage of our cultural evolution.

The natural leader acts in terms of this basic pattern. He satisfies his communication drive primarily by telling others what he wants and how he wants it. His primary concern is making others understand him, not understanding others. Taken with the other characteristics of this stage, this kind of communication is successful. People need a sense of purpose and direction; they want to know what their work is. The leader tells them.

Soon, however, one-way communication proves deficient. People reciprocate in the centric mode, and as little information flows up as comes down. A widening gap separates the leaders and lower ranks of their followers.

CONTROL BY INSPECTION

The natural leader acting in the spontaneous centric mode intuitively obeys this need to check everything himself. He tries to inspect all the work done for him, evaluating what is done, not in terms of what others want, or objective standards, but rather, in terms of his own preferences.

If the leader is skilled and knows what he wants, this kind of control can be excellent on a short-term basis. Since he is technically oriented, he maintains excellence in technology. Mistakes are quickly caught and corrected and this gives immediate success in the competitive marketplace.

There is no alternative for this control by inspection until sound and rational plans are developed on which to base control by exception; therefore, this first stage is maintained at least until planning is mastered. However, control by personal observation is both limited and limiting because the leader can control only those activities of which he is informed. Also, others are required to conform to his way of doing things and must clearly centre their efforts on his needs and objectives. This minimizes initiative and creative thinking opportunities and erodes spontaneity and enthusiasm.

When people first combine their efforts in a group endeavour, the group is not cohesive; there is little teamwork. At this stage, the spontaneous centric mode can be uniquely effective because the uncoordinated, divergent, and unschooled efforts of the members of the group are forcibly welded into a functioning entity by the technical orientation, centralized decision making, personalized organization, one-way communication, and control by inspection exercised by the leader. The most successful leader of a new, immature or uncohesive group is one who, knowingly or intuitively, can exercise leadership force. Leadership force is the active power brought to bear by a leader to secure desired results. Leadership is most effective when people can be enouraged and inspired to work because they want to, not because they are forced. However, when the situation requires, an effective leader must be able to compel the necessary action. The following principle of leadership force is intuitively applied by the natural leader.

PRINCIPLE OF
LEADERSHIP FORCE

The greater the divergence of the individual objectives of the members of the group, the greater the leadership force required to ensure cohesive action

Divergent objectives can be reconciled through persuasion or by redefining the overall unifying objective. The greater the willingness to cooperate, the less the leadership force required. In relative terms, however, it is also true that leadership force proportional to the divergence must still be exercised to secure cohesive action.

THE TRANSITIONAL STAGE

There are certain readily identifiable structural and motivational changes in the work of the leader who has outgrown natural leadership. If he is to survive and remain successful as a leader, he must make *the transition between the spontaneous centric and the rational radic modes*, termed the *cenrad transition*. To understand this, we must keep in mind that the impetus for change does not arise in the leader. He finds that acting in the spontaneous centric mode is highly satisfying and personally rewarding; his preference is to retain it. However, the principle of human reaction is operative and the centric mode of the leader generates increasing centric response by his followers. This reaction takes time. While the group is young and not very cohesive, members of the team react well to the strong leadership force exercised by the leader. With time and experience, however, their attitude becomes, almost literally, 'Up to now, we submitted to a firm hand because we knew this was the only way the group could work as a unit. But now we've learned the rules and understand and accept the overall objectives. We're ready to make our own decisions. Let us use our own imaginations and ideas in getting the work done.'

Although the leader may not change, the oganization is ready to move on. As the enterprise matures, the data base expands and deepens, facilitating confident planning and control so that extemporaneous action is no longer mandatory. It is possible for the leader to delegate because he can control; he need no longer decide everything himself. Policies are understood, procedures are established, and rationalized structure and operation become possible.

Too often, however, the spontaneous centric leader does not change and each increment of growth creates unrest. People become dissatisfied; the work becomes stereotyped. Waning interests leads to diminished effort; costs increase and efficiency deteriorates. The symptoms are easily identified.

DISSATISFACTION OF PEOPLE

The mode of the centric leader evokes increasing reciprocity in similar terms from other members of the organization. Continually impelled to work aggressively towards their own objectives, to secure their own rewards, and to identify their own territory, even as is the leader, the other members of the organization become increasingly frustrated. The energy which might have been used to work towards organizational objectives does not simply disappear. The person who does not feel he is accomplishing his own objectives, who cannot find a satisfying place in the organization, or who believes he is inadequately rewarded is driven to displacement activity. He may use the energy in his private pursuits' as a public official, or through activity in a club or other undertaking. He may initiate projects which interest him, but which have little relevance to the organization's objectives, and invest the best of his time and energy in them.

If the frustration continues, the displacement activity may become ritualized as part of the organization's culture. For example, in one metal manufacturing company, groups follow a formal ritual of establishing their own work pace and hold to it without regard to company standards. Whenever new standards are posted, the same three men go to the cloakroom. When they return, one of them starts the new standard down the line by word of mouth. Those who transgress are invariably warned first; if they persist, the word 'scab' is painted on their cars, and, if this does not bring them around, they are sent to Coventry and subjected to unrelenting petty harassment.

Since most people spend a large part of their lives in the work environment, and derive much general satisfaction and well-being from it, there can be little question that the impact of the spontaneous centric mode carried beyond its period of utility is a primary factor in the eventual deterioration of most organizations.

DECREASED INNOVATION

Since the reproductive drive cannot be expressed directly at work, people must find cultural substitutes, usually of a creative nature. This creative potential will either be directed to innovation which contributes to the organization's objectives, or to activities which may have an opposite effect. In the first, relatively free-wheeling burst of organization growth, this creative energy often has free expression. Under the natural leader, however, authority and controls are centralized and the opportunity for innovatory activity is gradually restricted. As this centralization hardens and controls become rigid, the spark of innovation dies. However, the need remains and is increasingly diverted into undesirable channels.

ORGANIZATIONAL PROLIFERATION

The more natural leadership and the spontaneous centric mode are outgrown, the greater the burden of responsibility and authority concentrated at the top levels. To relieve this burden, the natural leader appoints assistants and creates staff agencies; the more he insists on doing himself, the larger the supporting organization he needs to carry out his dictates at the operating level. At intermediate levels of organization, managers become relay and confirmation points for communications and decisions passing from top to bottom levels. They help sustain the personal grasp of the top man; however, as this process continues, the spontaneous centric leader finds it increasingly difficult to maintain effective contact with the operating levels because he relies increasingly on the judgement and opinions of those at intermediate levels, and not those actually doing the work. Communication slows down, the organization becomes monolithic and inflexible, more and more people are needed to do less and less work, and these people derive less satisfaction from the work they do.

This organizational proliferation is in close accord with the genetic drives of top executives. Their teleological needs are gratified because the organization's objectives are uniquely their own, and not shared with lower levels. Their security and territorial needs are given full play by continued centralization of authority and controls. Since the short-term results tend to be successful and highly rewarding to them, they see the proliferating organization as a symbol of their own success, and may actually encourage it rather than show concern over it.

INCREASED EXPENSE FOR LOWER PRODUCTIVITY

During the early phase of spontaneous centric leadership, a strong, self-oriented individual makes most of the decisions that shape day to day action. To the extent that he is outstanding, these decisions bear his personal stamp. As a result, action is rapid, decisive and dynamic. Sales and profitability tend to increase with gratifying speed.

As the organization moves beyond the personal grasp of the strong, centric leader, a number of adverse conditions develop. The addition of unnecessary personnel multiplies overhead costs. Disinterest and apathy at the operating level discourage productivity. The ratio of indirect labour to direct labour tends to increase sharply.

As people at lower levels find their basic drives thwarted, they are increasingly driven to find substitute activities. Since their managers show little understanding or consideration of their needs, their reaction is increasingly centric. An aggressive person who cannot identify his own work and responsibility tends to take on whatever work he likes and can commandeer. This empire building further increases expense and reduces efficiency. The consequences are most direct in a competitive business enterprise, for profitability begins to deteriorate. First, individual product lines and, later, the enterprise as a whole lose their competitive position.

CREATION OF BUREAUCRACY

As the spontaneous centric pattern of action becomes habitual, the organization becomes bureaucratic; that is, it is typified by authoritarianism, needless proliferation of work, positions, and red tape. Since people do not have authority to make their own decisions, they fall into the habit of checking everything they do. They look for shared responsibility so that the blame can be shifted elsewhere if mistakes occur. To ensure that people act in the way they should, that is, in the manner intermediate levels believe the top leaders want them to act, rules and procedures are developed to cover most actions. The channels of communication are overburdened as leaders at the top attempt to remain cognizant of the problems at the operating level on which they must make decisions.

Once established, the pattern of bureaucracy persists. It enables the protagonists to satisfy their basic needs through substitute cultural activity, even if, at the expense of the organization, each person pursues his own personal objectives, puts his mark on his own territory, and finds safety and security in this artificial world.

THE TIME OF TRANSITION

The leader who has mastered professional management skills recognizes the need for the early centric approach. If he has not established this mode spontaneously, he does so consciously in the rational centric mode. He can best form a unified, cohesive group by an initial technical orientation, centralized decision making, one-way communication, personalized organization, and control by inspection.

The professional manager knows that he will have to shift to the centric mode, either rational or spontaneous, when new people first join the group, when he organizes new groups, and when unexpected emergencies occur. However, he also recognizes that his leadership can endure only if he begins to lay the groundwork for change. To establish the foundation he needs for personal confidence, purposeful early action, and initial success, he must begin with the centric mode, but must shift to the radic mode to start the principle of human reaction acting for him rather than against him.

The professional begins, then, by shifting to the rational centric mode. He is centric for a carefully determined purpose. He begins to establish plans, to rationalize the organization, to select and develop strong people.

THE MANAGEMENT LEADERSHIP STAGE

As people continue to work together, cohesiveness develops and technical proficiency improves. As they become more competent, develop confidence, and begin to understand the larger issues that concern them, they, too, are ready for a new mode of leadership; in fact, the group will remain effective only if the leadership mode does change from predominantly centric to radic. It is important to note that the mode of leadership can shift only as the manager successfully plans, organizes, leads, and controls. Also, the leadership mode must be changed at a pace and in a manner to fit the needs and receptivity of each individual and situation. The characteristics of the management leader are outlined below.

DOMINATION OF GROUP OBJECTIVES

The management leader knows that he will gain the greatest returns for himself by putting the principle of human reaction to work for, instead of against, his best interests. He can harness the great energy that resides in the basic human drives by helping people to integrate their personal objectives with those of the organization as a whole. When people learn to put group objectives first and the leader knows how to ensure their sharing in the greater rewards this brings, their teleological needs are satisfied on the most enduring basis, for every shared accomplishment leads to greater motivation.

The leader acting in the rational radic mode knows this. He understands that people will not knowingly abandon personal goals unless they believe that greater gain lies in accepting and working towards what is best for the group as a whole. The management leader sets the pattern by first clarifying his own role and objectives. When he realizes that he will gain most through others by putting the objectives of the group first, he willingly subordinates his own objectives, and indoctrinates other members of the group to do the same.

MANAGEMENT EMPHASIS

The management leader is a specialist. Just as we can identify the professional functions of doctors, engineers, and lawyers, we can also determine the professional functions of the management leader. To secure most effective results through and with others, he specializes in the management functions of planning, leading, organizing, and controlling. To the extent that he is expert in these functions, he can maximize his own efforts through the efforts of others. If the leader does not specialize in these functions, he finds himself using most of his strength and ability to do the work of others.

Conscious specialization in management work breaks the management-technical dichotomy which has hampered the manager's efforts. By staking out management territory, he is satisfying his territorial urge and delineating clear-cut parameters within which he can channel cultural substitutes.

DECENTRALIZED DECISION MAKING

The management leader knows the decisions he should make and those that can better be made by others. He establishes the conditions that make delegation possible and consistently pushes authority down to the operating levels. Under this kind of leadership, people are given opportunities to make decisions relating to their work. The manager who finds the security, power, and responsibility he wants in management work secures great personal benefits from delegation, for the more he can get others to do for him, the greater the personal rewards and satisfaction he earns.

LOGICAL ACTION

The management leader thinks through and takes the rational steps necessary to attain his objectives. He proceeds purposefully, making the most effective use of all available resources. This action not only gives him the ability to deal better with the vagaries of the future, but also helps those with whom he works to understand his objectives and contribute more effectively.

Acting logically, the manager uses the rational tools available to him. He understands and applies management concepts and principles. He masters and uses a common vocabulary of management so that he can communicate easily and meaningfully with other managers. He knows, however, that he can proceed no faster than his people can follow, so he moves carefully from the rational centric mode with short-term, highly flexible plans to the rational radic mode with long-term, stabilized planning and control.

Logical action is most difficult to maintain because it is contrary to the spontaneous centric action which accompanies all the basic drives. Logical action, therefore, is in itself a learned cultural urge and carries all the attendant problems. It is never as strong as the primitive spontaneous action which it has displaced; as a result, when pressure or emergency arises, there is a constant tendency to revert to the spon-taneous mode. The professional manager knows this and does not try to act logically at all times. He disciplines himself to think and act logically when he wants to set limits, to develop habits, and to create organizational discipline. Within these parameters, he relies on his instincts to govern his routine and repetitive actions.

RATIONAL ORGANIZATION

Instead of building jobs haphazardly around individual personalities, the rational radic leader logically arranges and groups the work to be performed. He makes sure that each person has challenging, satisfying work to do and that all efforts are directed towards profitable results. In itself, this is one of the best ways of satisfying the normal human needs. The greatest obstacles to accomplishing rational organization are the individuals who see this as dismemberment of their own territories. As is to be expected, they fight this both overtly and with the cultural substitutes they can find. Many a manager, for example, has found that his logical reorganization did not work because the people involved either spontaneously or purposefully confused orders, delayed deliveries, or ruined work. When the rational organization did not seem to be succeeding, the manager regressed to the old form.

The management leader who knows how to develop a rational organization ensures the greatest productivity by the fewest people at the least cost. The end result is greater material and psychological rewards for all.

Here, also, the manager begins his actions at the centric stage where the group members are, not at the radic stage where he would like them to be. He realizes that he must catalyse change in his organization if he is to succeed, so he begins with existing deficiencies and moves carefully to achieve desired improvement.

TWO-WAY COMMUNICATION

The efficient manager knows how to get other people to understand him, but he devotes just as much effort to understanding the ideas, needs, and requirements of those with whom he works. Using this approach, he is able to discover emotional obstacles that others may have, and can work around them with minimum loss of time and efficiency. In addition, the others on the team will understand him better, and more effective teamwork will result.

Two-way communication is difficult to establish and maintain. For one thing, it requires the manager to share information which he considers to be his own property. Such communication is effective in the long term only if others in the group are educated to use radic communication techniques so they can respond in kind.

CONTROL BY EXCEPTION

The management leader acting in the rational radic mode sets limits so that others know what is expected of them and can decide for themselves whether or not they are obtaining the desired results. Then he can concern himself only with those things that are not progressing according to plan. Thus, he can exert maximum control with minimum effort. More important, he gives others the tools they need to evaluate their work and correct mistakes. This practice, in itself, provides one of the greatest incentives to continued effective action; not only do staff members achieve greatest satisfaction from their work, but also, the manager is freed for the creative and most productive parts of his job.

The ability to exercise controls confers on the accountable manager the leverage he needs to maintain an existing centric mode or to make the change to a radic. But letting others assume control he had formerly exercised himself is most difficult. For instance, it means that he gives up some of his power; he shares his territory and divides his personal objectives. To proceed successfully, the professional manager knows that he must first have firm confidence in his ability to satisfy his own personal needs. He does this by clarifying the power he wants to retain, the territory he will continue to treat as his own, and the objectives which he considers his personal commitment. This means that he must develop his own plans, organize his own job, and reserve the responsibility and authority he needs as a basis for concentrating his attention only on exceptions—thus permitting others to have full responsibility and authority for everything else.

THE OMNIMODE

The professional in management is flexible and versatile in using the leadership modes. He recognizes that each person must have individual leadership and that the mode must be shifted to fit the need. *A manager is acting in the omnimode when he is able to move at will from one mode to another in order to meet identified needs.* Within the same group, different individuals

40

require variations in the style of leadership. Some fall easily into a radic environment and respond to the shift from centric to radic as quickly as it can be accomplished. For many reasons, others remain centric, often for prolonged periods. With them, the leader will remain rational centric until he gains their confidence and the principle of human reaction begins to exert its influence.

At times, the leader will find that certain individuals cannot change, or, because of the conditions involved, his skills are not adequate to meet the need. When this is the case, he will remain with these people in the rational centric mode, proceeding with change only as his initial attempts meet with success.

In using the omnimode, the following sequence of moves from spontaneous centric to rational radic produces best results. When the professional manager is in spontaneous centric, his first need is to find a common ground with the individual or group he wants to lead. He does this by shifting to rational centric. In fact, no matter what the mode of others, on first contact he always moves to rational centric to draw the energy he needs from initial satisfaction of his genetic drives.

To move to the rational radic mode, he must secure common acceptance of objectives made in the best interests of the group. To do this, he shows by word and deed that he understands the objectives and needs of others, but makes clear that objectives which are in the best interests of the entire group will represent a compromise by each of part of his special interests.

Once there is agreement on objectives, he can begin to shift to other aspects of the radic mode as the situation requires, keeping in mind that the only way to change modes is to perform the work necessary to act in that mode. He works to develop initial plans, and recognizing that this is a time-consuming process which requires effort, he formalizes organization, institutes improved methods of communication and motivation, selects and develops competent people, and exercises effective controls. The vital need is to be able to shift, as required, from radic to centric and back again.

After he has decentralized authority, the professional manager can move with confidence and precision to recentralize authority with one individual when this is required. Without distorting the overall structure, he can personalize organization to meet the developmental needs of individuals. Although he may have sound plans, he is able to move intuitively in a crisis, without being strapped to a predetermined course of action. While he usually controls by exception, he is able to resume control by inspection to regulate a failing operation if needs be. When all the facts are in and he has weighed and decided, he is able to maintain one-way communication to ensure that action is in the overall best interests of the organization.

The omnimode is as flexible, as changing, and as responsive as people themselves. It makes great demands on the manager in strength, integrity, and courage. *The ability to exercise the omnimode is the mark of the true professional.*

SUMMARY

(a) The personalities of managers are as varied as the personalities of men in other professional fields. Successful managers learn to evolve in the way they act from the spontaneous centric mode to the omnimode.

(b) The following are characteristics of the spontaneous centric leadership stage. (i) The leader promotes his personal objectives above those of his group. At first the results are good, but later, group productivity falls off. (ii) The leader stresses his technical specialism, which will initially encourage productivity, but will finally impoverish the jobs of his subordinates. (iii) The leader reserves decision making for himself. Highly effective at first, such centralized decision making defeats the purpose of delegation. (iv) The leader uses intuitive action to solve problems, and can be supported only by a limited number of people who can follow his spontaneous moves. Once the organization enlarges, such action is increasingly difficult and costly to sustain. (v) The leader uses personalized organization to achieve results. In a new organization, there is always so much work to be done that strong individuals can perform much unrelated work. With the introduction of new individuals, however, problems of overlapping, duplication, and frustration result. (vi) The leader conveys his ideas in one-way communication with his group. Initially, this action is necessary and often effective; past a point, however, it blocks understanding between the leader and the members of his group. (vii) The leader controls the group by personal inspection. Initially, mistakes are caught quickly and corrected; later, this method minimizes initiative, creative thinking, spontaneity, and enthusiasm.

(c) Leadership force is the active power used by a leader to secure desired results. The greater the difference among the objectives of the individuals in a group, the greater will be the leadership force required to enforce cohesive action.

(d) The action taken by the leader in the spontaneous centric stage usually forces him into the cenrad transition. He either begins to fail in his leadership position, or he begins the transition from the spontaneous centric mode to the rational radic mode. The need for this transition is marked by definite characteristics exhibited by the group. People become dissatisfied; innovation decreases; the organization proliferates; there is increased expense for lower productivity; bureaucracy is created.

(e) The rational radic leader can be recognized by the following seven characteristics. (i) He develops group objectives so his actions will produce maximum returns. (ii) He specializes in the management functions of planning, organizing, leading, and controlling to maximize his own efforts through the efforts of others. (iii) He delegates responsibility and authority to his subordinates to gather greater satisfaction and rewards for himself and the members of his group. (iv) He logically plans his actions to deal better with the future and help those with whom he works to understand his objectives and to contribute more effectively to the group objectives. (v) He logically arranges and groups the work to be performed to establish a rational organization. This satisfies the basic territorial drives of all members of his group. (vi) He establishes two-way communication for better understanding in the group. (vii) He sets limits so that he can exert maximum control with minimum effort.

(f) The management leader has the ability to move at will from one mode to another to meet identified needs. This ability to exercise the omnimode and to recognize its worth is the mark of the true management professional.

4. THE WORK OF THE PROFESSIONAL MANAGER

Managers frequently fail to measure up to their true potential because they diffuse their energies in work that others could better do for them. How can a manager determine how best to allocate his effort? First, he needs to know what work he should be doing. To identify this, we establish that a manager has a unique organizational position. He has four interfaces which so place him organizationally that only he can have the objectivity, perspective, and balance to satisfy the varying and sometimes conflicting needs of his subordinates, peers, and superior. We can see this in Fig. 4.1.

Logically, we would expect the manager to accomplish his objective of securing results through and with others by performing that work which others cannot do for him. Because of his position, he must think through and develop understanding of his own role as related to that of others with whom he works—subordinates, peers, staff groups, and his own superior. We conclude, then, that his work should consist largely of doing those things that his subordinates do not have perspective or objectivity to do for themselves.

This, however, is only one side of the coin. For while the manager is a leader in that he has other people reporting to him, we must remember that, in turn, he reports to his superior. Thus, he is also a follower—a member of somebody else's team. Not only this, but he also has other managers on his own level—his peers—with whom he must maintain effective working relationships if he is to get his job done.

44

This multiple role can bring a host of opposing forces into play. If he wants to be an effective follower, a manager's first loyalty must be to his own superior and to others on his own level. Yet, often as not, all these people will have interests at variance with those of his own subordinates. This fact illustrates why we have a man in the middle at all. He is needed to reconcile the interest of his subordinates and his superior; he is the catalyst that makes teamwork possible between two separated organizational levels and he fulfils his role as a catalyst by performing the work that only he can do—the work that neither his boss nor his subordinates are organizationally placed to perform for themselves.

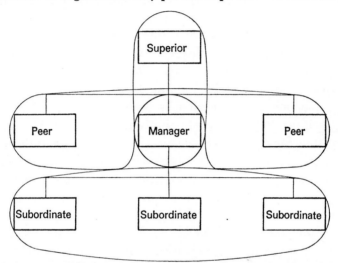

Fig. 4.1 Multiple interfaces of the manager. Only he has overall objectivity with relation to positions of subordinates, peers, and superior.

THE WORK OF THE PROFESSIONAL MANAGER

Determining the work he *should* perform is the first important task of a manager. He may already have a list of responsibilities or a job description. His salary, in fact, may be based on a comparison and evaluation of his job with those of others. He may have kept a time diary and know precisely how he spends each of his hours on the job. While these approaches are commonly used, they fail in their most important purpose because they establish what he *is* doing, not what he *should* do. Since a manager tends to spend large parts of his time and effort on his least important tasks, it is obvious that the first step in making most effective use of his time is to establish, with clear and verifiable logic, the important responsibilities he should have.

45

We can study management in an orderly and rational fashion only if we organize our information in a logical way. Applied to the work a manager performs, this means that he should have some system for dividing the work that he does into categories which can be precisely defined. To the extent he uses the same system of classification used by other managers— both within and outside his organization—he can compare his work with theirs.

The sciences and other disciplines have also experienced this classification problem. From the days of Aristotle, attempts were made to classify the million or more different types of plants and animals. An acceptable taxonomy appeared only after Linnaeus abandoned arbitrary choice and developed a classification based on identifying the unique characteristics which distinguish each category.

Classification of categories ranging from chemicals, cells, atomic particles, and proteins to personality types and neuroses has been an indispensable first step in systematic study and analysis and has provided the foundation for exponential advances in technology and the sciences. However, this foundation has not been laid for management. We lack a system for sorting, categorizing, labelling, and defining new and old management information. A commonly understood classification of management work is a tool which will prove indispensable to the progress of the management profession. Such a taxonomy will facilitate the communication and dissemination of new management knowledge and will provide the basis for a logical definition of management terms.

A system of classification for the work of management offers great benefits. It would enable managers to compare their jobs with others and, thus, to make sure they are doing all the important work they should. If we used such a system, it would quickly enable us to understand new advances and improvements in management and, because we were working in similar terms, to use them with confidence and precision. Such a system would enable us to sort out our thinking so we could come to focus on the critical responsibilities which a manager must master if he is to manage professionally.

The need for a commonly understood taxonomy is highlighted by a large department store chain, which initiated a management by objectives programme. Store managers worked with headquarters staff to develop comprehensive annual objectives, which were neatly typed and placed in folders. At the end of the first year, the regional managers conducted reviews with their store managers about their reported results. In each case, the review failed because the changing economic and market conditions made it too difficult to hold store managers accountable for commitments made a year earlier and, in most cases, the managers had not been able to find enough money in their budgets to achieve their objectives. Management of the chain, accepting the common interpretation that setting objectives was enough to manage by, had failed to recognize that no objective is better than the programme, schedule, and budget necessary to carry it out—a fact which any logical analysis and classification of management work would clearly establish.

THE LOGIC THEME FOR THE CLASSIFICATION

In an attempt to satisfy this need, we have developed a taxonomy of work which establishes categories based on the essential characteristics of management work. The logic theme used to identify this work has four steps: (a) Determine the objective, the result to be accomplished through the work that is done. (b) Identify the largest categories of work that must be performed to achieve the objective. (c) Define each category of work in the clearest, most simple terms possible. (d) Select a suitable semantic label for each category.

In developing this logic, we have established two standards: (a) The work in each category will have a common objective. (b) Work assigned to any category will be more closely related to the other kinds of work in that category than to work in any other category at the same level of the hierarchy.

THE HIERARCHY FOR MANAGEMENT WORK

Work is performed in bewildering variety. To bring order to this universe, a graded series of groupings of progressively smaller compass is needed to segregate one kind from another. We first developed a hierarchy for management work in 1957.[8] A more complete set of categories based on later experience is as follows:

Class
Order
Function
Activity
Segment
Element

These categories appear to be ample for the complete classification of work.[9] Experience indicates that 80 per cent, or more, of all taxonomic allusions will be listed under the function and activity categories.

CLASSES OF WORK

Using the classification technique, we define work as the application of energy to accomplish objectives. The objective of work is to apply energy to change the nature or condition of things so as to accomplish desired objectives.

We determine the primary categories of work through analysis of the ways in which energy can be applied to cause these changes to occur. We can identify a number of classes of work, such as mechanical work, electrical work, chemical work, genetic work, and human work. We will not attempt, here, to develop these further because our concern is to establish a framework for management work, which is an order within the class of human work, as in Fig. 4.2.

CLASS	ORDER
Mechanical work	
Human work	Management work
	Technical work
etc.	

Fig. 4.2 Classes and orders. The class of human work subdivides into the orders of management and technical work.

ORDERS OF HUMAN WORK

Human work is the application of a person's mental and physical effort to achieve objectives. Following our logic, the objective of human work is to achieve results through the application of mental and physical effort. There are a number of possible breakdowns of human work, but the most useful and realistic recognizes a salient fact about human work that is central to our understanding of management: humans secure results in two ways—directly through their own efforts and indirectly through the efforts of others. If this is accepted as a suitable basis for the next subdivision of human work, then two orders of human work can be identified, defined, and labelled: technical work and management work.

48

Technical work is the direct application of physical and mental effort to resources, to secure results by the person doing the work. It can be performed with or without the direct aid of a machine, just as mechanical work can be performed with or without the direct intervention of humans. Management work is the application of physical and mental effort by a person in a leadership position to secure results through *other* people.

FUNCTIONS OF MANAGEMENT WORK

Our next step is to subdivide the order of management work into its functions. See Fig. 4.3. Using our logic theme, the objective of management work by a person in a leadership position is to secure results through other people by the application of physical and mental effort. The largest categories of work which a person in a leadership position must apply to secure results through other people could be determined by subdividing on such bases as the required skills, the characteristics of the work, or of the materials and tools used. However, none of these is definitive. The very clear, differentiating factor, and the basis for the classification logic, is that the position of the manager has certain unique characteristics which set it apart from others and give him perspective and objectivity with regard to the needs and objectives of his subordinates and the group as a whole. He is the communications channel and transfer point between his subordinates and his own superiors.

The following are the four functions defined as the major categories of work necessary to achieve the overall objectives of management work. The planning function is the work a manager performs to predetermine a course of action to be followed. The organizing function is the work a manager performs to arrange and relate the work to be done. The leading function[10] is the work a manager performs to influence people to act to accomplish objectives. The controlling function is the work a manager performs to assess and regulate results.

AREAS OF DISAGREEMENT ABOUT FUNCTIONS

Other investigators and writers agree substantially on the planning, organizing, and controlling functions, as defined, which follows from the basic work of Henri Fayol. There is most disagreement on the nature of the leading function. The usual approach has been to identify two or more 'people' categories, such as 'staffing' and 'directing', or to overlap the category with the planning, organizing, or controlling functions. First developed in 1959, the leading function, as defined, seems to be as acceptable a 'people' category as any.[11] The important conclusion, in this case, is not the semantic label, but rather the work to be done and the objectives to be achieved.

Classes of Work (incomplete listing)
Chemical
Electrical
Genetic
Mechanical
Human
    Orders of Human Work
    Technical (see Figure 4.4)
    Management
        Functions of Management Work
        Planning
            Activities of Planning Function
            Forecasting
            Developing objectives
                Segments of Developing Objectives Activity
                Establishing key objectives
                Establishing critical objectives
                Establishing specific objectives
            Programming
            Scheduling
            Budgeting
            Developing procedures
            Developing policies
        Organizing
            Activities of Organizing Function
            Developing organization structure
                Segments of Developing Organization Structure Activity
                Establishing functional organization structure
                Establishing divisionalized organization structure
            Delegating
            Developing relationships
        Leading
            Activities of Leading Function
            Decision making
            Communicating
            Motivating
            Selecting people
            Developing people
        Controlling
            Activities of Controlling Function
            Developing performance standards
            Measuring performance
            Evaluating performance
            Correcting performance

Fig. 4.3 A taxonomy of management work. This shows five of the categories for classifying management work: classes, orders, functions, activities, segments.

Coordination has been suggested as another function of management work. However, every act that can be labelled a coordination function constitutes identifiable parts of the planning, organizing, leading, or controlling functions. Therefore, we can conclude that coordination is the act of timing, integrating, and unifying by performing some, or all, the work of management.

There has been much disagreement about the separate identity of planning and controlling. Some feel that they are part of the same function. However, the distinction in management work is the same as that in the genetic work of the cell; the application of energy necessary to determine purpose is different from the application of energy necessary to regulate the action taken to achieve that purpose; therefore, we conclude that planning and controlling are different functions.

A number of authors have concluded that some functions of management work are continuous; in particular, that deciding and communicating are parts of all the other functions. While deciding and communicating are performed in concert with other functions, they are no more 'continuous functions' than is pharmacology a 'continuous discipline' because drugs are used in obstetrics, gynaecology, surgery, anaesthetics, and other fields of medicine. In fact, if decision making and communicating are continuous, then, to a substantial degree, so are all the functions and activities.

For example, a manager motivates, selects, and develops people to do the work of forecasting, budgeting, delegating, measuring performance and other activities; relationships must be established if people are to work effectively together. A manager plans when he organizes, leads, and controls; he controls when he plans, organizes, and leads. In a similar sense, chemistry is not part of biology because the biologists use chemicals, nor is chemistry continuous with biology for the same reason.

ACTIVITIES OF THE PLANNING FUNCTION

The objective of planning function is to predetermine a course of action to be followed. The planning function has been subdivided into activities by establishing the largest categories of work that must be performed to predetermine a course of action. Ambiguities arise in developing the logic theme, for everything that takes place before action occurs could be considered planning. Thus, organizing and much of leading could also be planning. The distinction lies in the phrase 'to be followed'. Planning is not for any action, only goal-seeking action we commit ourselves to follow. The skills required for planning do not differentiate it from the other functions; its *objectives* do. Using our logic theme, all work that must be done to predetermine the course of action to be followed should be grouped as planning.

This grouping develops seven activities necessary to accomplish the objective of the planning function. Forecasting is the work a manager performs to estimate and predict future conditions and events. Developing objectives is the work a manager performs to establish the results to be achieved. Programming is the work a manager performs to determine the action steps necessary to achieve the results. Scheduling is the work a manager performs to determine the time required to accomplish the action steps. Budgeting is the work a manager performs to allocate the resources necessary to carry out the steps within the time limits and so achieve the desired results. Developing procedures is the work a manager performs to standardize the work that must be performed uniformly if the objectives are to be achieved. Developing policies is the work a manager performs to establish standing decisions to apply to repetitive questions and problems that arise in the accomplishment of objectives.

Attempts to apply a rigorous logic to the planning process in recent years tend to corroborate this analysis. PERT (Programme Evaluation Review Technique) varies primarily in semantics, using 'event' for 'objective', 'activity' for 'programme', 'activity time' for 'schedule' and 'PERT/cost' for 'budget'. PPSB, or the Programme Planning System of Budgeting, also follows a similar logic, varying primarily in semantics.

ACTIVITIES OF THE ORGANIZING FUNCTION

The objective of the organizing function is to arrange and relate the work to be performed so that it can be accomplished most effectively by people. The logic theme differentiates between the arrangement and relation of the work and the motivation of the people who do the work, in the same manner that medicine differentiates between the doctor who deals with physical problems and the one who is primarily concerned with mental and emotional maladies. The logic also differentiates between organization positions and the incumbents of these positions, a distinction as vital as that between a car as a vehicle and its driver as a person.

We can establish three major categories of work as activities of organizing. The developing organization structure activity is the work

52

a manager performs to identify and group the work to be performed so it can be accomplished most effectively by people. The delegating activity is the work a manager performs to entrust responsibility and authority to others and to establish accountability for results. The developing relationships activity is the work a manager performs to establish the conditions necessary for mutually cooperative efforts of people.

ACTIVITIES OF THE LEADING FUNCTION

The objective of the leading function is to influence people to take action to accomplish plans. Using our classification logic, we establish five activities. The decision-making activity is the work a manager performs to make the decisions necessary for people to act. The communicating activity is the work a manager performs to create understanding among people so that they can act effectively. The motivating activity is the work a manager performs to inspire, encourage, and impel people to act. The selecting people activity is the work a manager performs to find and choose people who are to take action. The developing people activity is the work a manager performs to help people improve knowledge, attitudes, and skills so that they can act most effectively. These activities of leading are based on management work which is done primarily in relationship with the people who are to act, and which requires a personal interface to be performed effectively.

ACTIVITIES OF THE CONTROLLING FUNCTION

The objective of the controlling function is to ensure that the predetermined course of action is carried out and subsequently improved. Four activities are identified. The developing performance standards activity is the work performed by the manager to establish the criteria by which work and results are measured. The measuring performance activity is the work performed by the manager to record and report performance and results. The evaluating performance activity is the work performed by the manager to assess performance and results. The correcting performance activity is the work performed by the manager to rectify and improve performance and results.

SEGMENTS

Only two activities, as yet, have been subdivided into meaningful segments. The first segments are subdivisions of the developing objectives activity of the planning function. The second consists of the subdivisions of the developing organization structure activity of the organizing function.

SEGMENTS OF THE DEVELOPING OBJECTIVES ACTIVITY

The objective of the developing objectives activity of the planning function is to establish the results to be accomplished. We can subdivide this activity into three segments. The establishing key objectives segment is the work the manager performs to establish the primary, continuing results which the enterprise is organized to accomplish and which determine its nature and purpose. The establishing critical objectives segment is the work the manager performs to determine the most important, continuing results that must be accomplished to achieve the key objectives. The establishing specific objectives segment is the work a manager performs to determine the measurable, time-limited results which must be accomplished if the critical objectives are to be reached.

SEGMENTS OF THE DEVELOPING ORGANIZATION STRUCTURE ACTIVITY

The objective of the developing organization structure activity is to identify and group the areas of work to be performed so that they can be accomplished most effectively by people. We can establish two subdivisions of the work necessary to achieve this objective.

The first segment, establishing functional organization structure, is the work a manager performs to identify and group the work to be performed in terms of the nature of the work itself. The second segment, establishing divisionalized organization structure, is the work a manager performs to identify and group the work to be performed in terms of the end results to be achieved by the work.

CLASSIFICATION OF TECHNICAL WORK

Management work cannot exist of itself; it must be the planning, leading, organizing, and controlling of other work. A manager works so that he may help others. A man operating an extrusion press produces toothpaste tubes which are end products of value in themselves; a teacher helping a student to master calculus helps produce a mathematical skill which also has its own intrinsic value. On the other hand, a manager who does the work necessary to plan, organize, lead, and control the

54

efforts of a dozen extrusion press operators, or, one who manages the teaching staff of a university, works so that others may achieve the end result. Technical work is specialized work applied to secure results directly from resources.

FUNCTIONS OF TECHNICAL WORK

Technical work does not subdivide in the consistent pattern that is true of management work. Some functions of technical work, especially those in formalized sciences or professions, can be classified in near-universal terms wherever practised. For example, the medical services function will have such similar activities as surgery, obstetrics, paediatrics, radiology, pathology, and pharmacology in virtually every part of the world. However, the classification of most functions of technical work varies from one country to another and even among different types of enterprises or within the same enterprise in the same country. As a case in point, subdivision of the marketing function of technical work depends on such factors as technology and culture; for example, market research, advertising, market forecasting, sales service and distribution are common activities of the marketing function in the United States, but the breakdown is quite different in Russia and Britain. Again, the purchasing function of technical work tends to have different activities in a city school system compared with a steel mill or a religious institution. Research as a function of technical work has a different breakdown in governmental health care services, contrasted with a university, a large chemical company, or a research institution. In fact, the classification of technical functions can vary, even within different parts of the same organization. To illustrate, the buying function in a large merchandising group has different activities in the shoe, ladies' fashion, and menswear departments of the same group.

VARIATIONS IN TECHNICAL WORK CATEGORIES

Much of this variation in technical work categories is haphazard and even illogical. It has been built on the strong personalities of outstanding individuals and continues to be viable only because of the compensating strengths of the people involved. A major opportunity for improved efficiency, reduced costs, and more human use of human beings lies in recognizing the essential logic of these work processes and in establishing a rational pattern through proper classification. Since technical work does not follow a standardized format, a classification must be developed for each enterprise. This can be accomplished by following the technique used to classify management work.

To illustrate, the key objective of the Universal Company is to build a growing, profitable and progressive business in the development, manufacturing and marketing of speciality chemicals for chemical processing industries throughout the world. Using the logic theme to identify the primary categories of work necessary to accomplish this objective, we determine the three functions of technical work. The research and development function is the work necessary to discover,

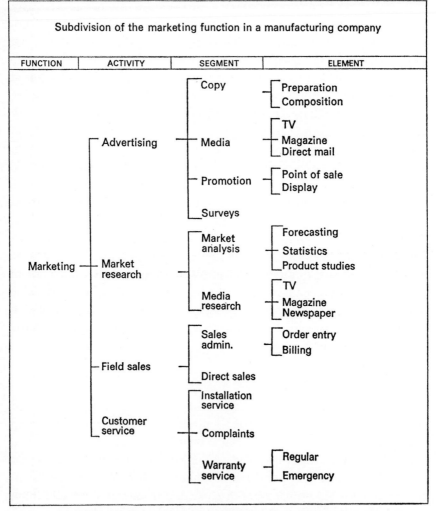

Fig. 4.4 Classification of technical work. This chart shows the subdivision of the marketing function in a manufacturing company.

create, and improve speciality chemicals. The manufacturing function is work necessary to convert raw materials into saleable products. The marketing function is the work necessary to find potentially profitable customers, persuade them to buy, and service the sale to ensure satisfaction. The classification is continued until the final category is identified and defined. Figure 4.4 shows the subdivision of the marketing function in a manufacturing company.

WORK CLASSIFICATION FOR THE IDEAL ORGANIZATION

The classification developed in this logical fashion will tend to differ from that used in practice. Most likely, the organization that is in force has evolved haphazardly around strong personalities. Classification in terms of our rigorous logic results in an ideal organization which can be used as a standard with which to compare an organization which actually exists.

Differences between the ideal and the actual, point to variances which are potential sources of unnecessary expense, personal friction, human inefficiency and dissatisfaction. Sound practice indicates that careful change of the existing organization towards the ideal will both stabilize and improve the entire basis for operation.

THE PRINCIPLE OF ORGANIZATION LEVELS

A manager at the first supervisory level has minimum opportunity to delegate management work because his subordinates are technicians and are not expected to be proficient in management skills. Also, as we have noted, if his subordinates are not skilled in the work they should be doing, the manager usually ends up by doing it himself. This can be stated as a principle:

PRINCIPLE OF
ORGANIZATION LEVELS

The lower his organization level, the more technical work a manager tends to perform

At successively higher organization levels, a manager is primarily concerned with managing other managers. He has increased opportunity to delegate management work to subordinate managers, and also has available a broad range of staff services. In consequence, the higher his organization level, the more of his total time a manager is expected to devote to purely management work.

At top levels, the chief executive ideally should devote at least 90 per cent of his time to management duties and no more than 10 per cent to technical work. As shown in Fig. 4.5, foremen at the first level of supervision ideally should devote no more than 50 per cent of their time to technical work and the other half to managing. Here, we see the difference between the ideal and actual performance of management work. At top levels, managers typically spend 50 per cent or less of their time and effort managing, where, ideally, they should be spending 90 per cent. At successively lower levels the percentage diminishes until at the first line of supervision the typical foreman will be spending no more than 10 per cent of his time managing, whereas, ideally, he should be spending 50 per cent.

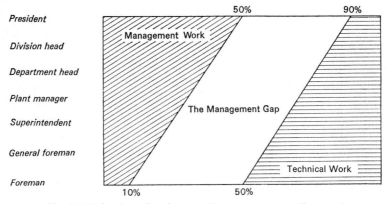

Fig. 4.5 Ideal and actual performance. The management gap illustrates the difference between ideal and actual performance of management work.

This difference between what *can* be achieved and what actually happens is the management gap. Usually, it is fairly consistent from top to bottom. It can be corrected only when managers at each level, starting at the top, concentrate on the management work they should be performing and build a strong organization to which they delegate full responsibility and authority for technical work.

VARYING PROPORTIONS OF TECHNICAL AND MANAGEMENT WORK

The amount of technical work a manager performs varies with the situation. When he is new to the job and uncertain of his own capabilities and those of his subordinates, the manager tends to do some technical work to make sure it is performed properly. When a new subordinate joins the team, the manager tends to take over parts of his job, giving up the responsibility and authority as the subordinate shows the requisite competence to assume it.

In building his team, the manager trains and develops his people; he counsels and coaches them so they can assume more and more of the technical burden. As the work changes, as people come and go, as emergencies arise, the manager may take back temporarily some of the technical work he has delegated. There is always the danger that he will retain it unless he keeps in mind the need to renew his concentration on management work. This requires unending vigilance and self-discipline, but is the surest path to outstanding management performance.

TRANSITION FROM TECHNICAL TO MANAGEMENT EMPHASIS

Often, the realization that there is a difference between management and technical work is a revelation. Once he sees the need for change, however, the manager must recognize that the shift in emphasis takes time. Most managers require a minimum of three to seven years to master management skills, to build a strong team that will assume the proper share of the operating load, and to develop sound managerial relationships with their superiors, others on their own level, and staff agencies. During this interim, an appropriate and workable balance must be maintained. While this transition is being effected, it may be necessary to place major emphasis on technical results. Delegation of technical work will proceed slowly, but it must be pursued relentlessly. Understanding and discipline are mandatory, but the mastery of true professional competence in management is well worth the effort.

THE PRINCIPLE OF MANAGEMENT RESULTS

The primary concern of every manager should be the performance of the management work assigned to his position. To the extent that he concentrates on management *per se*, the manager can multiply his results by what he can get others to do for him. What is more, by confining himself as largely as possible to the work he should be doing, he avoids the temptation to perform his subordinates' work for them. As a result, they are called on to undertake important and challenging activities of responsibility and authority and not merely perform detail and routine. This, in itself, is the most potent source of deep and enduring job satisfaction. We can state this as a fundamental truth which will apply in all situations as follows.

<table>
<tr><td>PRINCIPLE OF
MANAGEMENT
RESULTS</td><td>*A person in a leadership position tends to secure most effective results through and with others by performing the management work of planning, organizing, leading, and controlling*</td></tr>
</table>

Carrying this principle to its logical conclusion, the primary concern of management development and education should be to improve the abilities of managers to plan, organize, lead, and control. Managers should be compensated for performing these kinds of work.

THE PRINCIPLE OF TECHNICAL PRIORITY

Management work is largely mental; it requires concentration. Most people prefer to do things, rather than think about them. Technical work is largely doing, while *thinking* is the essence of management.

A manager will tend to give priority to technical work for clear-cut reasons. Since he has usually come up through a technical specialism, he is more familiar with the technical work, and more comfortable with it. Often, he is more expert in it and becomes impatient with the mistakes of his subordinates. When he does the work himself, he can be sure it meets his standards. The following principle summarizes this tendency.

<table>
<tr><td>PRINCIPLE OF
TECHNICAL
PRIORITY</td><td>*When called upon to perform management work and technical work during the same time period, a manager will tend to give first priority to technical work*</td></tr>
</table>

The nature of the operation influences the amount of technical work the manager does. The more specialized it is, the more likely the manager is to act as a master craftsman in some respects and personally handle the most difficult technical problems and assignments. However, the manager often does this by choice rather than necessity, because he lacks faith in his people. This may cause him to overlook the fact that his subordinates have the necessary background or training and need only an opportunity to learn how to handle the really difficult jobs themselves.

In writing position descriptions for managers, the technical work a manager is expected to perform himself should be clearly specified and differentiated from the technical work he delegates.

In the following excerpt from a field sales manager's position description, for example, the manager himself is required to handle governmental and institutional key accounts; this is his reserved technical selling work. All other field selling, however, he is required to delegate.

| KEY ACCOUNT SALES | *Sell to designated key governmental and institutional accounts (reserved)* |
| FIELD SALES | *Identify and contact potentially profitable customers, sell to satisfy their identified needs and follow up to ensure satisfaction (delegated)* |

If subordinates obviously are incapable of doing the technical work, it is up to the manager to see to it that they receive the necessary training and development. If he does not consciously discipline himself to perform management work, he will find that most of his time is devoted to technical work.

The amount of time and effort a manager devotes to management work in part depends on the standards and the personal example set by his own superior. If the superior appraises his subordinate's performance in terms of management results, management will receive prime emphasis. If technical proficiency is the basis of performance evaluation, non-management work will receive first attention. Thus, the importance given to management work—and the attendant organizational efficiency which results from proper emphasis on management work—is, in the end, the responsibility of top management.

SUMMARY

(a) The organizational position of the manager gives him unique objectivity, perspective and balance with regard to the needs of subordinates, peers and superiors. Because of this position, the manager is best placed to perform the specialized work of management.

(b) A taxonomy of work establishes categories into which all work can be divided. Management is an order of human work. It can be subdivided into functions, activities, segments, and other categories.

(c) Following the logic theme of identifying the objective to be achieved and then defining the primary categories of work necessary to accomplish that objective, four functions of management work can be identified and defined. Planning is the work a manager does to predetermine a course of action. It is made up of the activities of forecasting, developing objectives, programming, scheduling, budgeting, and developing policies and procedures. Organizing is the work a manager does to arrange and relate the work to be performed so it can be accomplished most effectively by people. Activities of organizing are developing organization structure, delegating, and developing relationships. Leading is the work a manager does to cause people to take action. The activities of leading are decision making, communicating, motivating, selecting and developing people. Controlling is the work a manager does to assess and regulate the work in process and the work completed. The activities are developing performance standards, measuring performance, evaluating performance and correcting performance.

(d) Technical work is non-management work which is applied directly to resources. Technical functions and subdivisions can be identified, but they are not universals as in the case of management work; they vary with different industries and in different countries.

(e) Several principles are stated to identify fundamental truths which apply to management and technical work. The principle of management results establishes that management effectiveness depends on performance of planning, organizing, leading, and controlling work. The principle of technical priority makes clear that a manager tends to give preference to technical over management work if he has a choice. He must strive continually—and should be encouraged by top management—to give proper emphasis to the performance of management work.

5. PLANNING WORK

Planning is a vital tool for any manager, for it is his means of commanding the future, rather than being commanded by it. Planning is the means of moving to the rational radic mode. When he plans, a manager thinks through with his subordinates the results that are most desirable, the action that has the greatest probability of accomplishing those results, the timing and the resources that will be needed. This not only improves the overall effectiveness of the action he takes, it also helps to involve people.

A sound plan both helps to coordinate action and serves as a basis for control. If we want to check on performance and results, there is no better standard than knowing what we set out to accomplish in the first place.

By a systematic approach to planning, a manager can ascertain the capabilities of his work force and utilize resources to accomplish the most desirable results. Most important, a sound plan is a means of ensuring that people continually address their major efforts to the most important work, rather than the least important, as is the spontaneous tendency.

WHY MANAGERS DON'T PLAN

In spite of its value, few managers are expert in planning. Those that are usually stand out. We don't plan because it requires thinking and we usually prefer to take spontaneous centric action, rather than go through the frustrating and demanding labour of moving to the rational mode.

63

Managers who begin planning with enthusiasm often fall by the wayside because their first attempts are uncertain and unproductive. They fail to realize that planning is complex mental work. A further problem is that there are few universal techniques in planning. Most managers hammer out an approach that works for them and find it extremely difficult to pass on their skill to others.

THE ACTIVITIES OF MANAGEMENT PLANNING

Management planning is made up of seven major activities: forecasting, developing objectives, programming, scheduling, budgeting, developing procedures, and developing policies. The characteristics and differences of these planning activities can be clearly established.

A forecast is an estimate or prediction of what will probably happen in the future. Based on the best data available, the forecast predicts the trend, event or situation that will have a good probability of occurring. The forecast says, 'This will probably happen.'

An objective is a commitment to achieve a result. It defines clearly what this result is to be and implies that the individual or the company has committed itself, in the sense that it is prepared to use the resources necessary to achieve the result. The objective says, 'We are committed to cause this to happen.'

A programme is the sequence of action steps necessary to achieve an objective. It states what is to be done. The programme uses resources of time, materials, tools and facilities, manpower and money. The programme states *what* will be done to cause the objective to happen.

A schedule is the time sequence necessary to carry out the programme steps. The schedule is determined by the programme, but is independent of it in that it can be changed without altering the programme.

A budget is an allocation of resources. The budget is usually stated in terms of money, a symbolical representation of the manpower, materials, tools, and facilities that must be used to carry out the programme within the constraints of the schedule, so as to accomplish the objective. The budget thus represents the cost of the objective.

A procedure specifies the way in which particular work is to be performed. The purpose of the procedure is to standardize the work so that everybody who performs it will do it in the same way. The procedure says, 'Do it this way.'

A policy is a directive to do something. It is a command from top management for all concerned to act in the manner specified by the policy statement. A policy does not spell out the end to be accomplished; it specifies a means of accomplishing this end. The policy says, 'You *shall* act in this way.' In this sense, policies are established only after objectives are defined.

The essential differences among the areas of planning which are most often confused can be readily identified in Fig. 5.1.

MANAGEMENT PLANNING ACTIVITY	Establishes	Involves Resources	Kind of Situation		Applicability to Enterprise	
			Repetitive	One -Time	All	Part
Forecasting	Probable happening			X	X	X
Developing objectives	Results to accomplish	X	X	X	X	X
Programming	Action steps	X		X	X	X
Scheduling	Time sequence for action steps	X		X	X	X
Budgeting	Resources required	X		X	X	X
Developing procedures	Standardization of work	X	X		X	X
Developing policies	Standing decisions	X	X		X	

Fig. 5.1 Management planning activities. This shows the commitment and consequences of each of the seven activities of the function of planning.

THE EVOLUTION OF PLANNING

The ability to plan is a cultural characteristic and subject to the evolutionary principles we have already described. Our teleological drive requires that we have a mental image of action before we can undertake it; therefore, in a sense, everybody plans because each person predetermines the action he will follow. However, as we have noted, there is a difference between spontaneous and rational predetermination of action and this distinction is operative in the evolution of planning.

Most planning is in the spontaneous centric mode. We react to a current problem or situation and move immediately to correct it, without thinking through the end results we really want. This spontaneous planning tends to be immediately successful; it is rewarding because it succeeds. Since it provides prompt rewards, we reiterate the

65

pattern until it becomes habitual. This can be beneficial if not overdone, for spontaneous planning is adequate for the greater part of our actions, because only 10 to 20 per cent of the things we do are critical in terms of the results that are important to us. If we think through and move logically to accomplish this 10 to 20 per cent, the larger number of less important results falls into line.

The vital need for every manager is to identify and then treat differently those areas in which carefully thought through results should be logically developed, and those areas in which action based on precedent, intuition, and common sense will be appropriate.

We have identified the typical characteristics of the spontaneous and rational modes of planning; these are discussed below.

THE SPONTANEOUS CENTRIC PLANNING MODE

When he is first called on to do planning work, a manager will act spontaneously and intuitively and in terms of his own special interests; he does not stop to predetermine the course of action he should follow, but his action is guided by the memories and lessons of previous experience stored in his subconscious. His teleological drive works constantly for him.

INTUITIVE

He is intuitive at this stage, but if he is dealing with problems in which he has a sound background and depth of experience, his subconscious serves him well and many of his choices and conclusions are outstanding.

CENTRALIZED

As for all spontaneous action, both advantages and disadvantages exist with this type of planning. Acting in the spontaneous centric mode, the planner centralizes in himself most authority for making planning decisions. In his own mind, he knows clearly what he wants to do. When one person can keep the total plan clearly and vividly in his own mind and require that all action be coordinated to achieve it, he can accomplish quick and substantial results with minimum overlap and wasted effort. To the extent he lets others make decisions for him, or subordinates his own deep convictions to permit others an opportunity to try out their own ideas, he weakens the main thrust. While in an older, matured

66

organization, this diffusion of effort may be an investment in human enrichment, in the new, young enterprise it can result in harmful diversion of limited energy and resources.

SHORT RANGE

During the spontaneous stage, the planner rarely thinks far ahead. The problems and conditions to which he reacts are almost always immediate obstacles that stand in the way of achieving the objectives he visualizes; short-range action is immediately effective. But, because this short-range planning breeds unexpected emergencies and crises, it becomes less and less effective in time.

THE NEED FOR TRANSITION

No matter how capable he may be, the planner who persists in the spontaneous mode eventually finds it difficult to do most of the planning and thinking for everybody else. As his organization grows, problems become broader in scope and more diversified, and it is increasingly difficult for him to keep abreast. Obsessed with the problems of the present, he has little time or energy to be concerned about the distant future.

As they continue to work for a spontaneous centric planner, people become dissatisfied. They may complain about the 'lack of opportunity', but what they really mean is that they have little chance to make their own plans and see them work out successfully.

If competition exists, it highlights the inadequacies of spontaneous centric planning. If most of the leaders in competing organizations shoot from the hip and do little thinking ahead, they all suffer common disadvantages. However, if one or more leaders begin to think logically about the future, if they analyse past experience to learn what lessons it can teach, and anticipate future needs, problems, and opportunities— if they plan logically and effectively—they will outshine competition. Rational planning moves ahead and takes competitive leadership with it.

To become professionals, managers must learn to change to the rational mode, progressing from rational centric to rational radic.

THE RATIONAL RADIC PLANNING MODE

Leaders learn to plan in the same way that they master other skills. It takes much time and effort to become a good planner. Just as no skill is learned simply by acquiring knowledge from a book, planning also demands continued application on the job. The rational radic planner can be identified by these characteristics.

LOGICAL

The manager who develops to become a professional in planning, supports his intuition and personal experience with logical, disciplined thinking. He thinks through the conditions under which he expects to operate in the future, determines what results he can reasonably expect to achieve, develops alternative courses of action which he appraises and assesses, and finally, chooses the alternative offering the greatest probability of success.

FORMALIZED

In the rational mode, the planner formalizes his approach by putting into writing his planning premises and the plans themselves. This facilitates communication; it also makes it more difficult to change his plans at whim. This encourages both stability and consistency, which are important if other people are to maintain confidence in the plans and to follow them.

DECENTRALIZED

The planner who uses the rational radic mode knows that his plans are only as good as the willingness and ability of other people to carry them out. He delegates authority both for the planning itself and for carrying out the plans to the people who are actually doing the work because people who are closer to the real problems understand them better. What is even more important, when people make their own planning decisions they develop an emotional ownership and generate real enthusiasm in making their plans work.

Although in the rational mode the planner tends to decentralize his planning, he also recognizes that he cannot simply let people do what they want. He provides reasonable limits and controls within which others can safely make and carry out their own plans.

LONG AND SHORT RANGE

The rational planner thinks ahead as far as he can project his ideas because, by anticipating future requirements, he can undertake immediate action with greater confidence and certainty.

Long-range plans are vital because they provide the framework within which people at the scene of action can make their own short-range plans with confidence and precision; but short-range plans are equally necessary because they ensure precise and well-coordinated action on the part of those who carry them out.

APPROPRIATE REWARDS FOR ALL INVOLVED

While the spontaneous planner secures greatest satisfaction for himself, the rational radic planner helps everybody involved to secure maximum satisfaction, both in making plans and in carrying them out. By establishing broad, long-range plans within which others can have great freedom in developing their own plans, the rational radic planner helps others to do more for themselves and, at the same time, he is ensuring, in terms of the principle of human reaction, that they will do more for him.

HOW TO MAKE THE TRANSITION FROM SPONTANEOUS CENTRIC TO RATIONAL RADIC PLANNING

Knowledge is a first requirement in making this transition, but it is equally important to convert knowledge to the necessary skills. This requires self-discipline, for old habits must be changed and new ones developed, together with continued application on the job, accompanied by careful audit of the work that is done and systematic coaching and review.

Since it is difficult to make a great leap forward, the best approach for a manager is to begin logical planning in the rational centric mode as close as possible to where he is now. He should start by projecting the definite results he wants to achieve in the immediate future—a day, week, or month. He should make these short-term objectives realistic so that he will have a high probability of achieving them and can secure the full understanding and agreement of those who will carry them out.

The manager must announce his plans so there will be a definite commitment and expectation. As results are achieved, he must make sure that those who carried out the plan are given recognition for their success. This will encourage repetition of the rewarding pattern and, if maintained, will help develop the rational radic mode.

As short-term plans are accomplished and the organization exhibits facility in their use, the time period should be extended to a monthly, quarterly, and annual basis, in that order, and then to three-, five-, ten-year, and longer periods.

As soon as skill is developed and the manager has amassed enough information to make longer-range projections, he must begin to think through long-term objectives. Although at first they will be tentative, objectives for three, five, and even ten years should be established at the first reasonable opportunity.

In making the transition to rational planning involving both short- and long-range considerations, a key requirement is to recognize the vital importance of adequate data about the past and the present. As a rule of thumb, we have found that a plan extending for one unit of time into the future requires a factual knowledge of three units of time in the past. For example, to establish a sound one-year budget, we should have validated information about similar budget items for at least three years in the past.

We have also discovered that there is a predictable pattern in the experience required to plan effectively. For each year we want to project into the future, we should be able to look back three years. Thus, to develop a one-year plan with confidence and reasonable precision, we need at least three years of past history on which to base it; for a ten-year plan, we should be able to review thirty years. Until we acquire the requisite background, our planning tends to be more tentative and changeable than will be the case later. Also, we need to work through at least one full cycle of any plan in order to be competent in its use. Thus, we must work through the first one-year plan before we can hope to master it. This may seem discouraging, but it is realistic. The pattern is summarized below:

	Hard data required for the past period of	Real competence to be expected only during
ONE-YEAR PLAN	3 years	2nd and successive years
THREE-YEAR PLAN	9 years	4th and successive years
FIVE-YEAR PLAN	15 years	6th and successive years
TEN-YEAR PLAN	30 years	11th and successive years

Even after a manager has moved solidly into the rational radic mode, he must keep in mind the need to shift to the rational centric when new people enter the group, when emergencies occur, or when environmental changes dictate a sudden shift in direction or emphasis. At times, people will grow slack in planning performance and the manager will be tempted to let them get by with substandard work. This is a time of trial. The manager must act in the rational centric mode to get the outstanding planning performance he needs from his subordinates.

He may counsel, coach, and secure participation as much as he can, but he must remember that his people look to him for satisfaction of their teleological and security drives and that he can best provide this by giving them firm guidelines, patient but unyielding insistence on high quality, and demand for the best they can offer. Their spontaneous centric tendency is to resist, and if the manager yields they will get transitory satisfaction. But he must remember that the only way to achieve the highest and best results over the long term is through rational planning, and, as the manager, he has the responsibility of seeing that it is maintained.

THE SCOPE OF PLANNING

In moving to the rational radic mode, an integrated structure of planning should be developed for the organization as a whole. Each level of management should do the planning work that only it can perform. The planning work done by any one manager should not duplicate or overlap unnecessarily the planning done by any other manager.

THE HIGHER THE LEVEL, THE BROADER THE SCOPE

Top levels of management, including the board of directors and chief executive, establish the rational radic pattern. They are so placed in the organization that they have the best perspective and objectivity for the overall needs of the company. Top managers with their staff agencies can best consider the total needs of all organization components and future opportunities for the entire organization.

Top-level plans require integration of all viewpoints, both internal and external. To be realistic, they should be based on the capabilities and requirements of lower operating levels. This means that enterprise planning proceeds best if top managers constantly have before them the tentative plans of lower levels, if they reconcile and integrate these with the needs of shareholders and the public, and finally, if they authorize the course of action best designed to satisfy all three groups and give purposeful guidance to the enterprise as a whole.

Because of its perspective, top management should devote most of its planning effort to long-range forecasts, objectives, budgets, and policies. Lower levels are most concerned with shorter-range objectives, programmes, schedules, procedures, and budgets. Because top levels of management plan further ahead, they plan more broadly and with more alternatives. When the time for commitment arrives, top executives and staff are most likely to narrow their choice to the alternative with greatest probability of success.

LONG-TERM AND SHORT-TERM PLANNING

The action we take now, greatly restricts our potential range of action in the future. To ensure that we have the latitude required for future action, it is important that we recognize the difference between long- and short-term planning. Long-term planning is sometimes called strategic planning and short term, tactical. The term 'strategy' has been used in so many contexts, usually undefined, that it has lost much of its meaning.

LONG TERM

A long-term plan looks as far ahead as possible and builds a picture of the desired end results. Once we know where we are going, the process of charting the intermediate steps is greatly simplified.

How far ahead should long-range plans be projected? This will differ with the type of enterprise. Some organizations can look ahead fifteen to twenty years, others find their sight blurs at a range of five to seven. A useful rule, here, is if the cost of carrying out a plan is justified by an anticipated economic return over a period of time, the decision involving the expenditure should be projected at least as far ahead as the period needed to secure that return. For example, if a company buys a new machine, it will be necessary to use that machine over a substantial number of years to justify the investment. In planning for the machine, it is, therefore, necessary to consider the full period involved. If the machine is likely to be outmoded when it is only half paid for, added thought should be given to shorten the period of payment, or to devise some other means of securing adequate return on the investment.

Consideration of long-term implications often puts a different perspective on short-term decisions. For example, a business enterprise may be able to save money immediately with the smallest possible investment in equipment and facilities and still satisfy its customers. But after five or ten years pass, this short-term saving may cost dearly.

SHORT TERM

A short-term plan determines what to do in the immediately prescribed future. Planning for tomorrow and next month differs in several respects from planning for three- or five-year periods. The short-range plan calls for immediate commitment of resources; if the organization is of any size, the plan sets in motion a series of events that is difficult to slow down or stop. Because it must be carried out in the near future, the short-term plan must be communicated effectively. People may operate efficiently with little knowledge of the five-year plan, but their spontaneous, intuitive teleological drive demands that they have clear understanding of what they are to do tomorrow and next week if they are to act effectively at all. The short-term plan must be more precise; it has relatively little flexibility, is generally difficult, and often expensive to change.

TRANSITION BETWEEN SHORT- AND LONG-TERM PLANS

Today has a habit of moving on and engulfing tomorrow. Short-term planning eats up long-term planning unless special provisions are made to advance the long-term plans as rapidly as the short-term ones are accomplished, and to effect a transition between the two. This is accomplished by reviewing long-range plans periodically, at least once or twice annually. At each review, the long-range plan is extended for the length of the review period. For example, if five-year plans are reviewed annually, each year the forecasts, objectives, programmes, and budgets are projected an additional year, while the short-term plans are also moved ahead one year. This rolling coverage ensures smooth transition from one planning phase to the next.

THE STEWARDSHIP CONCEPT OF PLANNING

The stewardship concept of planning requires each manager to be held fully accountable for his own component within the framework of the organization. He spends money for manpower, materials, facilities, and tools. He works to secure well-defined results which, in turn, make a measurable contribution to the attainment of overall objectives.

The stewardship concept requires that if he is to be accountable, the manager must act like a proprietor. Instead of looking to others to unify and integrate his plans, he takes the initiative in coordinating at his own level. Only after he is satisfied that he has done as much as he can, does he submit his completed plans to his superior for approval. Like any independent professional, he must show initiative and self-sufficiency in setting a course that will enable his people to move forward to their common goal with certainty and precision. He must be on the alert to spot roadblocks and to take advantage of the opportunities that present themselves. The stewardship concept is both challenging and rewarding. It helps the manager to focus his teleological drive on objectives that are personal and important to him.

PRINCIPLES OF PLANNING

Much can be learned from the experience and mistakes of others when undertaking planning work. The following principles summarize fundamental truths which every manager can apply with confidence.

THE PRINCIPLE OF PLANNING STABILITY

The further we project a plan into the future, the more uncertain we are of accomplishing it in exactly the way we stated it. Changing conditions may require us to modify our objectives, as well as programmes, schedules, and budgets. Since most long-range planning is done at top levels, this demands flexibility at the point where it is most difficult to achieve.

PRINCIPLE OF
PLANNING STABILITY

The stability of a plan tends to vary inversely with its extension

The further ahead we project our plans, the more generalized, less detailed and specific they should be. This sets up difficulties at once. We satisfy our teleological drive with short-term, concrete, and tangible plans; generalized, intangible, and long-term ones can create tension and frustration. This can be overcome by providing very specific and concrete short-term plans which will support the long-term plan and help people secure the teleological satisfaction they seek. Coordination of short- and long-term plans is vital. If the future is so uncertain that it seems impractical to set a specific plan for as little as a year, it may be better to develop several alternative, but very concrete plans rather than let everything hang in the air.

One diversified manufacturing company uses this principle by preparing three budget alternatives to anticipate future unpredictables in the major cost elements of its budget. The working budget is predicated on the continuance of existing trends. The budget alternatives allocate expenditures in terms of potential maximum and minimum levels of business, such as a 10 per cent loss or a 12 per cent improvement in sales revenue. The budget alternatives go into substantial detail on such critical items as personnel, maintenance, inventories, engineering, and salaries. The company finds this allows it to think through contingencies such as a recession or a sudden spurt of business at a time when the basic decisions can be made without pressure for sudden or impulsive action.

THE PRINCIPLE OF PRESENT CHOICES

The plans and decisions we make today restrict our potential. For example, the quality and type of people we select today will largely determine the kind of company we will have in the future. The product plans we make now determine the markets we can enter next year. Because the planning decisions we make have such long-range implications, it is important that they be made in context. Before we decide what action we will carry out tomorrow, we must determine whether that action will help or hinder our overall progress.

PRINCIPLE OF PRESENT CHOICES	*Current decisions tend to limit future action*

Failure to understand this principle can often lead to disaster. In periods of recession, for example, many companies first slash advertising budgets as an easy way to reduce costs. Historically, the data show that those who cut their budgets are the first to lose position when customer demand picks up, as it inevitably does. Those that hold to their advertising commitment are often in the best position to ride the crest when the tide turns and sales improve.

THE PRINCIPLE OF POSITIVE ACTION

The best way we know to achieve what we want to happen is to identify clearly the end results we want to reach and to take one small step after another until we reach our objective. To master the future, we need to make sound plans now and carry them out as if they could not fail. This is contrary to action in the spontaneous mode, which yields short-term results by taking advantage of opportunities as they happen. Sticking doggedly to a predetermined objective which offers the probability of greater long-term rewards pays off, although it requires greater tenacity and discipline.

| PRINCIPLE OF POSITIVE ACTION | *The probability of a future event occurring tends to increase as effort is applied systematically towards its realization* |

If the objective being sought is tangible and specific, the teleological drive supports this principle. It is important to make the first steps successful, as this reinforces the action and will help maintain momentum in spite of temporary setbacks.

THE PRINCIPLE OF COMMENSURATE EFFORT

Many a manager, in reviewing his day's efforts, finds that he has expended pounds of effort to accomplish ounces of results. This can be true in all areas. If costs are unreasonably high, we may concentrate on conserving paper clips and overtime when we could achieve fifty times the savings by eliminating unnecessary positions. We may undertake an expensive accident prevention campaign in all units of the company when personal attention to a few accident-prone people would give us better results at a fraction of the cost.

| PRINCIPLE OF COMMENSURATE EFFORT | *Effort applied should be commensurate with the results desired* |

As a case in point, a parts distributor with several hundred branches and offices decided to automate mail handling as a means of cutting costs. The initial plan called for the purchase of 300 automated postage meters, letter openers, and sorters. When the value of the objective was costed out, it was discovered that it would take seven years to recover the cost of the automated equipment. With the principle of commensurate effort in mind, a study was made of the minimum requirements warranting capital investment for new equipment. This showed that automation was impractical for locations that scheduled less than twelve hours weekly in mail handling. This eliminated 220 branches and offices from the automation programme. Varying investments were then calculated for different savings potentials, with the result that those locations handling more than 2000 pieces weekly bought automatic meters and openers, but only those handling 15 000 pieces or more weekly installed full automation. These investments were fully justified by the savings.

THE PRINCIPLE OF RESISTANCE TO CHANGE

People resist change. However, if the change is gradual and only slightly different from what they are doing now, the resistance will be minimal. Radical changes give rise to greatest resistance, for they require us to abandon what we know and have accepted. This thwarts our teleological and structural drives and calls into play the security drive. If we want to minimize resistance to our plans, we should design them so that new plans can fill the void at the rate at which people can understand and accept them.

PRINCIPLE OF RESISTANCE TO CHANGE	*The greater the departure of planned changes from accepted ways, the greater the potential resistance by the people involved*

Resistance to change can be minimized through effective communication and by giving people an opportunity to participate in making the decisions that lead to changes. If we want things to proceed smoothly, we should follow the rule that the greater the changes to be made, the more effort must be devoted to communication and participation. Whenever possible, when making changes, we start where people are now and change only at the rate that they can understand and accept.

TYPES OF OBJECTIVES

The teleological drive is the application of energy which causes us to develop an objective before we act. Since objectives must be formed before action can take place, it is helpful to know the different types of objectives and how they influence the action that occurs.

SUBCONSCIOUS

Subconscious objectives are normal and natural; based on our stored memories and experience, they are spontaneous, centric, and emotional responses to a problem or situation, but they are not very useful guides to purposeful action unless they are translated into specific verbal, graphic, or physical representations of the results to be achieved.

VERBAL

A verbal description of the objective is more useful, but since the verbal description depends on memory, its effectiveness deteriorates. For example, if our objective is to earn promotion to a better job, we might tell someone, 'We're going to work for a better job as a department head,' and describe in detail what kind of job we want. Within a week the picture is blurred, because the ability to use words as objectives depends on how precisely we can translate the words into something that can be seen, touched, and measured.

GRAPHIC

We can best visualize the results we want to achieve in the form of physical objects which can be seen or touched. The physical representation serves as the best objective because it provides, in complete detail, the result we want to achieve. It requires no translation of verbal symbols, no exercise of the imagination.

EFFECTIVENESS OF TYPES OF OBJECTIVE

The difference in effectiveness among the various types of objective is emphasized in the field theory work carried out by the psychologist, Kurt Lewin. His conclusions, rooted in fundamental reinforcement theory, provide practical management applications. Lewin[12] points out that the objective which a person strives for and its achievement are two distinct entities. No matter how much a person may desire to achieve an objective, it is not reached until the steps necessary to accomplish it are completed. An objective is effective to the degree it prompts fast and effective action. Verbal and graphic representations, Lewin says, though more desirable than vague and subconscious feelings, may not be valid indicators of objectives or the means of achieving them, because their sense may vary from situation to situation or person to person. Through the graduated continuum of imagined to verbal to graphic forms, these two concepts of objective and achievement converge more and more on each other, with a material representation the most effective in final integration of goal and achievement. Lewin cautions against abstract or weak representations of desired objectives, stressing that the aspiration to achieve them can deteriorate unless the objective is quickly reached.

We can conclude that the better we are able to translate our personal objectives into material objects, or into representations of material objects which we know from first-hand experience, the more effective those material things will be in motivating us towards fulfilment of the objectives.

THE PRINCIPLE OF TANGIBILITY

This characteristic of the teleological drive makes clear the conditions for successful action of any kind. We relate this to the process concept of human drives and state it as a principle as follows.

PRINCIPLE OF TANGIBILITY
The more tangible an objective, the more direct and specific the effort to achieve it tends to be

In making use of this principle, the important requirement is to convert objectives, whenever possible, into statements related to tangible and material *things*, rather than intangible *ideas*. For example, an objective, 'to be profitable' is useful only when it is finally related to such concrete things as '£100 000 increase in sales volume per month', or '34 new Class B accounts per quarter', or '15 per cent reduction in travel expense'. This points to the necessity of culminating any system of objectives in a statement of the tangible, measurable results desired. We will keep this very much in mind as we set about the development of objectives in the next chapter.

SUMMARY

Planning enables a manager to command the future, rather than be commanded by it.

(a) The function of planning is made up of the seven activities of forecasting, developing objectives, programming, scheduling, budgeting, developing procedures, and developing policies. All these must be performed for complete and adequate management planning.

(b) The practice of planning evolves in keeping with other management work. The spontaneous planning modes are effective in the short term and for small, young organizations. The rational planning

79

modes are imperative for larger, diversified and more mature organizations.

(c) Long-term planning considers possibilities five, ten or twenty years in the future and affects short-term decisions. Short-term planning specifies the action to take in the immediate future, such as tomorrow or next month, and can help or hinder long-range plans. Smooth transition between long- and short-term plans is accomplished by periodically reviewing and extending both the short- and long-term plan.

(d) The stewardship concept of planning requires a manager to be accountable and to act like a proprietor in planning for his component.

(e) Several principles can be used to improve planning effectiveness. (i) The principle of planning stability states that the stability of a plan tends to vary inversely with its extension. (ii) The principle of present choices states that current decisions tend to limit future action. (iii) The principle of positive action states that the probability of a future event occurring tends to increase as effort is applied systematically towards its realization. (iv) The principle of commensurate effort states that effort applied should be commensurate with the results desired. (v) The principle of resistance to change states that the greater the departure of planned changes from accepted ways, the greater the potential resistance by the people involved.

(f) Different types of objectives can be developed. In order of increasing value for compelling effective action, the types of objectives are: subconscious, verbal, graphic, and material. The principle of tangibility confirms that the more tangible an objective, the more direct and specific the effort to achieve it tends to be.

6. HOW TO PREPARE A PLAN

If a person wishes to master the practice of professional management, a prime rule is never to embark on a new day without a plan which is part of a monthly, quarterly, and annual plan. Thinking should be projected at least that far ahead to take rational radic action. Every enterprise should have an overall plan which directs the organization and all its components. If a manager is in charge of one component, he will want to integrate his objectives with the overall plan.

Even though an overall enterprise plan is desirable, a manager can proceed without it. Any manager can improve his work and results by planning for his own area of accountability. He uses the same technique in developing a plan for his own position, whether or not it is integrated with an overall plan.

The following steps are the ones a manager should follow to develop and use a plan for himself and his group. This is his position plan. It requires that he, first, develop his objectives, second, support these with a programme and schedule, and then, calculate a budget so that he will have the resources he needs.

DEVELOPING OBJECTIVES

Objectives are the keystone of a manager's plan. His objectives establish the results he expects to accomplish and provide a guideline for what must be done to accomplish those results. We have identified three types of objectives, and the analytical steps used in developing them are shown in Fig. 6.1.

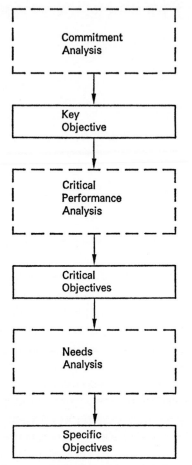

Fig. 6.1 Objectives. The three types of objectives and the analytical steps necessary to develop them.

We begin with a commitment analysis which enables us to identify the major commitments we will make and which, in total, constitute our key objective. *The key objective states the primary result we are organized to accomplish.*

Next, we determine which areas of performance are most vital to achievement of this primary purpose. These are our critical performance areas. From the critical performance areas, we derive our *critical objectives, which are the results we must achieve in each critical performance area to ensure outstanding performance* and thus accomplishment of the key objective.

We now analyse each critical objective by needs analysis to determine the important needs and deficiencies that must be satisfied to accomplish the critical objectives. Finally, we state measurable *specific objectives, which are the results we must achieve to satisfy our needs and to overcome our identified deficiencies.*

Both the key and critical objectives are continuing in nature; that is, they remain in effect except for periodic review and revision. Since they are relatively permanent documents, the initial effort necessary to develop them is a long-term investment in improved planning. To facilitate reference, as an index to major work assignments, and to promote sound organization, it is a good idea to incorporate the key and critical objectives in a position charter. This is a formalized statement of the primary commitments and obligations of a position.

HOW TO DEVELOP THE KEY OBJECTIVE

In developing his key objective, a manager begins by establishing the purpose of his organization—why it exists. He then states his purpose in concrete, understandable terms. If his group is part of a larger organization, it probably exists to contribute to the success of the larger entity.

To achieve its purpose, his organization must provide a product or service that other people want. The manager specifies exactly what he will commit himself to provide, to other clients or customers within his organization, or to external customers who will buy the product.

Now he has an important choice. He can provide his product or service to anybody who is willing to buy it, or he can focus on those customers or clients for whom he can do the best job. His chances of long-term success are much greater if he thinks through who his customers or clients should be and then uses his resources fully to satisfy them. He should specify clearly the customers or clients he will serve.

What should be his scope? An organization has the option of spreading everywhere, or restricting itself to a logically circumscribed compass. In developing his key objective, the manager should think through the geographic, organizational, or other limits of operations which he can most effectively serve.

Example: Statement of Key Objective

KEY OBJECTIVE: The key objective of the engineering department is to contribute to the growth and profitability of the Universal Products Company by creating and developing machines for the grinding, turning, boring, and shaping of metals to be marketed to industrial customers throughout the world.

HOW TO DEVELOP CRITICAL OBJECTIVES

The key objective states the overall result which the manager wants to accomplish. Clearly, everything he does is not equally important in achieving those results; probably 20 per cent of his work will make 80 per cent or more of the total contribution to the desired results. To concentrate his best effort on the critical action, he should establish his critical objectives. *The statement of the critical objectives specifies the continuing results he must achieve in critical areas of performance to accomplish the key objective.*

To develop his critical objectives, the manager first determines his critical performance areas. These are areas of his job most vital to overall success. As a manager, the critical performance areas will be the management and technical categories of work for which he is accountable. Next, he must think through and state in clear, concrete, and understandable terms the continuing results he must accomplish to do the kind of job he wants for each of these critical performance areas.

Now, the manager should state the evaluative standards for his objective. An objective will not be of much value unless he has acceptable evidence that it has been accomplished. Therefore, he should establish standards which will serve as constant guides for himself and for each person who is working towards the objective. The standards for critical objectives must relate to the objectives and must be continuing, not time limited.

Example: Statement of a Management Critical Objective

CRITICAL OBJECTIVE: Planning Performance.
To develop, establish and maintain a logical, efficient and integrated system of planning, including five-year and annual forecasts, objectives, programmes, schedules, and budgets, revised monthly and quarterly, with supporting policies and procedures.

Standards:

(a) The manager discusses forecasts of economic, technological, and market conditions with all his personnel—once each month.

(b) The manager develops written objectives, programmes, schedules, and budgets, secures understanding and acceptance of these plans by those with whom he works, and initiates and submits necessary revisions and improvements—once each month.

(c) The manager reviews company policies with his group and puts forward suggestions for revision—at least once each year.

(d) The manager maintains a procedures manual, and reviews all procedures and updates them as necessary—at least once each year.

Example: Statement of a Technical Critical Objective

CRITICAL OBJECTIVE: Design Performance.
To design products of outstanding value both to the customer and to the company.

Standards:

(a) Prescribed time, cost, and quality specifications are met.
(b) Products are suitable for efficient manufacturing.
(c) Customer requirements are satisfied.

HOW TO DEVELOP SPECIFIC OBJECTIVES

The key and critical objectives establish the most important, continuing results to which the manager should direct major attention and resources. He is now ready to focus on problems and results close at hand. Specific objectives are tools that help him do this. *A statement of the specific objectives specifies the measurable, time-limited results which must be accomplished to achieve the critical objectives.*

His specific objectives must be measurable. If he does not specify quantities, preferably in numbers, it will be difficult to establish meaningful programmes, schedules, and budgets and even more difficult to develop controls. Measurability can be in terms of units, e.g., 20 patient days, 5 per cent cost reduction, a ratio of 3.5 to 1. Trade or other defined criteria can be used, such as 'very fine quality' or 'mammoth size'.

A specific objective should be achievable. It is a mistake to state specific objectives that are clearly unreasonable. Some managers do this to stimulate effort, but people quickly recognize the gamesmanship involved. If a manager habitually overstates objectives, his people will also react in the centric mode and increasingly understate. While an acceptable compromise may be hammered out, the resulting acrimony is destructive. The basic problem is one of attitude. The manager's role is to shift into the rational mode and pursue a frank, sincere and honest approach that will result in mutually understood, accepted and, hence, achievable specific objectives.

Specific objectives are time limited and this parameter should be stated. Since the manager will determine the resources required to achieve the objective, he must use the time dimension to make his calculation. Also, if he includes in his specific objective the completion time, as well as the time of starting, it will provide an end point for the schedule which he will develop later.

One person should be accountable for each specific objective. Theories are offered about the virtues of diffused or multiple accountability, but in real life it is impossible to maintain a hard-hitting, productive, and satisfying effort unless each person has a clear delineation of his accountability. This reflects a basic human need, for each person instinctively wants his own clearly defined territory. If this is lost in group accountability, tension and uncertainty build up as we try to keep for ourselves the work we should do and the decisions we should make.

As a manager works with specific objectives, he will develop his own short cuts. However, the following is an approach which has proved itself in practice. The manager begins by conducting a needs analysis of his critical objectives. He does this by carefully reviewing each phrase in the critical objective and each of its standards. He looks for deficiency, maintenance, and special assignment needs. First, he asks himself, 'Where am I falling short in accomplishing this aspect of the critical objective?' As he thinks of each deficiency, he writes it down. He writes only the deficiencies; he does not, yet, try to determine what he will do about them.

In certain areas he will be satisfied to maintain the current level of performance. He notes these areas, identifying the level of performance that will be satisfactory.

Now the manager consolidates the needs he has identified, retaining only those he expects to use. Since he will next establish a specific objective to satisfy each of these needs, he combines those needs which logically belong together. At the same time, he eliminates or defers any needs to which he will not commit resources at the present time.

For each of the need statements above, he writes a quantifiable, achievable, specific objective which states the concrete results he will commit himself to accomplish. The manager should be very realistic; he makes sure the result is something that has a reasonable chance of accomplishment. And, *it must be quantified.* He does not leave the statement of the specific objective until he has been able to express some part of it in numbers or other measurable terms.

The specific objective should give a clear picture of the results he is committed to accomplish. Another person reading the statement should be able to understand and describe it to the manager in clear and precise terms. This is the most difficult part of writing specific objectives. A manager must work at it until he masters the knack of setting down concrete, challenging, and realistic results that are achievable and will produce the improvement he wants.

He now needs standards that will show that the specific objective has been accomplished. The best way to write such standards is to examine each phrase of the specific objective and ask himself, 'What will be acceptable evidence that I have accomplished this?' The manager writes down this acceptable evidence. It will become his standard. He writes as many standards as necessary to ensure that the results indicated in a particular specific objective have been accomplished.

The following example illustrates needs analysis, and the establishment of specific objectives and accompanying standards.

Example: Needs Analysis and Statement of a Specific Objective

CRITICAL OBJECTIVE: Design Performance.

NEEDS ANALYSIS:
Coordination of Specifications. Failure to prepare specifications to meet customer requirements satisfactorily. This is largely due to failure to find out more about the customer and his needs, and to lack of coordination between design engineers and sales product managers in establishing product specifications.
Personnel Resources. Inadequate backups for design engineer positions. There is too much reliance on detail men mastering design requirements and unwillingness to shake the boat by going out for college men.
Reporting. Completely inadequate reporting. Designers have no idea of their costs or time requirements. Too little about the customer's requirements is reported to the man working on the design.

SPECIFIC OBJECTIVE: Coordination of Specifications.
To have prepared specifications that will meet customer requirements satisfactorily.

Standards:

(a) Within three working days of entering the order, a set of customer specifications will be prepared that will state, in detail, function in industry terms, accuracy to three decimal places, capacity in units, both internal and external quality tolerances and finish.

(b) Provision will be made for maximizing the use of stock components and minimizing manufacturing costs, with alternatives and prices offered to the customer.

(c) The engineering and marketing departments will understand and agree to the specifications as witnessed by initials representing both on specification form #105.

(d) The understanding and agreement of the customer will be secured as to specifications, price and delivery, as witnessed by the customer's signature on the specification release.

(e) The customer will receive the product he orders at the specified time and price or, in cases of unavoidable nonconformance, he will be notified at once and his understanding and acceptance secured at that point. Failures in delivery will be kept to below 7 per cent of total orders; changes in price to 2 per cent. Failures to notify the customer will be 0 per cent.

(f) A written procedure will be developed, tested, and approved to cover.

Time Limit: Procedure to be effective by 1 April.

Accountability: Engineering department accountable for developing the procedure. Marketing and manufacturing departments to provide advice and service.

KEY POINTS IN DEVELOPING BETTER OBJECTIVES

The following points will be helpful to the manager in developing realistic, meaningful objectives. As is true of other aspects of planning, objectives are set for people. This is a basic consideration that should condition every step.

CONSIDERING PAST PERFORMANCE

Past accomplishments best indicate what we will be able to achieve in the future. Before looking ahead, we need to look backwards. If we know how and why we arrived where we are today, we can determine more intelligently our potential for the future. The first step in setting objectives is to review past operating results. How successful have we been in accomplishing previous objectives? Where did we fall short? Why? Will new factors enter the picture?

This review should include a comparison with performance in other units. How do our results compare with those of similar units? If there are differences, where do they exist? Past objectives should be studied and the degree of accomplishment analysed as part of this review.

SETTING REALISTIC LEVELS

There is often a tendency to set objectives at unreasonably high levels. The reasoning here is that if lofty goals are set, people will exert themselves in trying to accomplish them. This is valid if the objectives remain reasonable, but if they are set too high, they will frustrate people and discourage maximal performance. If, on the other hand, objectives are set too low, they lack challenge and will fail to spur high achievement.

In setting realistic targets, the manager should be guided by the advice of his subordinates. However, he must also bring to the situation his own knowledge of factors and conditions. This may encourage him to upgrade the targets beyond what subordinates think desirable. When this is the case, communication and understanding are vital if the objectives are to be accepted and serve as guides to productive action.

USING MEASURABLE TERMS WHEN POSSIBLE

Key and critical objectives are general, in that they will apply to more than one position; they are continuing, in that no specific date is set for their realization. For these reasons, it is impractical to quantify key objectives and difficult to find numbers for critical objectives. Critical objectives should be stated in measurable terms only if the quantification applies equally to all components affected and is continuing and not time limited in nature. Specific objectives should invariably be stated in measurable (quantitative) terms. The more concrete our objectives, the more clearly we can delineate planning steps to follow.

BUILDING IN AN IMPROVEMENT FACTOR

Improvement requires constant attention and encouragement. The best incentive to improvement is to upgrade objectives as often as we review them. Usually, this improvement factor is an added measure of performance that can be attributed to the personal stimulus of the manager—in other words, the added contribution he makes through the management work he performs.

TAKING PEOPLE ACTION

Objectives that are understood and accepted will best serve to guide and direct the actions of people. Every manager is accountable for securing the participation of his subordinates in goal setting; he may do this in several ways. One effective method is to ask each subordinate to set objectives for each key element of his job. The superior can then discuss and reach agreement on these. Participation can also be secured on a group basis. After subordinates have established their individual objectives, they may find it useful to discuss their conclusions with the manager and, thus, come to a joint agreement.

Communication is essential. People should be kept apprised of their progress towards objectives. They should know where they stand and where they are falling short. When deficiencies occur, the people who have set the objectives are in the best position to control and correct them. It makes good administrative sense to provide each accountable manager with the information he needs to analyse his own progress towards objectives and to take corrective action as soon as he sees that it is indicated.

DEVELOPING A PROGRAMME AND SCHEDULE

A manager's specific objectives give him a detailed statement of the results he should be working to accomplish. If the specific objectives are to be delegated to others on his team, he must be sure that he has their full participation and that there is understanding and acceptance of the final statements. Once this has been done, he can ask his subordinates to prepare their own programmes, schedules, and budgets for his final approval. After agreeing on the results to be accomplished, he can then logically ascertain the steps to be followed and the time and resources required. The more his subordinates are encouraged to think through and make their own decisions relating to the specifics, the more they will move towards rational radic action and the harder they will work to accomplish their own programmes and schedules within budget limits.

Whether he delegates or not, the manager will need to prepare his own programme and schedule. *The programme is the sequence of action steps to be followed in the order necessary to achieve the specifc objective. The schedule is the time sequence for each action step.*

HOW TO WRITE A PROGRAMME

The manager should have a programme for each specific objective. To develop his programme, he begins by writing out an abbreviated statement of the series of steps to be followed to accomplish the objective. He reviews the statement of the specific objective and the standards, then determines what action he will take to accomplish the results and meet the standards. He states the programme step titles in no more than three to five words each. In many cases, his programme step titles will summarize part of the performance outlined in the standards statement of his specific objective; however, the standards statement will not usually be complete enough or in the best sequence to serve as his programme steps.

When the manager is satisfied that the programme step titles show the sequence and priority of the steps that must be taken, he expands each, specifying exactly what is to be done and, where necessary, the name or title of the person who will carry out that particular step. Also, he specifies accountability for the programme as a whole.

If he is going to require specific reports at the completion of any of the steps, the manager notes this by using the initials of the person accountable. This simple notation will give him the control points he needs to maintain contact without getting personally involved.

HOW TO DEVELOP A SCHEDULE

Each programme step should be accompanied by a schedule, including a starting time and a completion time as appropriate. For a continuous programme, the manager would require only completion times for the individual steps. A useful approach is to use the minimax scheduling technique. First, the manager determines the greatest amount of time which the programme step could possibly take under normal circumstances. Second, he calculates the least amount of time. Third, he selects a most likely time between the two extremes and uses this as his schedule time.

The minimax technique often falls into disrepute because it can be manipulated to give the single estimate preferred. However, if his programme covers a new and untried situation with little data, or a complex project with many unpredictables, the manager may want to use the three-estimate calculation. He must keep in mind that if the estimates are not completely honest, the effort is wasted.

KEY POINTS IN EFFECTIVE PROGRAMMING AND SCHEDULING

In carrying out the mechanics of programming and scheduling, it is important for the manager to keep in mind the basic factors outlined below:

PROVIDING FOR IMPROVEMENT

A company must improve and upgrade its operations continually. It cannot long remain stationary and retain its competitive position. Every manager is accountable for bringing new thinking and innovation to his work. This means he should build an improvement factor into each programme step. He should ask himself and his subordinates, 'Is this the best way to do it? What other alternatives are available?' Continuing study of competitive methods, research findings, and other data will help maintain the kind of improvement that spells lasting success.

COORDINATING HIS OWN LEVEL

The programmes and schedules developed at each level should be coordinated at that level first. The manager himself knows best the extent to which his work directly affects other units. It is his responsibility to reconcile his interests with those of other managers at his own level. Matters that conflict or require a broader viewpoint should be referred to the next higher level. The completed programme and schedule should be approved by the next higher manager; only at his level is there perspective as to the needs of both subordinate and higher groups.

MAINTAINING STABILITY

Only a stable programme and schedule will withstand the pressures and demands of day to day operations. If the manager changes his mind at whim, his people will become uncertain, the work will falter and the programme and schedule will soon fall into disrepute. While programmes and schedules should not be considered inviolate or made inflexible, they should not be changed lightly. A high degree of stability is necessary to ensure confident action from all who work together.

Managers will overestimate time requirements as a matter of self-protection if they know that a staff group, or the boss, will automatically cut back the time allocated. Too often, schedules are arbitrarily cut on the assumption that, 'If he tries harder, he can finish sooner'. This inevitably leads to negotiation rather than calculation. The best solution is to avoid the cat and mouse aspects of scheduling by insisting on firm and honest commitments that managers are willing to stand by and that can be changed only by trade-offs that buy more time.

DEVELOPING A MANAGEMENT BUDGET

An objective is worth while only if the cost of accomplishing it is less than its value. While a manager cannot calculate all values in quantitative terms, he can determine beforehand what part of his total resources he will allocate to any given objective and its attendant programme and schedule. Management budgeting is the work of determining how best to allocate the resources of personnel, materials, tools, and facilities. For convenience, these values are generally converted to the universal denominator of money.

To develop his management budget, the manager must first value the specific objective; that is, he must determine how much the specific objective is worth to him when accomplished. Usually, the value can be calculated in monetary terms. If the objective is fairly standardized, he may already have a valuation in his records. He must try to fix a realistic money value to the objective and note this before he continues.

For each programme step, he calculates the units of man hours, materials, tools, and facilities that will be needed to achieve the programme within his schedule limits. For management programmes, man hours generally are the largest item. He should be able to estimate these and convert them to money.

The manager can now weigh the cost of carrying out his programmes within his schedule limits against the value of the objective. If there is too great a disparity, he will want to give second thoughts either to retaining the objective or to minimizing the programme steps and time requirements.

It is a fallacy to cut the budget without, at the same time, trading off programme steps or time. A manager can anticipate that 80 per cent of his objective will result from about 20 per cent of the programme steps. Therefore, he may find that he can easily eliminate part, or all, of the steps without seriously modifying the results that he wants to accomplish.

KEY POINTS IN EFFECTIVE MANAGEMENT BUDGETING

Every manager is accountable for the budgets developed for his unit. To ensure that this is done as effectively as possible, the following factors should be observed.

BUDGETING FROM THE BOTTOM UP, AS WELL AS TOP DOWN

Most of the money in the company is spent at the operating level. This is also where most end results are accomplished. First-line managers at the operating level have the best knowledge of what it should cost to attain operating results. For this reason, budgets should be built from the bottom up, as well as from the top down. Each subordinate manager should prepare a budget to cover the proposed costs of his unit. Since he does not have perspective beyond his own unit, however, and cannot determine the actual amount of money that will be available to him, he must reconcile this budget at his own level and then submit it to his manager for further coordination.

The process continues until the budgets are finally reviewed, reconciled, and approved at the top level of the company. It is here that the proposed total expenditures can be compared with the proposed income. It is here, also, that the best perspective can be exercised with regard to available resources and the relative needs of various parts of the company.

BASING BUDGETS ON PROGRAMMES

In many cases, managers establish budgets without having first programmed the activities they expect to carry out. When this occurs, the budget must be developed from historical costs or as a series of guesses. The budget is most useful as a management tool when it is used to determine the cost of programmes and to assess their relative value.

ESTABLISHING MANAGEMENT ACCOUNTABILITY

Every manager should be accountable for determining the budget covering his own operations. He should make a final decision concerning the budget that he submits to his own superior. Staff agencies such as the accounting or budget departments should not do the manager's budgeting for him. Their place is to offer him advice and service in the technical details and to help him follow approved budgeting procedures. If the accounting department is asked to develop a manager's budget for him, it is placed at a disadvantage. For one thing, the accountant does not have first-hand knowledge of the manager's operation. He has not prepared the manager's programme, and cannot, therefore, know what the costs should be. The accountant can do no better than prepare an accounting budget based on the historical record of past expenses. When this is the case, the budget is only an approximation and does not accurately reflect management needs. The accounting or controller's department can offer invaluable advice and service to the manager in helping him prepare his budget, but this should be the extent of its responsibility.

MAINTAINING INTEGRITY OF BUDGETS

Budgets are often treated so loosely that they quickly fall into disrepute. This is unfortunate, for the budget can be one of the most valuable of the manager's planning tools. When there is frequent occasion for complimenting managers because they have spent less than they budgeted, this may more realistically indicate the need for inquiry rather than congratulations. Budgeted sums are earmarked for specified purposes; when the money is not spent, it is being diverted from constructive uses. Overrunning the budget is equally serious. When the manager is spending more than he should, this points to poor planning and indicates the need for investigation and corrective action.

When held to budget accountability, the manager should be obligated only for his controllable expenses; that is, those expenses over which he has command or which he has agreed are chargeable to him. In many cases, managers are asked to pay overhead expenses even though they have little or no command over the expenditures. The best rule is to include the allocated expenses as part of the budget so the manager can estimate total costs; however, he should not be held to account for that over which he has no authority.

The following example illustrates the technique for programming, scheduling, and budgeting.

Example: Programme, Schedule, and Budget

(SPECIFIC OBJECTIVE: Coordination of Specifications.)

Programme steps	Account-ability	Schedule (completion dates)	Budget ($ or man days)
1. LIST REQUIREMENTS. Sales manager to prepare written list of industry and customer requirements.	JBP	15/5	2 man days
2. PREPARE SPECIFICATIONS. Sales manager to prepare written list of specifications from requirements, including details of function, accuracy, capacity, reliability, flexibility, and cost.	JBP	1/8	1/2 man day
3. RECONCILE WITH SALES. Engineering manager to prepare written report to sales manager after analysing specifications. In this, he either approves the written list of specifications by signature or recommends alternatives for presentation to customer.	ROL	1/9	1 man day
4. COORDINATE. Engineering manager to review final specifications list with staff specialist concerned and with division manager to secure understanding and agreement.	ROL	15/9	2 man days
5. SECURE DIVISIONAL APPROVAL. Engineering manager to prepare a written report to the division manager for final approval. The report will include the programme, schedule, engineering time and cost, and manufacturing cost.	ROL	1/10	1/2 man day

PROBLEMS IN PLANNING

Most of the manager's problems and errors in planning occur during his first few trials. However, experience indicates that he should anticipate at least one full year to develop a useful planning approach for his own position. If he extends this to his entire group, he will probably find that a minimum of three years is necessary to establish a smooth and efficient planning system.

The manager can anticipate a number of practical problems as he develops his planning approach. He will be his own greatest problem. His tendency will be to ignore the plans he has prepared and lapse intuitively into the spontaneous mode when problems occur or people come to him for guidance. At first, he will find that he makes decisions which are contrary to some of the things he has planned. He must acknowledge this mistake and go on from there.

96

Differences and confusion in vocabulary will undoubtedly become real problems at times. Past practice has left us with a plethora of obsolete terms; new developments are frequently attended by the coining of new words which are unnecessary because adequate terms are already in use. PERT and its companions are cases in point. PERT, or Programme Evaluation Review Technique, is a valuable and disciplined planning technique. However, it employs an arbitrary set of titles which duplicate standard terms. Such common terms, as forecast, objective, policy, and budget may be given widely different meanings; in fact, a forecast in one enterprise may be a budget in another.

A varied assortment of other terminology is found in planning practice. From military usage come the terms 'strategy' and 'tactics'. The 'strategic plan' is generally the overall, long-term plan, which includes the desirable objectives which the enterprise commits itself to achieve and definition of the resources necessary to accomplish them. The 'tactical plan' most often refers to the short-term plan embodying the objectives, programmes, and budgets designed to achieve the strategic plan.

Other planning terms with special meanings are common. Some are descriptive and necessary, some clearly redundant. 'Functional plans' most often refers to the objectives and supporting plans for the primary functions of the enterprise, such as marketing, engineering, and personnel, although 'development plans' can have a similar meaning. 'Financial plan' can refer to the plan for the finance function or, just as frequently, an estimate of revenues and expenditures for a given period, a *pro forma* operating statement or balance sheet, or a budget. Another term, 'operations plan' or 'operating plan', generally refers to the short-term plan, usually annual, particularly as it applies to the work directly performed, or with direct relation to, the product or service.

This hodge-podge of vocabulary is a hindrance in communicating, studying, and practising planning. As with other professional and scientific disciplines, a necessary first step to orderly and progressive development is precise definition of terms.

The manager may meet problems when his subordinates or superiors resist formalized planning because they feel it restricts a manager unnecessarily to defined areas. So penned in, an executive allegedly is prevented from undertaking important work he feels needs to be done or from innovating really creative activities of which no one else has thought. This is a fallacy, for a sound plan sets boundaries so that the members of a team working together towards their common objectives will not overlap undesirably in their efforts. Proper limits encourage creativity in the areas in which it can be most productive. To require a manager to avoid overlapping the responsibilities of another, no matter how innovatory his ideas may be, is no more than asking the violinist in the orchestra to stick to his music while the pianist confines himself to that for his own instrument. This can hardly be said to hamper the desirable creativity of either.

If anybody in an organization has new and creative ideas concerning another's area of responsibility, he should be encouraged and rewarded for offering and advocating these on an advisory and service basis; however, he should not be permitted to usurp previously assigned responsibilities and authorities.

SUMMARY

(a) Every manager should work within the framework of a written, understood, and accepted plan to guide his short- and long-term work.

(b) In developing a management plan for a position, it is first necessary to define the *key, critical,* and *specific* objectives. The *key objective* is the primary, overall, continuing result which a manager and his group are committed to accomplish. It is developed through the analysis of the various commitments necessary to achieve the overall purpose of the organization. The *critical objectives* are the continuing results to be achieved in critical areas of performance to accomplish the key objective. They are developed by analysing the critical areas of overall performance. A critical objective is continuing and general in nature and contains statements of results and standards. The *specific objectives* are the measurable, time-limited results which must be accomplished to achieve the critical objectives. They are developed through analysis of deficiency, maintenance, and special assignment needs and contain both results and standards statements. Specific objectives designate accountability and are time limited.

(c) A programme and schedule are tools to be used to reach the specific objectives. A programme is the sequence of action steps to be followed in the necessary order to achieve the specific objective. A schedule is the time sequence for each action step.

(d) A management budget is a tool which is used to allocate the available resources. This is often stated in money terms, but applies to the use of personnel, materials, tools, and facilities.

(e) Problems in management planning can arise because of the work habits of the manager, confusion in terminology, and resistance based on the assumption that planning limits creativity.

7. DEVELOPING THE ORGANIZATION

A key finding of behavioural research is the continuing impact of organization structure on human satisfaction. This is reasonable when we realize that people spend the larger part of their lives at work. Accordingly, the work itself serves as the source of actualization and frustration.

ORGANIZING FOR PEOPLE

When a manager develops an organization structure, he divides the total work to be done so that it can be performed by the people involved, and then integrates their effort so it is directed towards a common objective. As a manager, his task is to structure work so that people will enjoy doing it, their performance will be efficient, and he will be able to manage without becoming entangled in work others should be doing for him.

The first hurdle in structuring work is to separate the personalities of people from their work. What people do is, of course, strongly influenced by their personalities. It is elementary that structure affects behaviour, and vice versa. However, we cannot modify personal behaviour while changing the work to be done, any more than a physician can perform surgery and psychiatry at the same time. Both need appropriate attention in the sequence the situation requires.

The biological drives of people and organization structure are directly related. The basic management concepts and principles described in this book are rooted in these universal characteristics. As investigators from Freud to Birdsell have established, our drives have been programmed into our genetic structure through evolutionary adaptation and have a strong and persistent influence on our behaviour. A sound organization structure will be designed to channel these basic drives towards the desired objectives. A structure designed for people will have three major characteristics purposely built into it.

The organization structure will provide material rewards. People have a continuing biological drive to satisfy hunger and its derived cultural urges such as the acquisitive urge for the money that buys food, shelter, and other material goods. Just as the primitive hunter would quarrel or fight to get what he considered to be his fair share of the game he had helped kill, so each person in a modern organization wants fair and equivalent compensation for the work he does.

Organization structure provides material rewards by establishing positions which require important work. These call on the individual's best abilities and thus create for him the opportunity to earn the highest monetary returns for his efforts.

The organization structure will be designed to provide security for the people involved. People look for protection in the organizations to which they belong. There is no longer the onslaught of wild beasts or enemy tribes. However, there is the equally unsettling cultural threat of loss of status and uncertainty of employment. On the job, the security drive is translated into an urge for stability and predictability in our work. If a person is never sure what his work is, finds himself shuttled from one responsibility to another, or has his decisions countermanded, he will feel threatened and constantly under tension.

Security while at work is a result of logical, carefully structured work efficiently performed. Jobs are eliminated and people laid off most often because jobs are poorly designed and do not make their proper contribution to overall objectives. Security while at work also requires that an individual's territory is protected from trespass. On the job, the territorial urge impels us to protect our personal space, which is both the office or work area and the area of responsibility and authority that have been assigned to us. While we no longer physically attack invaders with knife and club, the emotional and verbal cultural substitution is as strong when others encroach on the work we believe is rightfully ours.

The security drive and its derivative cultural urges are satisfied in many ways on the job. We need to know that if we do good work, we will not be laid off arbitrarily. We want clearly defined responsibility and authority which we understand and accept and the opportunity to object if others initiate and perform work or make decisions which we feel are in our territory. Those who do not understand that the territorial drive is a strong and pervasive influence in organization, or who are acting in the spontaneous centric mode, may argue that people must be given more freedom, that they shouldn't be penned in by written job descriptions and objectives which may discourage their creative innovation or prevent them from doing work that should be done. In professional management practice, a sound position description or statement of objectives sets boundaries so that members of a team, working together towards common objectives, will not overlap undesirably in their efforts. This encourages creativity in the areas where it can be most useful.

The organization structure will be designed to help satisfy personal objectives. The work a person does on the job should lead directly to satisfaction of the purpose he sees in his own life. This helps satisfy his teleological drive, as well as providing the security he needs.

Integrating personal and organization objectives is believed to be very important. It is said to occur when the individual sees that his personal objectives are part of those of the enterprise as a whole, that the greater his contribution to organization objectives, the better his chance of satisfying his own objectives. While this type of integration would be helpful, it is often difficult to achieve because there is such a wide disparity between the individual's objectives and those of the overall organization.

The manager can bridge this gap in structuring the organization and can, at the same time, move towards the rational radic mode. Three steps must be taken. First, personal objectives must be known. If job expectations are discussed with a superior, they become a shared understanding and serve as a realistic guide. As we have established, personal objectives will be more meaningful and much more powerful as motivators if they are identified in terms of material things known from first-hand experience. Second, personal objectives must relate to job objectives. In practice, there is considerable overlap, for a formalized job objective becomes something to which we have made a commitment and is as real and may be even more motivating than a non-job objective. Job objectives are not integrated with personal objectives; rather, the job objectives become accepted as our personal objectives and are seen as the means to accomplish many of the non-job results we want. Third, progress towards objectives must be communicated. We need to know that our efforts are moving us towards the results we want. If we fall short, we want to know the deficiency so we can change or improve what we are doing.

Unless people know what work must be done to establish and integrate their personal objectives, are trained to do it, and have their progress evaluated, the work probably will not be done. For this reason, position descriptions should be created for each job. These should be discussed regularly with a superior. Each person should be required to participate in scheduled performance counselling sessions at regular intervals, preferably once every three months, during which he should have the opportunity to discuss and relate his personal objectives with those he has set up for his job.

Structuring the organization to satisfy these basic human drives is vitally important. While changes in leadership style, communication, job enrichment, and team building temporarily ameliorate deficiencies in drive satisfaction, they only treat the symptoms. To get at the causes, we must deal with the organization structure.

PRINCIPLES OF ORGANIZATION STRUCTURE

Many of the requirements for sound organization structure can be realized through application of the fundamental principles outlined below.

THE PRINCIPLE OF THE OBJECTIVE

We can do meaningful work only if we know its purpose. Our teleological drive prompts us to create a visual image or impression of the results we want before we can take action. As we have seen, this drive normally operates in the spontaneous centric mode, with subconscious objectives and intuitive action. Over the long period of human evolution, this mode has succeeded best for individuals. However, it is short term and has been self-defeating when applied to groups, for the principle of human reaction takes effect and the opposing spontaneous centric objectives inevitably come into conflict. Both our genes and our basic drives are directed to individual, not group evolution, which occurs through cultural urges which are relearned by each generation. This is why, although the human individual has maintained his identity with remarkable consistency, the predominantly spontaneous centric evolution of groups has made it impossible for any identifiable human group to maintain its identity for more than a few thousand years in the million or more years of human existence.

103

The principle of the objective establishes the fundamental truth that the organization will produce more if this spontaneous centric drive is harnessed and converted to a rational radic cultural urge that can be formalized and learned.

PRINCIPLE OF THE OBJECTIVE	*Organizational productivity increases as the work performed is directed towards tangible, understood, and accepted objectives*

The organization as a whole will produce more if each member is working towards objectives which he understands and accepts. The more tangible these objectives, the better they can be understood and accepted and the more positive the guidance they provide. This is clear if we keep in mind that the teleological drive can be energized with certainty and precision only if we visualize the concrete objectives we want to achieve. Vague objectives lead to vague and unproductive action.

THE PRINCIPLE OF SPECIALIZATION

People specialize by concentrating their energies on one specific field or area. Specialization is a cultural urge which is derived from the hunger, territorial, and aggressive drives. When a group of people work together to find food or the material objects which are its cultural equivalent, they quickly discover that everybody cannot do everything and the group still produce successfully. There is a practical need for each to limit himself to one part of the total task. Specialization and division of labour are the answer. The territorial drive comes into play because once we settle on an area or activity, we look upon it as part of our living space and develop a proprietary feeling about it. This not only leads us to concentrate our energy on our own territory, but also to keep others off. The aggressive urge prompts us to act in each case with vigour and emphasis.

In primitive societies, we can see early recognition of the need for specialization. Men will hunt for game, women for bulbs and roots, old people will chip out arrowheads and serve as look-outs. Each concentrates on his best skills and teaches them to younger members of the group. In the relatively few years that our industrialized society has existed, these cultural patterns have been intensified by the results they produced. When a person concentrates all his efforts on one kind of work, he will become more proficient in it. As he becomes expert and his competence

104

is recognized, he develops a mental image of himself as an important member of the group. This reinforces his tendency to specialize, for it rewards his application of this cultural urge.

Specialization satisfies our natural tendency to centric action, for it gives most immediate rewards. Least effort is required to develop our own skills; self-discipline is necessary if we are to share our abilities with others. Since it is easier for one person to work by himself rather than to make the extra effort necessary to participate jointly in work with others, once specialization is established it remains in the centric mode. This is why technical specialists, when promoted to managerial positions, want to continue their technical specialization. It requires an effort of will to shift the emphasis to specialization in management work.

PRINCIPLE OF SPECIALIZATION

The more specialized the work assigned to individuals within the limits of human tolerance, the greater the potential for efficient performance

The limit of human tolerance is reached when the work becomes so routine and narrow that the individual finds it mechanical. This limit varies with the individual. The key to maintaining optimum specialization, and yet keeping jobs interesting and challenging, lies in our understanding of the teleological drive and territorial urges as they apply to specialization. The teleological drive impels us to develop in our minds an image or impression of the result or objective we want to accomplish. Because of our natural spontaneous centric orientation, this must be an objective that we accept as our own. When a person is required to specialize in work for which he cannot visualize an objective, his basic teleological drive is thwarted. Tension is created, and the individual converts the energy into some other cultural urge which may be detrimental to the overall effort. On the assembly line, for example, he may damage parts or let imperfect work through to satisfy a vivid and tangible mental image of revenge and retribution. Work without a clear and tangible purpose is frustrating and potentially destructive.

The territorial drive provides further insight into methods for making jobs both specialized and interesting. In seeking living space we look for clearly demarcated limits, an area which others will not infringe. The cultural urge is to develop emotional ownership in an area of accountability, and not just in the work that is done. This means that our specialization should include all the related actions necessary to give us command

105

of enough responsibility and authority to enable us to find this emotional ownership we want.

There is often the mistaken assumption that each person must plan his own work and that it is undesirable to have 'planning' and 'doing' vested in different people. In the sense that no human action can take place unless an objective is first developed, either consciously or subconsciously, it is true that everybody both plans and does. Clearly, the more an individual can plan his own work, the greater the interest he will develop and the more effectively he will be motivated. However, there are many reasons why people should not always plan their own work, or some phases of it. For example, the machine operator can plan the set-up and in-process inspection for the part he is making, but he should not plan its configuration and dimensions, which depend on customer requirements and engineering specifications.

We can identify two distinct types of specialization:

(a) *Technical Specialization.* In this case, the primary concern of the individual is with a technical specialism. The salesman may specialize in selling work and the accountant in accounting. The more an accountant can focus his efforts on accounting, the more efficient he will become and the greater his productivity in accounting. The rule of technical specialization is: *a technical specialist should be required to concentrate his major efforts on his specialism.*

(b) *Management Specialization.* In this case, the concentration of primary effort is on the work of planning, leading, organizing, and controlling the efforts of others. A person in a management position is expected to multiply his relatively small personal efforts through what he can get other people to do for and with him. The more the manager concentrates on his particular work, the more effective he will become. The rule of management specialization is: *a person placed in a management position should be required to direct his primary efforts to the work of planning, leading, organizing, and controlling the efforts of others.*

When a person confuses his technical and management roles, he thwarts his territorial drive, for he cannot establish the clear-cut territory he wants for his own. Usually, he does not recognize what is happening and finds himself continually frustrated by his failure to fulfil either role satisfactorily.

The rules for specialization in technical and management work help the individual to establish the territory he wants for his own; they encourage him to channel and focus his aggressive urge on objectives which will bring him greatest long-term rewards and, in so doing, satisfy more fully the cultural equivalents of the hunger drive. Because his personal objectives can be identified and defined more clearly and concretely when he makes up his mind whether he is a manager or a technician, the rules also facilitate satisfaction of the teleological drive. However, because the change from the usual centric orientation of technical specialization to the radic orientation of management calls for extra effort and a long-term view, many managers fail to accomplish it successfully.

Currently, there is much talk that the days of specialization are numbered, but it is clear that specialization itself satisfies several basic needs; what is required is more understanding of management of the specialization process.

THE PRINCIPLE OF LOGICAL ARRANGEMENT

If people are left to themselves, their intuitive spontaneous centric orientation prompts them to shift their effort to the work they most like to do. Once their attention is centred on this work, they try to make it their property, absorbing whatever related activity they feel is desirable. This inevitably leads to imbalance. Some people do too much work, while others do too little. Work, thus arranged in terms of the personal preferences of the people involved, gives satisfaction and rewards to only a few. It leads to early success, for the strongest and most capable do the work they prefer. These people are rewarded and their centric action is reinforced, so that the personalized organization is perpetuated. When new people enter the organization, there are new demands and changing needs, but there is no logical basis for restructuring the organization. As a result, jobs continue to grow illogically, increasing in size and scope without real justification; positions increase, levels proliferate, and expense multiplies.

When work is arranged on a logical basis, with the structure designed to accomplish objectives, there is a rational basis for change. Each job is assigned as much responsibility and authority as the position can reasonably carry. In this way, the aggressive person is prevented from encroaching on other jobs. Instead of being encouraged to seek opportunities elsewhere, the individual is helped to concentrate on and improve his own job by investing in it all his energy and creative imagination. Also, such an arrangement prevents the poor performer from camouflaging his inadequacy. Once recognized, he can either be trained and

107

developed to do the work for which he is paid or transferred to another job more in keeping with his capabilities.

PRINCIPLE OF LOGICAL ARRANGEMENT	*Logically arranged work tends to produce the greatest accomplishment and highest personal satisfaction for the largest number of people over the longest period of time*

This principle involves application of the rational radic mode, for it requires understanding of the needs of others and a willingness to work within the limits of logically defined positions. Logical arrangement of work is the only way to prevent overlap, duplication, and friction in the long term. Within the limits of his position, each person can have maximum freedom to do his job in his own way and to inject into it his initiative, imagination, and creative ability. This gives free play to his basic drives and provides greatest long-term rewards.

THE PRINCIPLE OF BUSYNESS

If ten people are actually required to do the necessary work of an organization component, almost certainly twelve or fifteen could be easily engaged in the same activity. An individual who knows that he must appear busy, if he is to retain his job, will always find work to do.

PRINCIPLE OF BUSYNESS	*The more people in an organization, the more work they will find to do*

Busy work lacks a purpose, so it thwarts the teleological drive. Since it is not important, it gives little real or continuing satisfaction to the territorial urge. As a result, busyness leads to tension and frustration. The best solution to the busy work problem is a rational approach to organization, with each person carrying a full job of important work with authority to make most of his own decisions.

THE PRINCIPLE OF MAXIMUM SPAN

'Span' here refers to the number of people supervised by a manager. Some believe that a manager should supervise only a few people, so that he can develop much closer personal relationships, help improve morale, and motivate his people more effectively. However, managing a limited number of people will not use his full energies and he will begin

108

to take over the most meaningful work available to him, which is usually the most important technical work of his subordinates.

Another suggestion is that the span of supervision can be determined mathematically in terms of potential relationships. This theoretical treatment of the span of supervision is interesting, but does not apply in practice. Although a manager may have a hundred potential relationships, he will exercise only a few at one time. He rarely makes even half the contacts open to him.

Yet another approach to determine the span of supervision is to survey other companies to learn the number of people reporting to a specified type of manager. For example, if in a hundred companies, accounting managers supervise three subordinates on average, the assumption is that three is a typical span of supervision for accounting managers. The fallacy is that this average span can also represent inefficiency in many of the companies surveyed. Also, conditions vary greatly, depending on the stage of a company's growth, its type of products and markets, and the competence of its management; in consequence, the use of an average span as a standard is not too helpful.

Greatest satisfaction to the manager results if he has a busy and important territory and supervises more, rather than fewer, people. It is also easier to secure understanding and acceptance of overall objectives if the number of groups whose personal interest must be reconciled and integrated is kept to a minimum; the more groups there are, the greater the effort needed to coordinate their work. This diversion of effort to internal administration between groups, rather than direct application to overall objectives, is known as organizational slip and results in increased indirect costs. Many small groups carve out their own small territories in response to their territorial urges; they become isolated in protecting their own interests and are more difficult to convert to a radic orientation. Larger groups, with more people reporting to each manager, minimizes this.

PRINCIPLE OF
MAXIMUM SPAN

The more people each manager can effectively manage, the smaller the total number the organization will require to attain its objectives

In addition to the ability to manage, the following factors determine the number of people a manager can effectively supervise.

(a) *Diversity and Complexity of the Work.* The more complex and diverse the work supervised, the greater the likelihood that each person will

109

develop objectives dissimilar to those of others. Since each individual pursues his own objectives and protects his territory aggressively, more time and attention will be demanded from the manager to coordinate the total effort. For example, a foreman may be able to supervise twenty ditch diggers without much difficulty. However, another foreman with equal management ability might be hard pressed to supervise three electricians, a radio technician, a plumber, and two painters because their work is more diversified and more complex.

(b) *Dispersion.* The greater the geographical separation of the people, the fewer a manager can supervise. For example, while a sales supervisor can supervise twenty salesmen in one location, he will probably find it difficult to do a good job of supervising ten salesmen in ten different cities.

(c) *Volume of the Work.* The greater the volume of work, the greater, also, the number of problems and decisions forced to the top. This, too, is a limiting factor in the span of supervision. To illustrate, twelve data sorters in a telecommunications company reported to a supervisor. Each processed 2600 printed items per hour, averaging two problem items per hour which had to be discussed with the supervisor. The printer was modified with a laser head so that it printed 5400 items per hour, with similar problem ratios. The supervisor was overwhelmed with the problems referred to him, which had doubled. The group had to be split into two, each with its own supervisor.

THE PRINCIPLE OF MINIMUM LEVELS

The span of supervision is directly related to the number of organizational levels. For example, assume that twelve people are needed to operate twelve machines efficiently. If there is one supervisor for the twelve operators, only two levels are required. If two groups, of six operators each, are formed then each group will have its own supervisor and a superintendent to manage the two supervisors. In the second instance, three levels are needed to accommodate the same twelve people.

PRINCIPLE
OF MINIMUM
LEVELS

The fewer the levels of supervision within the limits of maximum span, the greater the potential effectiveness of the people involved

The number of levels of supervision should be kept to a minimum to prevent line loss, organization slip, and added cost. For example, if a manager is faced with a problem and has to go to his own superior for a decision, communication is swift. The superior is familiar with the circumstances and can deal with the problem quickly. However, if this superior, in turn, has to go to a higher supervisor, the latter will take time informing himself of the same facts that are already known at the previous two levels. If the superior's superior, in turn, must go to his superior, the process extends and lengthens.

As a generalization, the greater the number of organizational levels, the more communication between top and lower levels is weakened, distorted, and diffused. Since there is a relationship between levels and the number of people each manager supervises, the ideal situation is to have each manager supervise the maximum number of people he can, efficiently.

THE PRINCIPLE OF SPLIT GROUPINGS

A split grouping occurs when a natural and logical grouping of work is artificially divided so that the manager to whom the group reports is forced to become the technical coordinator. In Fig. 7.1, for example, we would expect the marketing manager to coordinate the work of the advertising and sales managers.

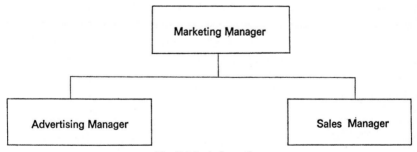

Fig. 7.1 Logical grouping.

If these technical activities report separately to the division manager, however, as is fairly common, he must function also as marketing manager to coordinate the split grouping in addition to his normal management responsibilities. See Fig. 7.2.

Split groupings force the manager to whom the groups report to spend a disproportionate part of his time handling technical questions and problems because only he has perspective and objectivity with respect

111

to the split parts. Usually, split groupings are unintentional, but they saddle the manager with much unnecessary technical work.

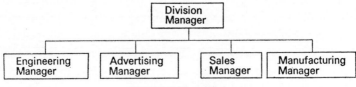

Fig. 7.2 Split grouping.

PRINCIPLE OF SPLIT GROUPINGS

Split groupings tend to force technical supervision to the next highest level

THE PRINCIPLE OF MANAGEMENT EMPHASIS

We are biased in favour of familiar things and those that yield greatest personal returns. This is supported by our intuitive centric tendency. Since we are most successful in those things for which we show greatest preference, the bias is reinforced.

If a manager supervises two different functions, such as engineering and research, after experience only in one, he will show preference to that one by favouring it in budget allocations, assignment of personnel, compensation, and other ways. The same holds true with geographic regions, product lines, and markets. In some cases, the preference may be negative, in that the manager leans over backwards not to show favouritism. In either case, it usually means that potentially profitable products or regions may not get the attention or resources they merit, or that functions which require the most help and guidance are neglected, while those which are self-sufficient get more attention than they need.

PRINCIPLE OF MANAGEMENT EMPHASIS

When supervising two or more differing functions, products, or geographic units, a manager will tend to show preferential emphasis in his decisions and choices; the closer to the line of operations he is located organizationally and the greater the differences in the units he supervises, the greater will be his preference

One drug company, for example, diversified into food. It found that the known and familiar drug lines received priority attention from its

112

key managers. The new and unfamiliar food products got the short end of budget appropriations, facilities, and personnel allocations. The company had to try to equalize the emphasis by using product specialists, then product managers, and finally, separate drug and food sales forces.

WHAT TYPE OF STRUCTURE SHOULD YOU HAVE?

Just as it is important for an engineer to know the types of bridges in use, and the advantages and disadvantages of each, a manager needs to understand the different types of organization structures.

There has been much misunderstanding about types of structures. An organization structure is a consistent pattern of grouping the work to be performed. Since work is done to accomplish objectives, the desirable structure is the one that will be most effective in accomplishing the objectives.

Much of the confusion about structure can be eliminated by recognizing that there are only two basic types. There may be combinations and modifications, but one pattern or the other, or a hybrid, can always be found. These types are: (a) Functional—organized in terms of the different kinds of work to be performed. (b) Divisional—organized in terms of the results to be achieved by the outcome of the work.

FUNCTIONAL ORGANIZATION STRUCTURE

In this type of organization structure, the grouping is in terms of the different kinds of work to be performed. See Fig. 7.3. At the operating level, this means that each position specializes in one kind of work; for example, plumbing, carpentry, painting, electronic assembly, or selling.

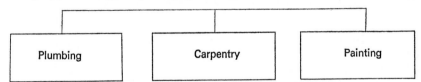

Fig. 7.3 Functional grouping. The grouping is in terms of the different kinds of work.

When we establish this kind of structure, we do so because, logically, we know that we will have most efficient and satisfying performance if people can specialize. All new plumbing work would be assigned to the plumbing man, for example, and it would be his responsibility to develop and improve his plumbing skills and to keep abreast of new developments in plumbing.

113

Each enterprise and each of its organization components tends to begin its existence with a functional type of structure. The reasons for this are straightforward: when the company is small, the functional organization is most economical to administer; it is most flexible and direct in its operation and requires fewer managers. The small, functional organization facilitates specialization. By throwing its resources into one specialized type of work, or by emphasizing the engineering, manufacturing, and sales of one specialized product, even the smallest company may be able to compete with the big corporation on quality, delivery, and price.

The functional organization is more economic because it requires only one group of manufacturing facilities, one sales function, and one set of managers; hence, capital and administrative expense are held to a minimum.

The disadvantages of a functional organization begin to appear as the company grows and diversifies. The functional organization meets these new demands by adding layers of organization, so that a constantly increasing organizational pyramid results. See Fig. 7.4. The larger the

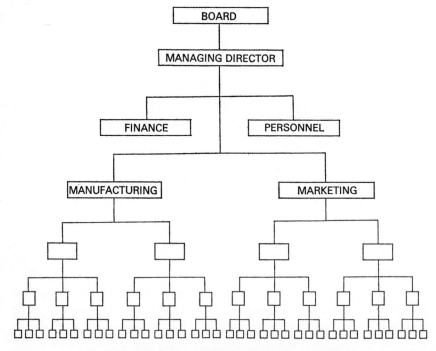

Fig. 7.4 Functional structure. Manufacturing produces all products for all geographic areas, marketing sells all products everywhere.

functional organization becomes, the more organization levels tend to be created. Line loss increases with each added layer of organization. More time is required for messages to be transmitted from the bottom to top layers of this organization. Policies and decisions slow down. Communications are weakened and distorted as they percolate from top to bottom. The organization grows more inflexible, slow moving, and cumbersome.

Problems of size are complicated by diversification. The greater the variety of the products and markets, the more complex and demanding the burden of decision making and coordination on functional management, the earlier that divisionalization should be undertaken. Dispersion —the geographic separation of plants, sales offices, and facilities—is also a contributing factor. If a company operates in several different countries, or in widely differing geographical locations, the demands on the functional organization will multiply and the need for change will be hastened.

DIVISIONALIZED ORGANIZATION STRUCTURE

As the functional structure becomes inadequate, the enterprise will begin to evolve to a divisionalized structure. Now, the work is grouped in terms of the end results to be accomplished. Different kinds of work are done by different people at different times, *but the accountability is for the completed end product, not just one part of it.* Divisionalization requires that the primary kinds of work necessary to achieve overall objectives be performed within the same organization grouping.

Divisional Groupings at the Management Level. Divisionalization can be identified most clearly at the corporate level; that is, the first level below the chief executive. With increased diversification, dispersion, and size, the enterprise as a whole inevitably outgrows the functional type of structure. Divisionalization then becomes the process of dividing the large, cumbersome, functional pyramids into smaller units regrouped in terms of the end results to be accomplished. Divisionalization can be accomplished on several bases. Most common at the *corporate level* are product and geographic divisionalization.

Product Divisionalization. In a product type of divisionalization, a company divides its large functional groups into smaller units, each grouped in terms of the product being manufactured and sold. As shown in Fig. 7.5, each unit forms a small product business within the framework of the company as a whole.

115

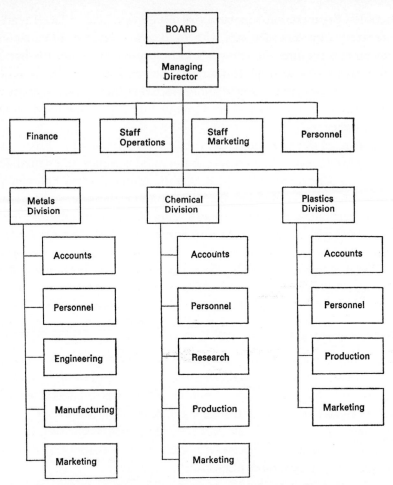

Fig. 7.5 Product divisionalization. The metals, chemical, and plastics groupings each have the functions they need to accomplish their own end results.

Product divisionalization focuses on the product itself the resources of one complete administrative unit. Manufacturing, sales, engineering, finance, and personnel are dedicated to the interests of one or a few related products. This increases emphasis on product development, market exploitation, engineering improvements and personnel development in terms of the needs of the individual product lines or groups.

On the negative side, product divisionalization is more expensive in the beginning because it requires added supervision and facilities. In particular, if it is to be managed effectively, it requires more capable managers and these are usually in short supply.

Geographic Divisionalization. When the company is making and selling much the same kind of product wherever it operates, but is widely dispersed geographically, the primary problem is to achieve a sharp focus on the differing economic, social, and political conditions in each of the geographic areas it serves. This emphasis can be accomplished best by subdividing the company into regional units, each relatively self-sufficient in manufacturing, marketing, or the other functions it needs to operate as a relatively autonomous business unit within the framework of the company as a whole.

In effect, geographic divisionalization sets up separate business units to cater to the needs of local markets. It facilitates the fastest possible service, undivided attention, and recognition of local needs and traditions. It also allows functional coordination within the region, provides a good basis for decentralization of authority, and creates more management positions, which encourage the development of managerial skills.

Disadvantages of geographic divisionalization include greater cost and shortage of people who have the management skills necessary to operate on an autonomous basis in the geographically separate regions.

Job Enrichment Structure. Job enrichment involves structuring operating positions on a divisional basis. Historically, this approach developed largely from work done by International Business Machines prior to 1946. It can best be understood by observing a machine operator at work. To operate the machine, it is necessary to set up his jigs and fixtures, do preventive maintenance and repairs, run the machine, inspect the product, and keep the area clean. All of these must be planned, either by the operator or a staff specialist. Figure 7.6 shows five kinds of work necessary to achieve the objective.

Fig. 7.6 Basic functional structure. One person performs each specialized job.

If different operators each do one kind of work, we have a functional organization. If one operator does all five kinds of work, we have an enriched divisionalized structure, as shown in Fig. 7.7.

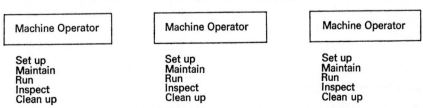

Fig. 7.7 Enriched by divisionalization. Each person performs all the work necessary to accomplish the overall objective and plans as much of it as is feasible himself.

Each alternative offers the advantages and disadvantages we have already discussed. If we divisionalize, each machine operator can be delegated far more responsibility and authority to plan and control his work than if our structuring is on a functional basis; in fact, the divisionalization will not be successful unless we *do* delegate more.

Matrix Organization. This is another type of divisionalization in which the work to be done is grouped in terms of projects or programmes—in this case, those which have a definite life span. Matrix divisionalization is most useful as a means of making effective use of highly skilled personnel who, because of cost and scarcity, must be spread over many projects.

Assume we are an electrical contractor designing and installing air-conditioning and heating equipment, usually on projects which require three to six months of work. We use design engineers and installation engineers. A functional structure is inadequate because the engineers must closely mesh their efforts at distant locations for months at a time. Product and geographic divisionalization do not work because the type of product and the geography are secondary to the needs of clients, which vary tremendously. We structure in terms of objectives of the project, assigning to each a team made up of the requisite skills organized only for the life of the project. As required, specialists are assigned from one project to another. On completion of a project, the specialists return to their functional group until reassigned, while the project managers start new projects. See Fig. 7.8.

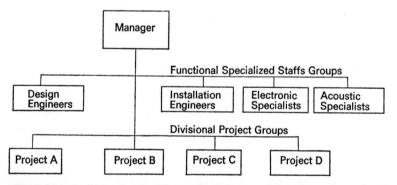

Fig. 7.8 Matrix divisionalization. The grouping is in terms of the projects to be completed.

Problems arise in determining who is accountable. While they work on a project, specialists are accountable to the project manager. The project manager is accountable for accomplishing the objectives of his project, by using all the specialized skills available.

The relationships become complex and difficult, and are tenable only if the basic pattern is understood and followed.

THE TECHNIQUE OF ORGANIZATION CHANGE

The following is a proven method of evolving an organization structure best suited to the long-term objectives of the company. It comprises the steps outlined below.

DEFINITION OF OBJECTIVES AND OTHER PLANS

Before changing the organization we must know the aims for which we are organizing. This calls for careful examination of key objectives and major long-term programmes and budgets. These plans specify expected product and market end results, growth objectives, and the requirements for people over the long term. If clearly defined objectives are not available, they should be developed before organization work begins.

DEFINITION OF THE EXISTING ORGANIZATION

To provide a basis for organization work, we need a clearly defined statement of the organization as it now exists. This can be secured through study of existing organization charts and position guides. If these are not available, they should be prepared. In defining the existing organization, the key responsibilities for each position should be identified first and then reconciled with the accountable manager.

DEFINITION OF THE IDEAL ORGANIZATION

The ideal organization is a theoretically perfect organization developed to accommodate the long-term objectives of the company. In establishing the ideal organization, we project as far ahead as our plans will permit and develop the ideal structure best designed to accommodate long-term requirements.

In developing the ideal organization, the organic pattern of growth should be followed. If the company has been diversifying and dispersing, and this process will continue, the ideal organization should anticipate the need for divisionalization and decentralization.

In establishing the ideal plan, we do not build it around the people currently in the organization. If we design an anticipated organization structure for the next ten years around the people we now have, we will inevitably find ourselves distorting the structure to fit the strength and weaknesses of our current personnel. The better approach is to establish a model or standard in the form of the ideal organization and to develop people to fit these logical requirements.

IMPROVEMENT OF THE EXISTING ORGANIZATION

With a clear picture of our current organization and a good idea of the structure we are aiming at, we can now streamline, clarify, and minimize. In the process, we will be able to eliminate overlap and duplication, minimize levels and maximize the number of people supervised by each manager. This improvement should be aimed primarily at strengthening the basic organization as it now exists. It should not contemplate fundamental changes in the structure; this is accomplished by our next step.

DEVELOPMENT OF PHASE PLANS

Phase plans are the interim organization plans designed to carry us from where we now are to where we want to be. Phase plans should be developed in terms of the people we now have. Frequently, a temporary modification of the overall pattern will be necessary to make most effective use of current job incumbents. When these individuals are transferred, retire, or leave the company for other reasons, a forward movement in terms of the ideal plan can again be undertaken.

Phase plans are short range and can often be predicated on impending personnel moves. Each time a phase plan is developed and put into effect, we look again at our overall long-term ideal organization and make required changes.

TAKING PEOPLE ACTION

Most of the problems of organization improvement lie not in design but in the people involved. The best way to take people action is to provide for the participation of the people who will be affected by the organization changes to be made. The more opportunity people have to contribute their ideas, the more strongly they will support the changes contemplated.

Communication is very important in taking people action. The rule is: give as much information as possible about organization changes to as many people as need it, as soon as possible.

SUMMARY

(a) The development of an organization structure must include a division of the total work to be done, so that it can be performed by the people involved, and an integration of their efforts so that they are directed towards a common objective. The work to be done should be separated from the personalities of the people involved.

(b) The principles of organization structure provide the basis for sound structure by taking into account the influence of the basic *drives* and *urges*. (i) The principle of the objective states that organizational productivity increases as the work performed is directed towards tangible, understood, and accepted objectives. (ii) The principle of specialization states that the more specialized the work assigned to individuals, within the limits of human tolerance, the greater the potential for efficient performance (iii) The principle of logical arrangement states that logically arranged work tends to produce the greatest accomplishment and highest personal satisfaction for the largest number of people over the longest period of time. (iv) The principle of busyness states that the more people in an organization, the more work they will find to do. (v) The principle of maximum span states that the more people each manager can effectively manage, the smaller the total number the oganization will require to attain its objectives. (vi) The principle of minimum levels states that the fewer the levels of supervision within the limits of maximum span, the greater the potential effectiveness of the people involved. (vii) The principle of split groupings states that split groupings force technical supervision to the next highest level. (viii) The principle of management emphasis states that when supervising two or more differing functions, products, or geographic units, a manager will show preferential emphasis in his decisions and choices; the closer to the line of operations he is located organizationally, and the greater the differences in the units he supervises, the greater will be his preference.

(c) While there are modifications and combinations, the two basic types of organization structure are functional and divisional.

(d) The functional organization is structured in terms of the different kinds of work to be performed.

121

(e) The divisional organization is structured in terms of the objectives to be achieved as the outcome of the work. This grouping can be identified most readily at the management level and is a method of retaining the advantages of functional organization while dealing with increased size, diversity, and dispersion. (i) In product division-alization, the large functional groups are divided into smaller units which are then grouped in terms of the product being sold or manufactured. (ii) In geographic divisionalization, the organization is divided into regional units which have their own manufacturing, marketing, and the other functions necessary to operate relatively autonomously. (iii) Job enrichment should be considered when organizing, to ensure that basic drives will be satisfied. It can be accomplished by assigning a total task to a person, rather than just one specialized part of it. This calls for divisionalization of the work, with both the inherent advantages and disadvantages.

(f) An organization change involves defining plans and objectives, the existing organization, the ideal organization, and phase moves. The existing organization can be improved by minimizing levels and maximizing the spans of supervision. Phase plans should then be developed to handle short-term problems in terms of the existing people. As many of the people should be informed of as much of the change as soon as possible. Organization change requires planning and time.

8. DELEGATION—THE EASY WAY TO MANAGE

The key to a manager's success is his ability to get others to do work for him by delegating responsibility and authority. *Delegating is the work a manager does to entrust responsibility and authority to others and to create accountability for results.* Delegation is a process of sharing with others the work and decisions the manager would otherwise have to carry out himself. This requires skill and self-discipline, but is absolutely necessary so that the manager can multiply his limited strength through that of others.

PROBLEMS IN DELEGATION

Managers usually find it easier to talk about delegation than to accomplish it. Problems arise because delegation is in opposition to some of our basic drives. When we give up work and authority, we must also give up objectives to which we have a strong emotional commitment. This is in opposition to our spontaneous centric teleological drive. To the extent we lack confidence in ourselves and others, varying degrees of insecurity result from delegation, bringing the influence of the security drive into play. When we delegate, we must share part of our territory and this often runs counter to both our territorial and acquisitive urges. For these reasons, delegation requires self-confidence and understanding of what is involved.

Frequently, the manager does not delegate because he fears the job will not be done properly. This applies particularly to technical work in which he is himself an expert; he feels he can show his expertise and secure recognition only by continuing to do an outstanding technical job.

The manager may be reluctant to delegate because he expects his people to work and make decisions precisely as he would, if he had time and energy to do everything himself. We often see the 'paragon phenomenon' when a person who is highly skilled in a specialism, such as sales, becomes a manager in that specialism. He then sees himself as a paragon of the ideal salesman. 'The way I used to do it' becomes the standard. The manager belittles the abilities of subordinates, he sees glaring faults in their sales approaches because they do not do their selling work the way he did when he was a salesman.

The manager who is expert in delegation overcomes these problems by establishing clearly understood plans and standards, indoctrinating his people to carry work through to completion, then disciplining himself not to interfere even though everything is not being done the way he would do it himself. He knows that results are the final measure and there are many different ways to arrive at equally satisfactory results.

Delegation often breaks down for failure to define responsibility and authority. If a manager does not know what work he is to perform, if he does not understand what authority he has, then he will be unable to delegate. As a case in point, a large suburban department store had almost its entire stock of television sets stolen by thieves who backed a lorry to the loading bay and carted off all the sets on the floor. This occurred in the half-hour period between the closing of the store and the first rounds by the watchman. One thief apparently had remained in the cloak room until the store was locked, and had then opened the loading bay for his accomplice. The store manager called the department manager in to reprimand him, but was told, 'Checking the cloakrooms before closing is not my responsibility.' Questioning the watchmen and the caretakers elicited the same response. Delegation was improved by making each department manager accountable for all aspects of his operation, including checking facilities, until the sales force went off duty.

HOW TO DELEGATE EFFECTIVELY

The drive and tempo of an organization are largely determined by the timeliness and content of the decisions that are made. Problems often arise because of uncertainty as to who has responsibility and authority. This is evident in many ways. Frequently, a manager has a valuable suggestion about some aspects of the business for which he is not directly accountable, but nobody seems able to make the necessary decision, so the idea dies. Managers often need help from technical specialists, but when they ask for it find that they are being given instructions instead of advice, which promptly aborts potentially valuable assistance. Committees, in particular, suffer from fragmented or unspecified authority. Many a group has come to enthusiastic agreement on an important course of action, only to find that nobody follows through and the effort is hamstrung. The wrong person making the right decision is sometimes no better than the right person making the wrong decision. Decision making cannot be divorced from the work to which it relates; a manager must know what authority he has, related to what responsibility.

Contrary to much that is written, the overwhelming need is not to provide for further sharing of authority, but, rather, for precise identification of those individuals who are accountable for making the final decisions and seeing that the important work is done. People who participate in decisions tend to work hard for the success of the decision; however, the contribution of ideas and suggestions which become part of the decision does not mean that accountability for the decision itself is shared. Only one person can be held accountable if there is to be meaningful control.

To delegate effectively, the manager needs a clear idea of the process that takes place. Analysis can best be made by determining the objective of delegation, then identifying the work that must be done to achieve it. The manager's objective in delegating is to get other people to do the work and make the decisions which they can handle as well or better than he can. Obviously to accomplish this objective, the manager must assign the work to be done. *Responsibility is the work assigned to a position.* The more decisions a person can make, the more rights and powers he can exercise related to the work, the more completely he can perform it by himself, then the more effective delegation will be. *Authority is the sum of the rights and powers assigned to a position.* The integrity of the delegation can be maintained only if the person concerned accepts *accountability, an obligation to do the work and make the decisions in terms of understood and accepted standards.* Below is a discussion of accountability, responsibility, and authority as they relate to delegation.

IDENTIFYING ACCOUNTABILITY

A primary need in delegation is to identify those individuals who are accountable for the most important work and decisions, and who have

125

responsibility and authority. These are the command points. If they are clearly identified, delegation is facilitated, for top managers can maintain control with minimum effort, and subordinates and peers can make suggestions and secure skilled help with equal facility. The manager at the command point can be evaluated on the quality of his decisions and the way he carries them out.

Each manager is a command point for certain work, that which he is accountable for accomplishing as part of his job. At the same time, he gives advice and help to others, does work for his superior, and is subject to the approval of others at levels above his own. These differing, and sometimes contradictory responsibilities and authorities can be clarified by defining the different types of responsibility and authority.

ASSIGNING RESPONSIBILITY

The objective of assigning responsibility is to have each person do his proper share of the work necessary to accomplish objectives. Work is assigned in two categories: that which is carried to completion by the person performing it and that which is performed for somebody else. This distinction is shown in our definitions of terminal and advisory and service responsibility.

Terminal responsibility is work a person is obligated to carry through to conclusion. Once assigned this type of responsibility, the individual initiates the work and determines what objectives are to be accomplished by it. He completes the work by carrying it through to a stage where no further effort is required.

As an example, the accounts manager for a large real estate firm needed a new accounts payable clerk. He sent in a request to the personnel department, complete with the required personnel specification form. Two weeks later, nothing had happened. When he was called to account by the finance vice-president, the accounts manager blamed the personnel department. 'Once I approved the budget for the salary, it was your responsibility to get the clerk,' said the vice-president. 'If the personnel department didn't deliver, as far as I'm concerned that's your fault.' The accounts manager was confused, for he had understood that it was the personnel department's responsibility to recruit and select employees. The key to the problem was failure by the vice-president to clarify the type of responsibility he had assigned. When pressed, he finally decided that he meant to assign terminal responsibility to the accounts manager to select his own personnel. The personnel department had advisory and service responsibility; if it did not present acceptable candidates for the accounts manager to choose from in the scheduled time, it was at fault; however, it was up to the accounts manager to use the department's help effectively, for he was accountable for selecting the people he needed.

Advisory and service responsibility is work a person does for others. It may be advice, i.e., suggestions and recommendations, or service, which is work a person actually does for others because he is more expert or knowledgeable. When he assumes this type of responsibility, he is accountable for the technical quality and content and for the adequacy and appropriateness of the advice and service he provides. He is accountable for his own work, but not for the completed work to which his effort contributes. This type of responsibility, exercised in a staff relationship, is frustrating unless it is spelled out clearly.

ASSIGNING AUTHORITY

The objective of assigning authority is to enable each person to make the decisions and exercise the rights and powers necessary to perform his work most effectively. Authority is assigned in two categories: that necessary to make final decisions and that necessary to ensure understanding and acceptance of final decisions made by others. Since a person's ability to do work is directly influenced by the rights and powers he can exercise, a manager must be sure, in delegating, to specify the type of authority he is assigning. This is often overlooked and gives rise to tension because the individual's teleological drive is channelled, on the job, by the authority he can exercise. If he is expected to carry work to completion, for example, and does not have the right or power to make final decisions, he will be frustrated and the drive will be diverted through some cultural urge to less desirable ends.

Command authority is the right to make the final decision. This means that a person does not have to go to another for approval. He makes the final decision and is accountable for it. He initiates the decision himself, or, if another person offers a recommendation, he decides whether to accept this. When a person has command authority, he also has the obligation to secure the necessary data and coordinate or reconcile differing points of view, as necessary to make the decision. He cannot further delegate command authority once it has been delegated to him without the understanding and agreement of his superior.

If a person has command authority and asks for help or consultation from others, he retains command authority as to how to use the advice or help, but he does not have command authority as to the content of the recommendation itself; that authority remains with the person making the recommendation.

Command authority generally will accompany terminal responsibility; that is, if a person is expected to carry work through to completion, he should have the authority necessary to make the final decisions related to it. Otherwise, he is, in fact, doing the work for somebody else who is making the final decision. If terminal responsibility does not carry command authority, probably the responsibility is greater than was intended. For example, the manager of the purchasing department of a transportation company was given command authority for the responsibility, 'Develop annual and five-year plans for the purchasing department, including forecasts, objectives, programmes, schedules, and budgets.' Actually, the vice-president of operations approved the plans and, hence, made the final decision with respect to them. The situation was clarified by changing the responsibility to read, 'Recommend annual and five-year plans for the purchasing department, including forecasts, objectives, programmes, schedules, and budgets.'

Recommendation authority is the right to offer recommendations and help and to understand what is done with the recommendations. The objective is to encourage people to make full use of the skilled technical help available to them, and to require that they also give serious consideration to recommendations offered. This encourages people to take a proprietary interest in work done for them by others and in decisions which are binding on them, but made by others. Understanding and acceptance (U/A) of the recommendation is accomplished by doing the work necessary to communicate what is done and by developing a willingness in the other person to support it as if it were his own.

If a person has recommendation authority, he must be consulted and his recommendation sought in specified areas. For example, the legal department of an industrial goods company has advisory and service responsibility and recommendation authority for all sales contracts. Therefore, the department is required to write or check sales contracts and must be consulted whenever such contracts are prepared; it has the right to understand and accept recommendations before they are put into effect. Acceptance does not necessarily imply agreement by the legal department of all terms of the contract; rather, it means that it is willing to consent to issue of the contract, even if it does not fully agree with it. For example, the sales department might incorporate contract

128

clauses which the legal department feels are too generous, but which it is willing to support.

Approval authority is the right to approve a decision before it becomes final. Realistically, approval authority is tantamount to command authority. Approval authority is specifically reserved for the responsibility to which it applies. Command and approval authority are often confused. This can become a problem, for when a person understands he has command authority he channels his energies into developing this territory. If his commands are countermanded, in effect he is forced to give up his territory, tension builds and the energy will seek outlet elsewhere.

As a case in point, the plant manager of a toy manufacturing company was held accountable for inventory of finished goods and charged for the cost until shipments had left his loading bay. He understood that he had terminal responsibility and command authority for manufacturing and inventory and that he was required to meet understood and accepted marketing and engineering specifications. However, the marketing department, which had a sales office in another city, had authority to approve order releases before the material could be shipped. At times, a large inventory of packed material would pile up on the loading bay because sales had not approved release of the shipping orders. The plant manager, who was charged for the inventory, became very disturbed for he believed he was being unjustly penalized. The situation was corrected by giving the plant manager command authority for goods through packing and placement on the loading bay and making him accountable for costs to this point. The marketing department had command authority and was accountable for the costs of holding inventory, and shipping to the customer; in fact, each salesman was charged for orders which piled up because of his failure to secure approval for release of the order.

Information authority is the right to receive specific information. This does not refer to routine reporting, but, rather, to notification of specific decisions as soon as possible after they have been made. Information authority does not require understanding and acceptance of the decision.

To illustrate, the personnel department of the central government office of a large city had advisory and service responsibility for recruiting university graduates to fill the needs of other departments. The personnel department was often handicapped because departments which needed graduates would wait until the last minute to send in their specifications. The personnel manager investigated and found that the critical factor was the annual budget. All expenditures for new appointments had to be approved in the budget. The personnel department normally did not receive copies of budgets until the consolidated budget was published; however, information authority was granted on salary budget allocations and the budget department sent regular reports as soon as these specific figures were approved. This eliminated the problem.

WHAT TO DELEGATE

Basic to successful delegation is an understanding of what a manager must do himself—and thus cannot safely delegate—and what he can entrust to others.

TECHNICAL WORK

Most technical work can be delegated. The manager of selling, for example, delegates all selling possible and the planning of his own sales effort to each salesman, and reserves planning, organizing, and controlling of the overall sales effort, and effective leading of the salesmen for himself.

Since the manager is often a specialist in the technical work he supervises, he may be the only one in his group qualified to perform certain parts of it. The purchasing manager, for example, may be an expert in value analysis. The manager should do this specialized, technical work himself only as long as necessary; he should be constantly alert for the opportunity to delegate the work to a subordinate.

ROUTINE AND REPETITIVE WORK

The routine and repetitive parts of planning, organizing, leading, and controlling should be delegated if others are logically placed to do this as well or better than the manager himself. In budgeting, for example, the accounts personnel can best do a cost analysis or a projection of cash flow for the manager. In selecting people, the personnel department can do most of the recruiting and interviewing for the manager. The general rule is to delegate routine and repetitive aspects of management work when possible. Initiation and final decision in the overall management functions and activities can never be safely delegated. Initiation means seeing that the work gets under way and is carried through.

Aspects of management and technical work which are routine and repetitive should invariably be delegated. Management should concentrate on performance of unique actions; that is, of work that must be

130

done differently each time it is performed. Routine and detail, if not delegated, will monopolize the manager's time and crowd out the opportunity for more creative and, in the long run, more satisfying management work.

WHAT NOT TO DELEGATE

The manager who knows what he cannot delegate will find this helpful in identifying the limits within which he can give people a high degree of freedom in doing their own work and making their own decisions. The manager cannot safely delegate final management decisions, decisions on overall technical problems, and work his team-members cannot perform effectively.

FINAL MANAGEMENT DECISIONS

The manager can never safely delegate final decisions on the overall plans that involve his own group, higher levels of management, and other units within the company. He also must reserve for himself final decisions on overall controls, organization, and leading. If the manager permits others to make these decisions, he is abdicating his managerial responsibilities.

Making the final decision does not necessarily involve doing the work leading to it. For the manager who will make the decision, the best approach is to require the accountable individuals to develop their own recommendations so that he need only study the alternatives and make the final decision. If the manager wishes to test individual viewpoints, he can do this through personal discussion. When the manager finds himself deeply involved in collecting information, sifting through data, or screening facts relating to final management decisions, he should search out team-members or staff agencies that can do this for him.

DECISIONS ON OVERALL TECHNICAL PROBLEMS

Problems will arise concerning the technical work carried on by subordinates. When these problems involve two or more team-members, or the group as a whole, the manager should reserve the final decision, because only he can give balanced consideration to all points of view and consider the requirements and prior decisions of higher levels of management and of staff groups with which only he has had contact.

131

The manager should encourage his team-members to coordinate efforts to find solutions to technical, as well as management problems to the point of final decision. When he places such complete reliance on others, he must anticipate their spontaneous centric reaction; their personal preferences and bias will colour their recommendations to him. However, this happens whenever people work together. The manager's best safeguard is to test the validity of both the facts and assumptions by careful questioning.

WORK THAT TEAM-MEMBERS CANNOT PERFORM EFFECTIVELY

If people do not have the capability or are not trained to do the work, delegation will not be successful. When new work is introduced, the manager often must do it himself, have it done by staff groups, or train people. When the manager himself does new work the first time, he should train others and delegate as soon as possible; otherwise he may find he enjoys doing it and finds reasons for not delegating.

DELEGATION STANDARDS

The manager who wishes to develop outstanding competence in delegation should measure his performance against objective criteria. The following standards provide helpful guidelines.

LIMITS OF RESPONSIBILITY STANDARD

Limits are established to give each person opportunity to develop fully his own responsibilities and to prevent encroachment on those of others. One of the key requirements in delegation is to ensure that each person feels secure in his responsibility. This helps him satisfy his territorial urge. A simple, but profound dynamic of human action is that each of us intuitively wants complete freedom to do our thing. We do not want to conform to rules if they infringe on our liberty. Yet, if other people also do precisely what they want and, in the process, overstep our prerogatives, we strive to protect our territory. Tension is generated and frustration or conflict results. The answer is clearly defined responsibility, authority, and accountability.

COMMENSURATE AUTHORITY STANDARD

Each person is delegated authority to make as many decisions as possible related

132

to the work he does. If a manager wants his staff to carry out their work with little intervention on his part, he should give them authority to make as many of their own decisions as possible. The more decisions the manager makes for his people, the more they will have to come to him and the less he will be able to concentrate on those things which only he can do. Authority should be commensurate; if the manager delegates his staff authority to make all their own decisions, he loses control. The manager must always reserve authority for planning, leading, organizing, and controlling.

SINGLE REPORTING STANDARD

Each person reports to only one manager for the same responsibility. A person who reports to two different bosses is inevitably confused in his objectives. He cannot satisfy both managers at the same time, or accomplish his objectives. As a result, his teleological drive and territorial urges are thwarted, for he can never have the satisfaction of working in his own territory or achieving clearly defined objectives. His security is also threatened, for he will not know which boss has the final decision. Also, the opportunities for buck passing, contradiction of orders, and duplication are many.

COMPLETE ACCOUNTABILITY STANDARD

Each person is fully accountable for the responsibility and authority delegated to him. The territorial urge makes us want to be accountable; we feel frustrated and insecure if we cannot anchor our aspirations to work which we feel is our own. If others infringe on our work, the territorial imperative comes into play and we attempt to protect our responsibility by subtle or direct means.

People must be held accountable when deficiencies occur and plans go awry. In an attempt to develop group solidarity, there is frequently an attempt to hold an entire group accountable. This is rarely successful, for if all are accountable, none is accountable. Individuals will put the blame on others; they will think of excuses and rationalize unless they are clearly and unequivocally accountable. This emphasizes that we are spontaneously centric and our drives and urges impel us to protect our own interests as we see them.

This standard also makes clear that the manager is always accountable for everything that occurs in his organization. If mistakes occur several levels below his position, he is still called to account by his own superior. Only in this way can the integrity of the organization be maintained.

HOW TO IMPROVE DELEGATION

In the course of his job, a manager is doing work and making decisions. Most likely, his job has grown spontaneously and, as a result, he is spending much of his time on work that others could do as well, or better, than he can. The same holds true for delegation. Unless he has analysed the work and authority he has delegated to others, his main effort is probably not properly directed. The following five steps will help a manager improve his ability to delegate:

(a) He should define his own responsibility and authority and then define those portions which he has delegated. These portions represent actual delegation.
(b) He should confirm his definitions by getting the U/A of his manager about what the superior has delegated to him, and the U/A of his team-members about what he has delegated to them.
(c) He should determine ideal delegation. That is, what he should delegate, in contrast to what he should be doing himself.
(d) He should compare actual to ideal delegation, identify discrepancies, and determine the steps he will take to improve his ability to delegate.
(e) Again, he should get the U/A of his manager about what the superior has delegated to him; also he should get the U/A of his team-members about what he has delegated to them.

THE ORGANALYSIS TECHNIQUE

The organalysis technique is a method for determining what ideal delegation should be, comparing this with the delegation that has actually taken place, identifying and evaluating the deficiencies, and planning the steps necessary to improve. Organalysis is carried out by giving each type of responsibility and authority a symbol or number and posting these on a matrix chart. This provides a graphic display which greatly facilitates analysis and improvement. The method is an application of linear charting as originally developed by Ernest Hymans and Serge Birne.

The first step in organalysis is to prepare the chart; then the manager posts it for actual delegation. He next posts ideal delegation, compares the two, and determines what improvement steps he will take.

The manager should prepare his chart, setting it up in similar fashion to that of Fig. 8.1. In the left column, he lists the titles for the management and technical responsibilities he now has. In the slanted vertical columns, he lists the titles of the positions with which he has relationships, beginning with his superior's superior and positions directly related to that. Then he should list his superior and staff or other positions directly related to that position. He next should draw heavy lines to show his own position, then follow with the titles of those who report directly to him, titles of peer positions, and finally, any others.

The following symbols and numbers should be used to show the type of *responsibility* and *authority* which have been delegated.

- ◯ Terminal responsibility
- ☐ Advisory and service (A/S) responsibility
- 1 Command authority
- 2 Recommendation authority
- 3 Approval authority
- 4 Information authority

First, the manager should list his responsibilities in the column to the left. Then, to show the delegation which now exists, he should post his

CHART SET-UP	POSTING CODE
• List management, then technical responsibilities	◯ Terminal Responsibility
• Col.1, title of superior's superior	☐ A/S Responsibility
• Col.2, title of immediate superior	1 Command Authority
• Col.3, title of *your* position	2 R/U/A Authority 3 Approval Authority 4 Information Authority
• Next: titles of those who report directly to you	
• Next: titles of related positions on your level	
• Last: all other related positions	

	General Manager	Marketing Manager	Field Sales Manager	Branch Sales Managers	Market Planning Manager	Personnel Managers (6)	Manufacturing Manager	Engineering Manager	Controller						
	1	2	3	4	5	6	7	8	9	10	11	12	13	14	15
SALES FORECASTS	3	(1)	(1)	[2]	(2)	[2]	[2]	[2]	[2]						
SALES BUDGETING	3	3	1	[2]	[2]				(2)						
FIELD SELLING		3	(1)	(1),[2]											
PRICING	(1)	(1)	[2]		[2]			[2]							
SALES CONTROLS	3	3	(1)	(1)	4										
CUSTOMER COMPLAINTS		4	(1)	(1)											
SALES TRAINING			(1)												
KEY ACCOUNT SALES		(1)	(1)												

Fig. 8.1 Organalysis chart—actual delegation. This is the chart of a field sales manager in a manufacturing company.

135

responsibilities and authorities on the matrix by placing the proper symbol or number in the box at the intersection of his position title (shown at the top) and each responsibility listed at the left.

He completes the chart of actual delegation by posting the responsibilities and authorities of others whose positions are named at the top of the chart.

The manager can now identify deficiencies in delegation by evaluating his actual delegation in terms of the standards for delegation. Discrepancies will be readily identified in the posting. The most common are outlined below:

(a) *The 1 is not in the circle: responsibility and authority are not commensurate.* Command authority should accompany terminal responsibility whenever possible. Normally, the superior retains command authority for overall plans, organization and controls that apply to all his subordinates, and decisions that apply to any two or more of them, or to his group and outside groups. In Fig. 8.1, the field sales manager is expected to make the final decision on sales forecasts, subject to two approvals, but the controller has responsibility for completed work on the field sales manager's sales budget.

(b) *There is more than one 1: more than one person makes the command decision.* If there is more than one 1, confusion will result. Subordinates will play off one decision maker against the other, depending upon whose decision is most favourable at the time. If the decisions are antagonistic, action will grind to a halt. In the example, the field sales manager and the marketing manager both have final say on the sales forecasts. The command point needs to be clarified.

(c) *There is more than one circle: more than one person has terminal responsibility.* Each terminal responsibility should be the obligation of only one person. When more than one person is expected to do the same work, confusion and waste are sure to result. Misunderstanding usually occurs because of failure to clarify who is accountable for carrying the work to completion and who provides advice and service. This is clear in the confused responsibility for sales forecasts in Fig. 8.1.

(d) *The square does not have a 2: the person who provides advice and service does not have the right to offer recommendations and to understand and accept the decisions that involve his work.* The person providing advice and service should not need to wait to be invited; he should have the right to initiate recommendations and to understand and accept the final decision concerning use of his advice and service. This is necessary because, almost invariably, the advice and service must continue after the decision has been made. Disinterest and resistance are almost guaranteed if U/A is not secured, especially if the person providing A/S finds his advice misused without his knowing about it.

DETERMINING IDEAL DELEGATION

The manager now has a clear picture of the existing delegation. The next step is to determine what ideal delegation should be. First, he must determine his management responsibilities, that is, the planning, organizing, leading, and controlling work required of him in his position. Then, he should list his technical responsibilities. Having done this, he identifies his reserved technical responsibilities, that is, the technical work he should perform himself because others logically cannot do it as well or better than he can. He writes the word 'reserved' in parentheses after each responsibility of this type. Finally he lists the technical responsibilities he has delegated, but for which he remains accountable. He writes the word 'delegated' in parentheses after each. There will be at least one delegated technical responsibility for each position he supervises.

The example below indicates that the field sales manager reserves key account sales as his own technical work, but delegates all other technical work.

Example: Steps in Determining Ideal Delegation

MANAGEMENT RESPONSIBILITIES:

Planning Performance. Recommend to marketing manager five- and one-year field sales objectives, programmes, schedules, and budgets revised quarterly and yearly, within the limits of approved sales forecasts and corporate policies and supported by approved procedures.

Organizing Performance. Develop current and ideal field sales organization structure, delegation and relationships, within marketing department guide lines.

Leading Performance. Make decisions within authority limits, develop sales communications, select, motivate, and develop employees with advice and service of staff groups.

Controlling Performance. Maintain performance standards for all positions, provide for prompt and accurate reporting of required information, evaluate and correct progress and results to ensure achievement of objectives.

TECHNICAL RESPONSIBILITIES:

Key Account Sales Performance. Sell to designated key governmental and institutional accounts (reserved).

Market Research Performance. Analyse consumer needs and wants, research and report media best suited to communicate product features and benefits and identify and forecast consumer demand (delegated).

Field Sales Performance. Identify and contact potentially profitable customers and sell to satisfy their identified needs and wants (delegated).

Sales Service Performance. Follow up sales to ensure satisfaction and referral (delegated).

Now, the manager should post ideal delegation of responsibility and authority on a prepared organalysis chart. An initial ideal posting is shown in Fig. 8.2.

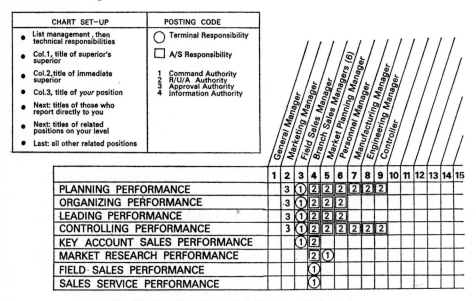

Fig. 8.2 Organalysis chart—ideal delegation. This is the chart of a field sales manager in a manufacturing company.

The manager should discuss the ideal posting with his team-members and those in peer positions, making changes as appropriate until he is satisfied that the posting represents the most logical, workable arrangement. He is now ready to discuss what he has done with his immediate superior. Finally, the manager agrees with his team as to the programme steps to be followed to achieve his objective of improving delegation from his superior to himself and from him to his team-members.

138

THE TECHNIQUE OF COMPLETED WORK

The technique of completed work is a means of forestalling the natural tendency of team-members to get a manager to do much of their work for them. It also helps to correct some of the deficiencies revealed by organalysis. It is a practical means of training people to be fully accountable when they have been delegated terminal responsibility and command authority. If the technique is to be successful, two cautions should be observed. First, completed work does not imply that the manager refuses to talk to people about their work after it has been delegated. Second, completed work is not accomplished simply by telling people, 'Here's the job. Now don't come back to me until you have finished.' Properly applied, the technique of completed work can eliminate much of the routine that consumes a manager's time. The important points are outlined below.

KNOWING WHAT IS WANTED

Before a manager can get others to do completed work for him, he must know exactly what he requires. The best way to do this is to think through the assignment and jot down the key points.

(a) *What Results Are Expected?* The manager should state clearly and concretely what objective should be accomplished when the job is finished and secure understanding and agreement on it.
(b) *What Are the Major Programme Steps?* Are there specific steps that must be carried out in a prescribed order? If so, the manager had better think these through or he will find that what is done differs from what he wants. Here, participation is vital.
(c) *What Is the Major Schedule?* If nothing else, he will want to specify the date on which a special job should be completed. If there are intermediate dates, he must be sure to think these through.
(d) *What Are the Limits?* The manager should specify budget considerations. This is the best way to control expenditures. U/A is critical.

STATING THE CHECK POINTS

To maintain effective control of the work he has delegated, the manager should require periodic check points for progress reports. He must think through questions and problems generated by the reports and jot them down so that he can discuss them later. U/A, again is vital.

139

SETTING THE EXAMPLE

Before requiring completed work of those who report to him, the manager must make sure he is practising this with his own superior and with others with whom he works. Unless he is setting a good example, requiring completed work of others will result in a poor response and hold him up to personal criticism.

TAKING PEOPLE ACTION

The technique of completed work is not a mechanical procedure. It requires a keen understanding of people and a careful approach in terms of human limitations.

(a) *Communicating.* If the manager wants completed work to be successful, he must make sure that his people understand what the technique is, why it is necessary, and how they can use it themselves to improve their own delegation.

(b) *Educating.* The best way for the manager to master completed work himself is to educate other people in the technique. This requires a careful step by step explanation of what it involves and practice in the method.

(c) *Participating.* The manager should encourage people to contribute their ideas and suggestions as to how to make completed work effective. He must remember that each time one of his people sees his own ideas incorporated in what is being done, that person develops an emotional ownership which commits him, more strongly than anything else, to helping the manager make his overall idea a success.

(d) *Delegating.* Once his team-members have learned the technique of completed work, the manager must give them authority to carry out their own work within this framework.

(e) *Reciprocating.* When people carry out a completed job effectively, the manager must not hesitate to give them a pat on the back. Even more effective is a brief recital of the job and its results at a staff meeting so that everybody will be informed of the success and will be motivated to improve efforts themselves.

EVOLVING TO EXCELLENCE

As with other professional management practices, success will not be full-blown. The manager must start where people now are and this is generally

140

at a relatively inefficient stage. By consciously extending his delegation, he can evolve to excellence in a predictable manner. The following techniques will facilitate this evolution.

(a) *Starting Easily.* Instead of trying to install the total technique of completed work all at once, the manager begins in the easiest manner by first requiring people to provide their own answers to each question they bring up. He practises this for a few days or a week. Each time a question is presented to him, he consciously responds by asking. 'What answer do you have?' or 'What do you think?' This will probably reverse a great deal of upward delegation.

(b) *Requiring Solutions, not Problems.* As soon as the manager and his people are in the habit of practising completed work on the matter of questions, they can go to the next most difficult area, that of problems and solutions. When a problem is presented to the manager, he should require a recommended solution before he gives active help. This demands management judgement. In an emergency, he may have to provide the solution himself, but he should gradually introduce, 'Please let me have your recommendation' and he will find that he has taken a major step in improved delegation.

(c) *Discussing.* The manager knows he will require check points and that he will provide active coaching. When people come to report, or when he is working with them, he helps them think the matter through for themselves. By inference or by expressing a personal preference, he may make the decision for them without realizing it. For a time, the process of helping other people to think for themselves will be frustrating both to the manager and to them. With perseverance, however, he will find that this is one of the most effective tools for easing the workload on himself and for building competence in others.

(d) *Selecting Assignments.* To assist in the process of evolving to excellence, the manager begins with simple, short assignments. As people become more proficient, he requires completed work on longer, and more complex assignments.

(e) *Extending the Check Points.* In the beginning, the manager requires people to check with him quite frequently. With practice, training, and confidence he will find that fewer check points will be required to keep informed of progress. When this occurs, he can minimize the person to person contacts and require a written statement, at intervals, to inform him of what has been accomplished. Eventually, he will reach the stage where check points halfway through, and on completion of the job, will be sufficient.

(f) *Suffering Mistakes.* If a manager gives people authority, they are certain to make mistakes. Some of these will be unimportant and others will be significant. The manager must keep in mind that the best way for an intelligent person to learn is to make mistakes and to profit from his experience. Patience is the key word. The manager should discuss people's mistakes with them. He must be sure they have figured out how to prevent the same mistake again. Then, he gives them their heads once more. If the mistake is serious, he may have to recall delegation for a time. But, unless he wants to do everything, he will have to train confident subordinates who can do the work themselves.

(g) *Requiring Completed Reports.* The final step for the manager, and the most difficult in the evolution to excellence in completed work, is requiring people to bring to him letters and reports which are complete except for the manager's own signature. He begins with rough drafts. He askes his people to bring him a rough draft of the letter or report ready for final discussion. Review of these drafts will give the manager a good idea of the ability of each subordinate to think clearly and to express himself concisely. If the subordinate is deficient, the manager will have to make up his mind whether he will help him to improve, or do the subordinate's writing for him. When the manager is satisfied with the rough drafts that are brought to him, he can then require final drafts. The manager should demand that the final draft be ready for finished typing and his signature. At this stage, he should refrain from making corrections on the final draft. He then discusses the deficiencies as he sees them and asks the subordinate to make the changes himself. Above all, the manager should not make changes in written material to fit his own style of writing. There are many acceptable ways of saying the same thing. So long as the letter or report is in good form, the manager should not demand that it be stated exactly as he prefers to write it himself. The final evolutionary stage in completed work is the presentation of the finished letter or report for the manager's signature. When he has accomplished this, he can be sure that he has attained a real standard of professional management.

SUMMARY

(a) Managers often fail to delegate responsibility and authority because they are prevented by their territorial urge and teleological drive. The paragon phenomenon works against the manager because he may belittle the efforts of his people who are working in his technical specialism. Adequate definitions of *responsibility* and *authority* are necessary to delegation.

(b) A manager can delegate several types of *responsibility*. Terminal responsibility requires carrying the work to conclusion. Advisory and service responsibility requires accountability for technical quality and content in the advice and service provided. Delegation of *authority* enables each person to make the decisions and exercise the rights and powers necessary to perform his work most effectively. Command authority gives the right to make the final decision. Recommendation authority is the right to offer recommendations and help. Approval authority gives the right to approve a decision before command authority makes the decision final. Information authority gives the right to receive specific information, but does not give any other right.

(c) Technical work and routine and repetitive portions of management work should be delegated. Final management decisions, overall technical problem decisions, and specific work that subordinates cannot perform effectively should not be delegated.

(d) Certain standards have been developed for effective delegation. (i) Limits should be established to give each person opportunity to develop fully his own responsibilities and to prevent encroachment on those of others. (ii) Each person should be delegated authority commensurate with the decisions that he is required to make related to the work he does. (iii) Each person should report to only one superior for the same responsibility. (iv) Each person should be completely accountable for the responsibility and authority delegated to him.

(e) The process of delegation can be greatly improved by the organalysis technique. It involves listing management and technical responsibilities for a position, then identifying for each the appropriate kind of responsibility (terminal or advisory and service) or authority (command, recommendation, approval, or information). Deficiencies in delegation can be identified and corrected by analysing actual and ideal postings in terms of established delegation standards.

(f) The technique of completed work enables the manager to avoid the pitfalls of upward delegation. It requires: (i) Determining desired results. (ii) Stating the check points. (iii) Setting the proper example. (iv) Taking people action. (v) Evolving to excellence.

9. MAKING BETTER DECISIONS

A manager's effectiveness is related directly to the quality of his decisions. The nature and quality of his decisions summarize his capabilities more fully than anything else he does. *Decision making is the work a manager performs to arrive at conclusions and judgements.* Decision making evolves from the spontaneous mode to the rational mode, as management competence and skills improve.

Decisions made in the spontaneous mode are intuitive, made without conscious thought or analysis; at the same time, they may be based on precedent. We often spontaneously do the same thing we have done in similar situations in the past. A spontaneous decision is often based on a hunch, an intuitive reaction to memories or previous conditioning. Even if the situation is observed or the facts reviewed, there is little attempt to determine what the facts mean or to make a logical judgement based on them.

Spontaneous decisions are based on precedents because this requires least effort; also, such action is easiest to rationalize. The fact that a decision turned out well and hence, presumably, was sound last week or last year often seems the best possible argument for making the same decision in a similar situation today. However, situations are rarely identical; all things change with time.

Spontaneous decisions are generally centric. While this is successful and quickly rewarding, it evokes increasingly centric decisions on the part of others as they attempt to protect their own interests.

Decisions made in the rational mode are based on systematic study and logical analysis of a problem. The facts are assessed, the alternatives weighed, and a decision is reached that gives proper consideration to the needs and interests of all concerned. Rational decision making uses full mental resources, emphasizes the creative aspects of problem solving, generates a consistent approach to thinking that minimizes the probability of error, and gives greater assurance of productive results.

PRINCIPLES OF DECISION MAKING

The following basic principles provide a sound basis for management decisions.

THE PRINCIPLE OF DEFINITION

Too often, time and effort are wasted because we do not think through what the problem is—or the objective.

PRINCIPLE OF DEFINITION	*A logical decision can be made only if the real problem is first defined*

We may not identify the real problem because we fail to take the time to determine the basic factors that must be changed to arrive at a satisfactory solution. If the problem calls for a solution, our drives activate a variety of cultural urges which prompt quick and instinctive action.

As an example, a processing company had canning plants in the east, mid-west, and on the Pacific coast of the United States. It made all the cans it required for its west coast needs at plants near Los Angeles and San Francisco. For some time, the company had excess manufacturing capacity at the San Francisco plant, and as a result, expenses mounted. Efforts to create a secondary market were unsuccessful. What to do with the excess capacity? Both eastern and mid-western plants had inadequate capacity and were buying cans from outside. Why not ship San Francisco cans to the Illinois and New York areas? The suggestion was hooted down. 'We'll be paying freight on too much air. Historically, tinplate has always moved from east to west, not from west to east. The freight will kill us.' As losses continued, the principle of definition was finally applied. An analysis was made and the real problem was identified as how to provide cans to mid-western and eastern plants at least cost to the company. Factual study of freight costs, tariffs, and burden absorption showed that empty cans could, in fact, be shipped

146

from west to east at a substantial overall saving to the company. The company was able to add some $750 000 to its earnings during the next fiscal year because of the savings and increased efficiency that resulted from the logical decision based on fact.

THE PRINCIPLE OF ADEQUATE EVIDENCE

A manager expert in decision making can back his conclusions with facts or reasonable inferences drawn from facts. When the facts underlying a problem are assembled and understood, the decision will often be so obvious as to seem to make itself.

PRINCIPLE OF ADEQUATE EVIDENCE	*A logical decision must be valid in terms of the evidence on which it is based*

A successful restaurant operator, seeking to start a chain, contracted to build a new restaurant in a suburb. When the restaurant was completed, the operator found that three other new restaurants were under construction on the same side of the street and within four blocks of his new building. He had failed to check newly issued building permits and discovered too late that his potential market had shrunk to less than a break-even level. Clearly, if he had amassed adequate evidence, his decision would not have been the same.

THE PRINCIPLE OF IDENTITY

From a different perspective, the same object will appear to be different to different people. A budget deficit means different things to the accountant, the salesman, and the engineer. The relative importance of the same facts may differ from year to year.

PRINCIPLE OF IDENTITY	*Facts may seem to differ, depending on the point of view and the point in time from which they are observed*

To establish the validity of our facts, we must try to use the varying viewpoints involved and determine the significance of the time period during which the event happened.

When making decisions involving two or more other people, we should be sure to get the point of view of each, carefully weighing their viewpoints and checking them with other sources before we make a decision.

147

Often enough, a subordinate's decision seems impractical. However, if we take the time to examine his viewpoint, we are frequently surprised to discover how reasonable his decision is in light of his reasons for making it.

USING THE RATIONAL MODE IN DECISION MAKING

A rational decision is the end product of a series of logically related steps. The following sequence will not guarantee that a manager's decisions will be right every time; however, it will improve the probability that his decision is the best available answer to the problem that really exists. The logical thought process is made up of six steps. The manager can improve his decisions by consciously following this sequence when the situation warrants the time and effort necessary for a rational decision. As is true with any new skill, his first few efforts may be awkward and unsatisfactory. However, practice will bring improvement and the reinforcement of success.

STEP 1: STATING THE APPARENT PROBLEM

When we first see a problem situation, or when it is first presented to us, the solution may seem apparent. Most often, we plunge ahead, only to discover that we are merely nibbling at the fringes of the problem and even, in some cases, working on the wrong problem. We also often observe only the symptoms of a problem and not the underlying causes. Then we jump to conclusions based on the superficial view. When this is the case, we treat the symptoms, not the basic problem.

To avoid this mistake, our first step should be to put the principle of definition to work. We should quickly review the situation and state the problem as it appears. We should jot it down, then discuss it with others who are concerned or involved with the problem. Since the problem as it appears is probably not the real problem, we then go on to the second step.

STEP 2: SEEKING THE FACTS

To identify the problem precisely, we must examine the circumstances surrounding it. It is rarely advisable to collect all the facts bearing on a problem. Some information may be more difficult or costly to secure than the situation warrants; too much ensures that the bulk of it will not bear on the most significant aspects of the problem. Fact gathering should be a clearly defined, sharply focused effort as implied by the principle of adequate evidence. We can focus on the most essential information by investigating systematically each of the decision-making factors discussed below.

We know that the same facts will be interpreted differently by different people, as stated in the principle of identity. To get around this bias, we should select individuals who will have opposing points of view. If we discover their viewpoints and why they hold them, we will have a more balanced picture.

The People Factor. The individuals involved in any problem will interpret the facts in terms of their personalities, preferences, and personal needs. Because the action we take will be predicated on what we can get people to do, we must know enough about the individuals concerned to anticipate their reactions.

We need to keep in mind that once a person has taken a firm stand on a matter, he will hold fast to it, especially if his emotions are involved. It is pointless to try to change attitudes in this fact-gathering stage. We must note what beliefs we are dealing with and proceed on the assumption that they will become more fixed, rather than change, as time goes by.

The Place Factor. The physical location can be significant. For example, one international company had the problem of staff going on holiday during busy seasons. The board approved a policy that all holidays would be taken between 1 May and 1 October or the privilege for that year would be forfeited. A cable from the Australian branch pointed out that this was the middle of winter in the southern hemisphere, and the busiest season. The policy was recalled and restated.

The Time Factor. Facts will differ with the time period in which they occur, as stated in the principle of identity. It is clear, for example, that a comparison of costs today with those of five years ago will be misleading unless we make adjustments for changes in the real value of money during the period.

In considering the time factor, we need to discover not only what implications time has for the problem itself, but, also, how it will influence the decision. We must find out how quickly the problem must be solved and to what extent the timing can be modified. Haste is to be avoided, for it leads to expedients and wasted resources.

The Causative Factor. Discovering why the problem situation occurred will best define the real problem. One approach is to compare similar situations to determine why the problem occurs in one, but not another.

149

For example, the Glasgow office of an international import company had continuing problems collecting large sums owed to it by West German companies. The accounts became so pressing that the controller from the London headquarters investigated. After a week of interviews, he still could not find the cause. Finally, he compared the Glasgow procedures with those of the London office, where the problem did not exist. He discovered that London always sent its letters and invoices in German to its German customers; Glasgow corresponded in English. The time lag reflected the natural tendency of the German clerical staffs to push the foreign communications aside until they could find somebody to translate for them. Once the cause was found, the real problem was evident.

Causative factors can often be identified by asking the people directly involved. Often, several different individuals will have a partial idea of the causative factor. Bringing them together for a short group session will have a synergistic effect; their pooled thinking may give a clearer picture of the real cause.

STEP 3: IDENTIFYING THE REAL PROBLEM

The most important part of decision making is to identify what the problem really is. This is a continuation of step 1 and a stringent application of the principle of definition. *The best method for identifying the real problem follows from the logic that every problem is an obstacle that stands in the way of reaching an objective.*

There are two parts to this step. First, the manager must determine his objective in the problem situation. He must think through, as clearly and precisely as he can, the measurable results which, if accomplished, will solve the problem to his entire satisfaction. At this point he should not concern himself with how to do it, he should just nail down in words what he will have *after the problem is solved*. Once the objective has been named, the problem can be identified in terms of 'how to' achieve this objective.

For example, a metal manufacturer designed a new tool that required a modification of his existing moulding machines. Careful analysis of customer requirements and production specifications yielded the objective, 'To provide the manufacturing department with a 500-ton moulding machine that will satisfy customer requirements and meet manufacturing capabilities.' The real problem was identified by adding

150

'how to' and was stated as, 'How to provide the manufacturing department with a 500-ton moulding machine that will satisfy customer requirements and meet manufacturing capabilities.'

The second step for the manager is to establish the standards that will tell him when he has accomplished the results he wants. Here he asks himself, 'What will be acceptable evidence that the manufacturing department has been provided with a 500-ton moulding machine that will satisfy customer requirements and meet manufacturing capabilities?' The following standards would answer this question. (a) Mean time between breakdowns is a minimum of 1000 hours. (b) Meets established manufacturing specifications. (c) Has fluidic controls. (d) Costs between $60 000 and $68 000.

A full statement of the real problem now becomes, 'How to provide the manufacturing department with a 500-ton moulding machine that will satisfy customer requirements and meet manufacturing capabilities, so that mean time between breakdowns will be not less than 1000 hours, established manufacturing specifications will be met, fluidic controls will be provided, and the cost will be between $60 000 and $68 000?'

The manager has now determined the specific objective that will have the greatest probability of eliminating the problem situation. In doing this, he must give proper consideration to scope and timing. Much effort may be wasted if he tries to solve problems for other people, or to extend his solutions beyond his scope or area of accountability. At the same time, he may belittle potential results if his problem solving is not sufficiently radic to take into account the needs and capabilities of other units. A manager has his own area of accountability, but this accountability extends beyond the centric interests of his own unit. A professional manager considers his problems and solutions in terms of their implications for other units and the company. He times, unifies, and integrates his own actions with those of his superior and with other units that are likely to be affected by what he does.

Timing Is Important. The right solution at the wrong time is no better than the wrong solution at the right time. We can give full consideration to the time element if we make sure the problem we state encompasses two aspects, the real problem as it exists now and how it will exist in the long term. Once we have identified the difference, we can begin to look systematically for both short- and long-term solutions. Unhappily, the best possible answer for today's problem may be precisely the worst answer for that problem as it will appear a year or two from now.

Deciding Too Soon Is a Mistake. Once a decision is known, people act as if it has already been implemented. The final decision should be withheld until there is a reasonable probability that action can be taken on it. If the decision must be postponed, it is far better to develop reasonable alternatives and make the final choice only when action can be initiated. *Indecisiveness Is Equally Bad.* Decisions that are made timidly, or too late, lead to inconclusive or hasty action, increased mistakes, and higher costs. When we hesitate to decide, we are really making a decision to do nothing.

As Chester I. Barnard, former president of the New Jersey Bell Telephone Company, put it, 'The fine art of executive decision-making consists in not deciding questions that are not now pertinent, in not deciding prematurely, in not making decisions that cannot be made effective, and in not making decisions that others should make.'

STEP 4: EXPLORING THE ALTERNATIVES

Once we have in mind a clear picture of the results we want to achieve, our natural tendency is to go directly to a solution. However, this encourages us to repeat an action we have taken earlier in similar circumstances, and we do not take the time to think through fresh, creative, and more effective action. Our need is not to mimic, but to improve on what we have done well in the past. Each decision should be a step forward, not a matter of marking time.

Other companies may offer solutions to similar problem situations that may serve as alternatives to the problem. A search of the indexes of business, professional, and management magazines may lead to articles that will provide useful alternative ideas. Staff groups and others involved in the problem should be called upon for suggestions in developing alternatives. Brainstorming is a valuable technique in developing the alternatives. One method is for the manager to get two or three people together who have a personal interest in the problem; if they do not understand the background thoroughly, he should explain it to them. He then asks them to suggest as many alternative solutions as they can. He should write them down as quickly as they are offered. There should be no discussion or critical comment on any suggestion until they are all down. Then the manager can sort the good from the bad, narrowing the selection to his final choice. The key to successful application of this technique is the manager's ability to elicit free and creative suggestions and to withhold criticism or comment so as not to inhibit imaginative suggestions.

Two points should be kept in mind when developing and assessing alternatives. First, of the many alternatives available, the manager can safely assume that only one or two will give real promise of significant success with reasonable expenditure of effort and resources. These may not be the most complete solutions, but they will probably enable him to reach his stated objective most effectively. He should eliminate the other possibilities and focus on these.

Second, the more opportunity to incorporate their ideas and suggestions the manager gives people who will be expected to carry out the decision, the greater the emotional ownership they will have in the decision and the harder they will work to make it succeed. Since management decisions are carried out by other people, the alternatives should be assessed with the questions, 'Which of these will get best acceptance? In which of these alternatives can I most effectively involve the people who will carry it out?'

STEP 5: SELECTING THE BEST SOLUTION

The point of decision for the professional manager is rational selection of the best among his alternatives; he will have greatly simplified his problem at this point if he has established standards that tell when he has achieved the desired results. With these criteria in mind, he can determine which alternative gives the greatest probability of success. This becomes the best solution.

The manager can anticipate that there will be some dissatisfaction with his decision, no matter what it may be. He will be tempted to procrastinate. This is fatal. When the time has come, the decision must be made. Nothing is so discouraging to subordinates as to have a boss who vacillates, who makes a decision and changes it, or who cannot get up the courage to plunge into the water. It is almost certain that less harm will be done by an imperfect decision than by a long, drawn-out vacillation. If the manager knows his objective and takes positive action, his momentum will enable him to correct mistakes and to retrieve lost ground. If he fails to act, however, events move and very soon the circumstances have changed so that the decision he has been steeling himself to make is no longer the best one.

If a manager feels he cannot decide, it is far better to come out with a crisp 'No' than to leave the issue in doubt. This at least will free others for action within their own spheres of authority so they can take the more limited alternatives that may be open to them.

In a sense, everything up to now has been preparation, for we are finally in a position to determine how to put the decision into effect. Often, we lose much of the effectiveness of the decision by walking away from it without determining a detailed course of action. While the manager may delegate most of this step, it is up to him to see that it is done. After making the decision, the following must be considered in outlining the course of action.

Considering Policies. Decisions must often be carried out within the framework of policies made at higher levels. It is important for the manager to establish clearly the limits of action before other people are given their assignments. Each individual is prompted to define his territory. His teleological drive presses him to work for his own purposes, not those of others. If limits are not set which reflect policy requirements, he will set his own to suit his personal preferences.

Developing Programmes. A sound course of action contains a statement of the action necessary to attain the end results. The manager must develop the sequence and priority of the steps to be taken. If the situation is unstable, or if new and unanticipated conditions are likely to arise, it may be necessary to develop alternative programmes that can be put into effect in case of later developments. When possible, it is better to pre-think alternatives, for when emergencies arise, our security drive pushes us to prompt, spontaneous action, which is undesirable if we are trying to make a rational decision.

Establishing Schedules. Time is always an important condition. Whenever possible, the manager should specify the date for the beginning and end of each programmed step. He must make sure that his people understand that they will be held responsible for accomplishment within these time limits. Unless people feel that the schedule is their own, they will not feel a personal commitment when they fail to meet the schedule. This is why participation is most important in programming and scheduling. So long as it fits his overall course of action, the manager should encourage each individual to determine for himself what he will do, and how he will do it, to reach the agreed goals.

Specifying Procedures. Some of the work to be accomplished may have to be performed in a standardized and uniform manner. In this case, the manager should develop and specify the procedures to be followed or make provision for using procedures already in effect. Unless they have a strong structure which dominates, people tend to follow the dictates of their own teleological drives and do things in the way which they prefer.

If work needs to be standardized, procedures which are understood and accepted will provide the necessary structure.

Determining Budgets. Almost always, there are expense limitations within which the action must be accomplished. The manager can best hold the cost down to the desired level by determining in advance what he can afford to spend in terms of people, materials, tools, and facilities. Converted into money, this is his budget. He should keep in mind that the budget is only as effective as the understanding and acceptance of the people who must live within it.

The sequence outlined provides a systematic approach to making sound decisions. The following basic considerations apply at every step and should be kept in mind by the professional manager.

DECENTRALIZING DECISION MAKING

Decisions at lower levels are short-range operating decisions, made in response to immediate operating requirements and emergencies. Because of this, they often are expedient, limited in viewpoint, and give little consideration to overall long-range management needs. Since lower level decisions are closest to the point of action, they directly influence operating results; once put into effect, they may commit the company as a whole to a course that will severely restrict its future freedom of action, as implied by the principle of present choices.

The implications of this are twofold. At higher levels, managers should make decisions that apply to two or more of the units reporting to them, or involve their own as well as other units. At lower levels, managers should try to see and understand the point of view of their superiors before making their own decisions.

When decision making is pushed downwards organizationally, much of the burden of routine details is taken from the shoulders of higher level managers. At the same time, people at lower levels are given greater command over their own work and, as a result, can be expected to show much greater interest and motivation from satisfaction of their teleological drives.

Availability of information is an important consideration in determining how far down the decision can safely be made. If the decision pertains only to one group, information should be available to the manager of that group. If two or more groups are involved, the manager accountable for both groups should be provided with the necessary information.

155

USING COMMITTEES IN DECISION MAKING

A committee should be used to assist a manager in decision making when a group of people can reasonably be expected to give better results than can a single individual. If a committee reviews and comes to an agreement on the real problem, this will help ensure that all pertinent viewpoints have been considered.

The committee may be useful in proposing and analysing possible alternative solutions. The alternatives can often be thought through most effectively on an individual basis by each member of the committee, and then reconciled by the committee as a whole.

Selection of the best alternative, which is the heart of the decision-making process, should be made by the accountable manager. However, the committee may express its opinions, to help ensure that he has considered all important viewpoints. If the members of the committee are expected to participate in carrying out the action, they also should be asked to participate in determining the course of that action.

Improperly used, the committee can waste much valuable time. It is a poor data collector. In analysis and decision making, a committee compromises at the lowest common denominator of the group.

COORDINATING DECISIONS

Decisions are often unbalanced because all viewpoints have not been considered; the managers involved have not coordinated fully at their own and subordinate levels. Decisions should be coordinated fully at the level involved. When a manager asks his team to participate in decision making, he should insist that they time, unify, and integrate their recommendations at their own level before putting them before him. The manager has the same obligation to his superior.

If the decision involves the manager's own and other groups, his superior will assume the authority for final decisions. The manager can be of great service to his superior in reaching a sound decision by apprising him of the nature of the problem, securing his permission to go ahead, then preparing a sound and balanced recommendation for his review and final approval. To do this, the manager will want to consult with other groups, develop alternatives with them, and consider their suggestions in the recommendations he prepares for his superior. If there is disagreement on important points, he should make sure his superior knows of this and is informed of the pros and cons.

156

SUMMARY

(a) Spontaneous decision making, without conscious thought or analysis, is often based on the past and is usually unsuccessful in the long term. Rational decision making is based on facts and sound logic and is followed by carefully determined actions. It is usually successful.

(b) The following principles provide a sound basis for management decision making. (i) The principle of definition states that a logical decision can be made only if the real problem is first defined. (ii) The principle of adequate evidence states that a logical decision must be valid in terms of the evidence on which it is based. (iii) The principle of identity states that facts may seem to differ, depending on the point of view and the point in time from which they are observed.

(c) Use of the following six steps to make management decisions will increase the probability of success: (i) The manager should establish the apparent problem, that is, the surface problem as it appears to him at the outset of the decision-making process. (ii) The manager should gather the pertinent facts, taking into account the factors of the situation, the people involved, the location, the time and the cause of the problem. (iii) The manager should define the real problem by determining his objective and then by establishing the standards that will indicate that he has achieved his objective. (iv) The manager should establish and examine the alternative solutions to the problem by using the ideas and suggestions of others. (v) The manager should narrow all the alternatives to the one that will give the greatest probability of success. If he cannot reach a decision, he should say 'No'; he should not leave the problem hanging in the air. (vi) After making the decision, the manager should establish a definite course of action to implement that decision with policies, programmes, schedules, procedures, and budgets.

(d) Decentralized and committee decision making can be useful if their limitations are understood. Decentralized decision making is most often short range because of the management level at which the decisions are made. Committees should be used only after the real problem has been defined and the data collected.

(e) At no time should the manager fail to realize that it is his responsibility to coordinate the decisions made for, and by, his group.

157

10.   MOTIVATING FOR RESULTS

A manager gets his results through other people. No matter how perfect his plans, organization, and controls, if people do not want to do the work required, if they cannot attack their tasks with interest and enthusiasm, the manager will not accomplish as much as he might. *Motivating is the work a manager performs to inspire, encourage, and impel people to take required action.* What kind of behaviour to motivate, and how to motivate it, are the key questions.

THE EVOLUTION OF MOTIVATION

We can best answer these questions if we keep in mind what we have learned from recent research findings. As genetic research has shown, we are born unfulfilled; all our lives we strive to become complete. Just as the acorn contains the blueprint of the oak, within the primal human cell is the tracery of what the brain and body will become. Our teleological drive constantly impels us to put forth physical and mental effort—or work—to attempt to fulfil our endowment.

We are always hindered in attaining the fulfilment we seek by the diverse factors of ecology and society that we call environment, which both shape us and are shaped by us. These factors present the challenge which determines how successfully we become what we are capable of becoming. Most compelling of these environmental challenges are those presented by other people. To the extent we wish to work with others,

158

every action carries its special burden of adjustment to their needs and wants; but every such compromise to the demands or needs of others means that we fail to satisfy to some degree our innate centric teleological drives. From a practical viewpoint, complete fulfilment of our potential is thus impossible, for we must continually modify the fulfilment we seek for ourselves as we adapt to the needs of others.

The reality of fulfilment lies in the process of growth towards the ideal, not in the consummation, for growth changes the ideal and, hence, it can never be realized. *Contrary to earlier ideas, we now know that fulfilment of a person's potential is a process, not an end in itself.* Looked at in this way, human evolution is a continuing process of progressive change towards fulfilment. This process is self-generating, for each new generation adds fresh energy to the system. It proceeds on an open-ended, ascending spiral, not in a closed loop.

Within this framework, history becomes an exemplification of the principle of human reaction. Each generation has relearned, through trial and error, the lessons of the past and intuitively adapted its culture to the changing needs of people.

INDIVIDUAL AND ORGANIZATION CONFLICT

Our genetic drives impel us to fulfilment and satisfaction as individuals, not as members of groups. These compulsions would doom any continued affiliation with others if they were not overlaid and subordinated by cultural urges, which enable us to function effectively as members of groups. Our cultural urges towards cooperation, sharing, concern for others, and subordination of individual to group purposes are acquired and are only as effective as our learning and practice of them.

There is, thus, inevitable and continuing conflict between the needs of any individual and those of the groups of which he is a member. This conflict is healthy and desirable, for it catalyses evolutionary progress towards cultural, and eventually, genetic changes which will equip us to function best as group members. As we have seen, the cultural conditions which make for a rewarding group membership can only be achieved if they also provide for satisfaction of the basic genetic drives. For example, it is emotionally impossible for a normal individual to give first priority to the needs and purposes of the organization of which he is a member if he cannot first find assurance that his own needs and purposes will be satisfied.

It is for these reasons that the centric mode must always precede the

159

radic. We can best think of the relationship of the individual and the organization to which he belongs as a symbiotic one, for, while they can be reconciled, the two have essentially dissimilar objectives. However, they must live together in harmony if they are to maximize their respective benefits. To understand the relationship, we will examine both organization and individual needs.

ORGANIZATION NEEDS

Whenever two or more people seek to work together as an organized group on a continuing basis, the following organization needs must be satisfied or the group cannot endure.

(a) Priority of the overall objectives of the organization as a whole.
(b) Provision of sufficient resources derived from the total effort to ensure accomplishment of overall objectives and the safety of the organization as a whole.
(c) Effective performance within the organization of all the work vital to accomplishment of overall objectives.
(d) Communication of information necessary for accomplishment of overall objectives.
(e) Maintenance of controls to ensure accomplishment of overall objectives.

Individual happiness and fulfilment depend on the satisfaction of basic genetic drives and cultural urges which are essentially individual, and not group oriented, and in fact, may be contrary to the needs outlined above. In practical terms, this means that the individual must be able to adapt to the needs of the organization, while the organization must know how to satisfy the needs of the individual,with the recognition on both sides that complete satisfaction is impossible and some degree of compromise is always necessary.

INDIVIDUAL NEEDS

By himself, or as a member of an organization, the normal individual will have greatest probability of satisfaction and fulfilment if he can achieve the conditions below.

(a) Satisfaction of his personal objectives.
(b) Adequate resources to provide food, shelter, and the material goods he feels he needs.
(c) A territory of his own which he can develop to his own satisfaction.

160

(d) Work which gives him fullest opportunity to use his talents and abilities.

(e) Freedom to do his work in the way he prefers and to make his own decisions.

(f) An environment which will enable him to feel important as a person and to enjoy the trust and confidence of those with whom he associates.

To these individual requirements must be added purely personal needs of status, sex, and power which vary greatly and which the individual must resolve within the context of those listed above.

THE LESSONS OF HISTORY

We can learn a great deal about how the conflicting needs of individuals and organizations are resolved if we study historical patterns. In every ancient civilization of which we know, the needs of the organization dominated and these were usually expressed in satisfaction of the needs of its leaders; in other words, the prevalent mode of motivation was spontaneous centric. As civilization advanced, organizations changed very slowly by natural selection, but invariably remained spontaneous centric in orientation. In each case, the principle of human reaction was operative as people eventually resisted and rebelled against this centric leadership.

In almost every generation, a few have seen the need for a different orientation and have voiced concern and admonition. As early as 600 B.C., Lao-tse, the Chinese philosopher, had this advice for managers which gives both the theme and the method of the rational radic mode. 'In managing human affairs,' he said, 'the first rule is self-restraint. . . . The wise man gives to others so that he will have more for his own. . . . When his work is done, his people will say, "we did this ourselves".' It is no accident that religious organizations have been the most enduringly successful of all human institutions and that every one of the major religions has some construction of 'Do unto others as you would have others do unto you' as a prime tenet of belief. It would seem that the oldest lesson is also the newest.

THE IMPACT OF TECHNOLOGY

The pattern of individual and organizational conflict can be traced clearly in modern industrialized societies. Here, the basic dichotomy between people and their institutions has been aggravated by the exponential multiplication of technology and the accompanying increase in formalized culture.

From the time technology began its greatest expansion in the nineteenth century, the spontaneous centric mode provided the driving force. Some leaders saw the self-defeating implications of this mode and advocated or accomplished moves towards the rational radic. These groping attempts have never been more than partly successful, for they have been individual and sporadic moves against the prevailing tide. However, in every generation there have been perceptive voices. For example, in light of today's new awareness of the importance of human assets, compared with financial, and the general advocacy of human asset accounting, it is interesting to note that in the early nineteenth century, Robert Owen, the successful British weaver and social reformer, compared the value of investment in machines to that in human beings and advised business leaders that they would get a far greater return by investing in their human assets through the training and satisfaction of their workers. However, the time was not ripe and the suggestion was regarded largely as an interesting curiosity.

Henri Fayol, a French mining executive before the Second World War, advocated consideration for human, as well as material resources. 'Social order demands precise knowledge of the human requirements and resources of the concern and a constant balance between these,' he said, in developing his principles of management. He recognized the importance of the radic mode for long-term success. 'In a business the interest of one employee or group of employees should not prevail over that of the concern,' he emphasized, and 'that the interest of the home should come before that of its members and that the interest of the State should have pride of place over that of one citizen or group of citizens.'[13]

THE INFLUENCE OF F. W. TAYLOR

Early in this century, Frederick Winslow Taylor saw the waste of human effort and of material resources. He stated, 'We can see our forests vanishing, our water-powers going to waste. . . .' and he deplored even more 'our larger wastes of human effort, which go on every day through such of our acts as are blundering, ill-directed, or inefficient. . . .'[14]

In advocating change, Taylor expressed the logic underlying a move to the rational radic mode. The first objective of management, he said, 'should be to secure the maximum prosperity for the employer, coupled with the maximum prosperity for each employee.'[15]

162

It has become fashionable to belittle Taylor and his work, equating his approach with the drabness, monotony, and conformity which accompany the early stages of mechanization. While he exhibited some of the attitudes of his period, Taylor's thinking marks a giant step forward in laying the groundwork for a rational radic approach to motivation. It was fortunate that Taylor's training led him to emphasize efficiency in the work itself, for this led to that improvement in material welfare which is a necessary basis for concern with cultural urges which are further removed from the insistent prompting of the primal genetic drives.

Taylor identified the spontaneous pattern of cultural evolution. He pointed out that the methods of work common in each trade had developed through 'an evolution representing the survival of the fittest', that is, the spontaneous centric mode. Workers learned successful methods through trial and error and rule of thumb and passed on their skills by word of mouth. Most managers had been first-class workers themselves, Taylor said, and they realized that the workmen knew better than they did how to do the work. However, although it was not recognized, the principle of human reaction was operative. Experienced managers realized that 'the workmen believe it to be directly against their interests to give their employers their best initiative, and that instead of working hard to do the largest possible amount of work and the best quality of work for their employers, they deliberately work as slowly as they dare. . . .' The best managers understood the problem, Taylor said, and recognized that 'the manager must give some *special incentive*' such as the opportunity for advancement, higher wages, shorter hours, better working conditions and, above all, 'personal consideration for, and friendly contact with, his workmen which comes from a genuine and kindly interest in the welfare of those under him'.[16]

Taylor went on to advance this philosophy by what we can identify as progressive moves to the rational centric and rational radic modes. He concentrated on the improvement of technology, so that there would be resources to support long-term concern for people and their welfare. And he constantly reiterated the vital importance of motivating people as the foundation to improved efficiency.

Taylor was by no means a voice crying in the wilderness. He reflected the best thinking of business leaders of the time. For example, Thomas J. Watson, Sr, founder of IBM, constantly reiterated a thought that has reappeared in recent behavioural science writings. Watson held that a manager's job is 'to be an assistant to his men—to bring the best out in them'.[17] Armco Steel Corporation in its *Policies* issued in 1919, affirmed its intention to follow the rational radic approach: 'Mutual Interest is the "cement" that binds a group of men and women together in every sort of productive effort. Without a true "Mutual Interest" there can be no serious applications, no real loyalty, no cordial cooperation, and little chance for concerted and effective effort.'[18]

MOTIVATION AS A SOCIAL PROCESS

This thread of rational radic thinking and action became stronger through several decades. Gradually, students and analysts of management began to visualize the overall process and to isolate its vital elements. During the 'twenties, Mary Parker Follett, both a psychologist and administrator, identified the organization as a social system and emphasized the need for practical methods of resolving conflict and integrating the needs and objectives of managers and subordinates in the administrative process.[19]

Chester I. Barnard believed that people in an enterprise must be motivated in terms of many complex influences which constantly impel them to action. His experience had demonstrated to him that motivation involved more than any one factor; it was not enough to improve methods, increase compensation, practise good human relations, or apply psychological findings. It required sensitive and realistic use of all available resources. Barnard analysed the pressures that cause people in an organization to act. He looked at broad, continuing, and impersonal factors such as governmental and legal requirements, formalized executive authority, and the need to satisfy overall objectives. People also act to satisfy the technical requirements of their skills and the technical standards of their departments. Barnard stressed that individuals are motivated in terms of what they understand, not by what really exists; the person who sees himself as a skilled worker on a superior team acts in terms of that understanding. Furthermore, Barnard stressed that people act in terms of the expectations of the informal organization, as well as the formal. Their personal conduct reflects more closely what their fellows expect of them than what the organization demands.

Barnard defined and summarized the role of the manager in creating a rational radic culture in the organization, 'The capacity of responsibility is that of being firmly governed by moral codes—against inconsistent immediate impulses, desires, or interests', and of, 'inculating points of view, fundamental attitudes, loyalties, to the organization or cooperative

164

system, and to the system of objective authority, that will result in subordinating individual interest and the minor dictates of personal codes to the good of the cooperative whole.'[20]

BEHAVIOURAL SCIENCE THEORIES OF MOTIVATION

Changes in motivational practice have been accompanied, and frequently influenced, by theory and research in psychology, sociology, anthropology, and other social sciences. Of particular interest to managers is the work of a group of behavioural scientists who have advocated a humanistic, participative approach on the assumption that this results in greatest human satisfaction, and whose theories now dominate the teaching of management.

As Warren G. Bennis, a leading behavioural scientist from the State University of New York at Buffalo says, 'The behavioural sciences have made stunning progress in management education. In less than one decade, they have not only infiltrated the field, they have secured a firm foothold in all the leading centres of management studies.' Not only this, he says, but 'the behavioural sciences have literally transformed management education and research, and they are currently challenging management's natural and penultimate target, management practice.'[21] This viewpoint has far-reaching implications. If it is true that behavioural scientists are most competent in both the theory and practice of management, and if they have developed a body of validated knowledge which managers can follow with confidence and success, their role may be to coach and counsel enterprise executives in the conduct of their businesses, as well as to educate managers in their profession.

The applicability of current behavioural science theories can best be assessed through an understanding of their antecedents.

The general theme is based on organismic theory, which develops the concept that the individual functions as a whole person and must be so understood. He is actuated by a master drive, self-actualization, which prompts him to become what he is capable of becoming. To this theme are added the ideas of Max Weber,[22] a German sociologist of the late nineteenth century, who analysed the bureaucracy he observed in Germany during this period and commented on its authoritarian, stultifying characteristics. The undesirable features of Weber's bureaucracy of pre-First World War Germany are extrapolated and applied equally to modern large-scale enterprise. Since this bureaucratic organization is said to blight the healthy human personality and prevent self-actualization, it is concluded that business and industrial organizations, in particular, must be changed radically to more favourable types. Although these improved types of organizations are not yet known, the general conclusion is that people will work most productively under a participative leadership style, which encourages personal satisfaction, teamwork, and trust and involves self-control, decision by consensus, and decentralization.

ORGANISMIC THEORY AND SELF-ACTUALIZATION

Organismic doctrine[23] is based on the idea of wholeness—that the whole personality is more important than the sum of its parts and can only be properly understood as a totality. For example, emotional problems cannot be understood as individual symptoms, but must be considered in relation to the total organism; people learn tasks best as a whole, rather than as discrete actions. A central theme of organismic theory is that each individual has the inner potential for becoming a whole person—a well-integrated, fully satisfied personality. Especially significant is the contention that an individual fails, not because of himself, but because of the bad influences or deficiencies in his environment.

This theory borrows from the thinking of Jean Jacques Rousseau, the Swiss-born French philosopher and writer who died in 1778. Rousseau, whose writings and ideas helped spark the French Revolution, believed that man was innately simple and good, but that the social institutions he created had made him grasping, deceitful, and contentious. His answer was to destroy the faulty culture and its manifestations and to build a new society which would be based on the compassion and goodness innate in each individual.

Organismic theory has tapped other doctrinal sources. From Gestalt theory it borrows the idea that the response of an organism can be understood only as a whole, and not as the sum of responses to individual elements in the situation. It reflects the thinking of Jan Smuts, the South African field-marshal and prime minister, who originated the concept of holism, which states that the organism as a whole has a reality separate from, and independent of, the sum of its parts.

Organismic theory asserts that people are motivated by an overall, master drive. Kurt Goldstein,[24] a German neuropsychiatrist who emigrated to the United States in 1935, conceived this to be a master motive which he named self-actualization. He developed the idea that drives such as hunger, sex, and power are means of actualizing oneself.

166

This concept was further expanded by Abraham Maslow, who added to Goldstein's conclusions the notion that needs are hierarchal, that we must satisfy our basic physiological needs for food, sex, and security before such psychological needs as recognition and status become foremost. These needs culminate in that of self-actualization. Maslow studied a group of people who had actualized their potential according to his criteria. He found that they had the following distinctive characteristics.

(a) They are realistically oriented.
(b) They accept themselves, other people, and the natural world for what they are.
(c) They have a great deal of spontaneity.
(d) They are problem-centred rather than self-centred.
(e) They have an air of detachment and a need for privacy.
(f) They are autonomous and independent.
(g) Their appreciation of people and things is fresh rather than stereotyped.
(h) Most of them have had profound mystical or spiritual experience although not necessarily religious in character.
(i) They identify with mankind.
(j) Their intimate relationships with a few specially loved people tend to be profound and deeply emotional rather than superficial.
(k) Their values and attitudes are democratic.
(l) They do not confuse means with ends.
(m) Their sense of humour is philosophical rather than hostile.
(n) They have a great fund of creativeness.
(o) They resist conformity to the culture.[25]

THE HAWTHORNE EXPERIMENTS

The behavioural science theories most often taught to managers stem most directly from the work of Elton Mayo and the Hawthorne studies, which were carried out at the Western Electric Company's Hawthorne plant in Chicago between 1927 and 1932. The importance ascribed to these findings is indicated by a popular text used in the business schools. This states that management thinking is undergoing a 'behavioural science revolution' based on 'the research of Elton Mayo and his associates'. The text continues, 'The Hawthorne studies provided scientific verification for the changing view of many students of industrial organizations' and 'set the foundation for later investigations'.[26]

Mayo, an associate professor at Harvard University, set out to study the effects of leadership, money, fatigue, and other physical factors on productivity. He assumed that good illumination and other desirable working conditions would improve productive output, but found that the productivity of girls assembling relays improved without regard to illumination, rest periods, or related factors. Startling as it appeared, the answer was in the motivation of the workers. Given a feeling of importance by being singled out for attention, their actions and attitudes a subject of friendly interest, the girls responded in terms of the principle of human reaction.

After extended observation and experiment, Mayo and his researchers concluded that social factors, not physical, had the greatest influence on willingness to work. People respond to trust and confidence rather than authority, they decided, and work more productively under friendly, relaxed supervisors who help them use their abilities to the full, rather than under the close control of authoritarian managers pressing for results. Money, it appeared, was a secondary motivator. This was a powerful and appealing message. It seemed to demolish much prevalent thinking about management and to open new opportunities for human fulfilment.

The Hawthorne findings were accepted with implicit confidence and triggered a long series of studies and reports which extrapolated from Mayo's findings to fundamental questions about the nature of management.

These threads were woven into a theoretical garment by Douglas McGregor, who based much of his thinking on Mayo's findings, and also revived Rousseau's idea that people are essentially good, but their institutions make them bad. He asserted that the typical enterprise manager is authoritarian and power centred, and gets results primarily through reward and punishment and tight control. McGregor characterized this manager as a theory 'X' type, who, he stated, believes that 'the average man is by nature indolent, lacks ambition, is inherently self-centred, by nature resistant to change, gullible and not very bright.' This, said McGregor, 'is a consequence of the nature of industrial organizations, of management philosophy, policy and practice.'[27] Contrary to mistaken management belief, McGregor asserted, people want to be creative, they prefer responsibility, they are eager to work. McGregor suggested that managers should adopt an ideal leadership style, which he characterized as theory 'Y'. This was based on the concept formulated by Goldstein, and expanded by Maslow, that

168

people want to actualize their potential. McGregor felt that people could be trusted to select goals which would contribute to the overall purpose of the organization if they could see benefit to themselves in doing so. In his theory 'Y', he emphasized the need to integrate individual and organization objectives and to help people feel an emotional ownership in their work.

The ideas expressed by Mayo and McGregor are reflected in much of the behavioural science and management writing of today.

Frederick Herzberg, of Western Reserve University, cites the Hawthorne studies as 'a landmark study in industrial relations'. He says, 'The behavioural scientist has debunked the concept of the "economic man".' He has shown the inadequacy of the environment which corporate management has created, with its 'rules, regulations, policies, organization structure ... its span and control, unity of direction, committees. In this industrial environment,' Herberg asserted, 'the job of achievement and creativity is an unsought pleasure.'[28]

Chris Argyris, of Yale University, advances the conclusion that business organizations psychologically hobble people because management has purposefully developed the pyramidal, hierarchal organization as 'a strategy designed to give the greatest influence over persons, information and instrumentalities to the higher-level positions'.[29]

Argyris has concluded that the necessary improvement cannot be accomplished within present organizations. With Max Weber, he feels that work specialization, span of control, the chain of command, and unitary accountability lead to dependent and submissive individuals who use a minimum of their real abilities and that this occurs inversely with organization levels, with the first-line worker most harshly penalized. He contends that most human problems would be solved if managers used a leadership style similar to that advocated by Maslow and McGregor.

Warren Bennis, citing the 'pioneering work' of 'Elton Mayo, with his emphasis on the significance of the human group', also feels that contemporary management practices are inadequate and penalize the human personality. Bennis says, 'Contemporary students of organization agree' that forms of organization in current use, such as division of labour based on functional specialization and the hierarchy of authority, are 'hopelessly out of joint with contemporary realities, and that new shapes, patterns and models will replace them'.

In company with Argyris, Bennis decries the inadequacy of the pyramidal structure characterized by chain of command, specialization, technical dominance, impersonality, and extreme proceduralization. Bennis, who equates modern management with the bureaucracy of Max Weber, foresees 'the end of bureaucracy and the use of new social systems'.[30]

The Hawthorne findings and their interpretations are so much a part of these theories that a critical evaluation is vital. Analytical studies now make it clear that the Hawthorne experiments were poorly controlled, imprecise and, as one critic says, 'scientifically illiterate'. Not only is this basic data under fire, but there is a strong view that some current thinking based on this data also has a special bias which colours widely-accepted 'scientific' conclusions.

Mayo and his researchers contended that their data demonstrated that relaxed, friendly supervisors caused people to produce more. After analysis of this same data, Professor Karl E. Weick of the University of Minnesota, stated, 'On closer inspection, the Hawthorne studies actually reveal the opposite relationship—because of higher productivity, the managers became more relaxed.'[31] Further research has confirmed this. Lowin and Craig have established that high producers by their performance strongly influence their supervisors to supervise less closely, to loosen up on controls and to be more considerate and friendly.[32]

Professor Alex Carey, of the University of New South Wales, made a detailed comparative study of the Hawthorne conclusions and the evidence on which they were based. He also determined that Mayo's data proved just the opposite to the conclusions he reached. Specifically, he says, 'The change in payment system alone . . . produced as much increase in output in nine weeks . . . as was produced in about nine months by change in payment system together with a change to genial supervision.' As Carey showed, instead of minimizing the motivating power of money and of authority and hierarchy, as most of today's behavioural scientists assert, the Hawthorne studies, in fact, demonstrate 'the value of monetary incentives, driving leadership and discipline'. Carey concludes by commenting on 'the gross error and the incompetence in the understanding and use of the scientific method which permeate the Hawthorne studies from beginning to end'.[33]

This incompetence in scientific method is disturbing enough. Of even greater concern, however, is the belief of some authorities that some precepts accepted unquestioningly by managers today are strongly coloured and distorted by an anti-authoritarian bias of some behavioural scientists themselves. This is summarized by Professor James A. Lee, in an article in the *Harvard Business Review*, where he said: 'The vast

170

majority of the behavioural theorists today are professors, whose strong autonomy needs and anti-authoritarian bias govern much of their research approach and ideal model-building. They bounce their theories off other faculty members and students, who are well known to have similar needs and biases; they use students for subjects for some of their studies, and they arrive at a recommended work environment in the image of the ideal university.'[34]

ARE SOME BEHAVIOURAL SCIENCE THEORIES OBSOLETE?

Serious doubts are beginning to appear among researchers and practitioners who have attempted to make the theories work in real life. This concern is expressed by Reed M. Powell and John L. Schlacter on the basis of field work they have conducted on the influence of participative management.[35] Their conclusion is that while there is some evidence that participation does help improve morale, there is 'no such relationship in evidence between participation and productivity'. Their research indicates that, while writers and theorists strongly advocate 'the new, "concerned and involving" theory "Y" type' manager, and almost unanimously agree that the authoritarian, control-centred manager is obsolescent, in real life he has continued to play the most effective role. Current participative techniques, these scientists say, tend to encourage development of divisive objectives which blunt the thrust of the entire team towards productive results. Their findings concluded that, 'while participative management techniques may produce involved, happy workers . . . as group members become more interrelated and as their influence upon one another increases, the formal directive leadership pattern within the group erodes'. Management thus sacrifices its capability to lead effectively in its attempt to give maximum autonomy and satisfaction to subordinates.

These studies are further substantiated by another behavioural scientist, Ralph Stogdill, whose work makes it clear that the conflict is as much between differing objectives as between the individual and the organization. The contention of the behavioural scientists for whom McGregor, Argyris, Likert, Bennis, and Herzberg speak is that the proper objective of the enterprise is to create satisfied and happy employees, who will, in turn, be productive because they are satisfied and happy. Stogdill's thinking, to which most practising managers subscribe, is that the proper objective of the enterprise is to survive and grow successfully, and, as a means to this end, to help people to actualize the best abilities they can use in the service of the enterprise. While the emphasis may appear to be subtle, it is vital. In a nutshell, a manager must decide whether his objective is to create satisfied and happy people or to help employees of the enterprise to work most effectively towards organization goals. If his primary goal is to help people actualize, as Stogdill says, 'he can be surrounded by loyal, happy workers but lose money on his operations'.[36]

BEHAVIOURAL SCIENCE IN BUSINESS

A number of attempts has been made to implement behavioural science theories in business and industrial enterprises. Professor James A. Lee comments, 'Theorist-consultants have studied attempts to produce change in a few socio-industrial subcultures. They have reported all the temporary successes and few, if any of the failures.'[37]

The Harwood Manufacturing Company, a textile manufacturing firm, is an interesting case of an enterprise which was literally managed by behavioural scientists. In the foreword to a book reporting the results, Dr Rensis Likert, of the University of Michigan, says, 'This volume reports an extraordinarily successful improvement of a failing organization through the introduction of a new management system. An unprofitable enterprise was made profitable, and a better place to work, in the short span of two years.' He goes on to say that 'General principles and specific insights emerging from . . . quantitative social science research . . . were used to plan and guide all changes. . . .'[38]

It is now clear that massive investments in new machinery, updated technology, improved production flow, and the wholesale firing of employees who were resistant to self-actualization were potent factors which may have been underemphasized. Sizable performance improvement occurred, but, since no controls were used, there is no way of knowing how much of this was the result of sensitivity training, participative management, and leadership styles and how much occurred because of more conventional measures.

After careful study of the Harwood data, Dr Frederick G. Lippert states, 'The findings are tinged with grey. One reason for the success . . . lies in the sheer amount and variety of resources put to work. The direct dollar costs of the change efforts on the human organization side were about of the same magnitude as the direct dollar cost of physical improvement. . . .'[39]

In the Harwood situation, participatory measures had significant

172

impact on improved productivity, but, it seems clear, coercive pressure which the scientists applied was even more potent. In one instance, low-producing machine operators were ruthlessly weeded out. During this period, the behavioural science programmes increased productivity by 3 per cent, but a rise of about 5 percentage points in average productivity was brought about by the termination of the low performers.

Dr A. Lowin, who also studied the Harwood data, discovered that, in one case, productivity went up after introducing behavioural science techniques, but grievances also increased sharply. Although grievances are usually taken as negative morale indices, the researchers asserted that this proved that the workers felt freer to present grievances in the more 'participative atmosphere'. Dr Lowin comments that the behavioural scientist's 'enthusiasm may be overextended'.[40]

THE BEHAVIOURAL SCIENTIST TAKES OVER

Encouraged by initial acceptance, some behavioural scientists have taken the position that if management cannot reform itself, they will perform the task for them by direct intervention in enterprises, where they will take positive action to bring about the kind of industrial society they believe to be desirable. The consensus of this thinking is voiced by Richard Beckhard, of Massachusetts Institute of Technology. Beckhard sees fundamental changes being accomplished in enterprises through planned intervention using behavioural science knowledge and methods. This will include establishment of new strategies, total change in the culture of the enterprise, and fundamental alteration of roles. Among the anticipated results will be to vest authority in those who have the most knowledge rather than those who have organizational accountability for results.[41] Since Beckhard, in company with Schein, Bennis, and others, considers the intervention of behavioural scientists central to effective change, presumably the authority of the behavioural consultants will supersede that of the chief executive and line managers who are much less knowledgeable in behavioural science methodology.

The scientists would learn to understand what they were doing by having managers in their client enterprises go through 'laboratory training'. As Schein and Bennis define it, this is an 'instrument whereby the normative goals and improvements set forth by organization theorists and practitioners of organization can be achieved.'[42] The enterprise itself serves as a laboratory, hence the term 'laboratory training'. Using laboratory training to discover the methods they will use, the behavioural scientists will guide management in engineering the new social architecture. The specific techniques to be used are primarily sensitivity training, T-groups, and personal counselling with top executives.

There are strong arguments against turning over the management of change in a business enterprise to social scientists, for this directly influences both survival and success. The measures advocated by Argyris, Bennis, and some other behavioural scientists, notably sensitivity training and T-groups, are very much under fire by competent practitioners. The Council on Mental Health of the American Medical Association has emphasized the hazards in inept use of sensitivity training, pointing to 'depression, psychosis, major personality disorganization and anxiety reaction' as possible by-products[43] and cautioning that psychiatrists with special training in small group dynamics or those with equivalent preparation should conduct the sessions. Many behavioural scientists do not have the necessary pyschiatric training, or have inadequate experience in group therapy.

Frederick R. Kappel, then chairman, American Telephone and Telegraph Company, summarized this in a speech at Michigan State University in 1963. 'The main source of knowledge about modern business is *in* business. It is not in the schools,' he said. 'Scholarship in the field needs a large component of knowledge based on first-hand, intimate acquaintance with business problems as they emerge in the heat of the day.' Kappel articulated a vital point when he said, 'I now make a businessman's plea to the professors . . . that you do all you can to make sure your facts always march ahead of your conclusions.'[44]

The final word was probably pronounced by Douglas McGregor after he had tried to implement his theories in real life as President of Antioch College from 1948 to 1954:

Before coming to Antioch I had observed and worked with top executives as an adviser in a number of organizations. I thought I knew how they felt about their responsibilities and what led them to behave as they did. I even thought that I could create a role for myself which would enable me to avoid some of the difficulties they encountered.

I was wrong! It took the direct experience of becoming a line executive and meeting personally the problems involved to teach me what no amount of observation of other people could have taught. I believed, for example, that a leader could operate successfully as a kind of adviser to his organization. I thought I could avoid being a 'boss', but I couldn't have been more wrong.[45]

CONCLUSIONS FROM SCIENTIFIC RESEARCH

Much of value is to be learned from the various scientific fields which can often be applied directly, or with minor modification, to management needs. Several conclusions can be drawn from current research. First, there is no scientific evidence that an ideal leadership style exists, or, in fact, that any given style is always best. Second, people who have full and challenging work, who can make most of their own decisions and who can relate effectively to their superiors, peers and the objectives of the enterprise, will tend to be happier and more satisfied at work than those who do not, although a direct relationship between satisfaction and productivity cannot be proved. Third, motivational needs of individuals differ and the manager must be able to assess these requirements and vary his approach to suit both the needs of people and of the situation. Fourth, profitability follows most surely if people are able to use their abilities to the full, find satisfaction in their work, and produce because they want to and are not driven to it. However, these conditions are always relative and changing and are satisfied by varying mixes of authoritarianism and participation and organization control and self-control—in other words, by the omnimode.

PRINCIPLES OF MOTIVATION

If we distil the great volume of fact, opinion, and conjecture that has been voiced, we can derive several fundamental truths or principles which summarize what we really know about motivation. These will serve as guides to professional managers concerned with encouraging and inspiring others to higher endeavour.

THE PRINCIPLE OF PARTICIPATION

Participation involves making systematic provision for consultation with subordinates in those matters directly related to their jobs. In developing participation, a manager asks his subordinates for their suggestions, recommendations, and advice in matters that affect their work.

*Motivation to accomplish results
tends to increase as people are given
opportunity to participate in the
decisions affecting those results*

The more opportunity people have to participate in the decisions that will affect them, the greater the personal ownership they will have in the work and the results they will accomplish. Time devoted to securing participation is generally a good investment if we want increased interest and enthusiasm in getting the job done.

Armco Steel Corporation provides an example of the application of this principle in introducing office automation. Armco wanted to automate its payroll and invoicing systems, but did not want to dislocate people or cause unrest and dissatisfaction in the process. To secure participation, Armco asked one plant manager to make a feasibility study in his plant, using his own staff to do the work. When the study proved successful, the people who had already participated in it were given the key assignments to install the new automated systems. People within the plant were trained to take over the new jobs that opened and a nine-month transition period was arranged to protect those who were changing jobs. The installation was not only completely successful with no disruption of personnel, but also saved $40 000 annually in this one plant.

Giving people a feeling of ownership in work is one of the best ways to ensure outstanding results. However, participation is not to be undertaken casually; it must not become abdication by the manager, or more harm than good may result. The following rules should be observed.

The Manager Remains Accountable. No matter how much his people participate, the manager must reserve the right to make the final decision. He must make this understood or he will be in danger of abdicating his accountability. When asked to participate, individuals tend to press their own special viewpoints. It is up to the manager to help them see the whole picture and to secure their acceptance and support.

Keeping Expectations Reasonable. Not every decision calls for participation. If people cannot contribute meaningfully, it is better not to ask for suggestions. When we enourage people to participate, they often develop the belief that their recommendations will automatically be accepted. This may be impossible and we should avoid raising expectations which we cannot satisfy. We should make it clear that, although we are asking for participation, we will make the decision that we feel will best reflect the needs and interests of the group.

Providing Either Answer or Action. Every suggestion that is offered merits either answer or action. We should do something about it or explain why the idea cannot be used. This can be a time-consuming process. The individual who has what he considers a first-rate idea will not be happy if it is turned down. The best approach, here, is for the manager to call together those who have participated, then announce the decision and why it was made. Questions and discussion should be encouraged. This will help those in potential opposition to talk out their resistance.

Once the decision is made, people should be given as much freedom as possible in deciding how they will put it into effect in their unit. This gives them a personal stake in its success. This feeling of emotional ownership can be almost as effective as financial ownership.

Giving Credit Where Due. When we announce our decision, we should be sure to mention by name the individuals whose ideas were incorporated. Even if we had the same idea ourselves, and possibly first, the radic approach is best. We will gain more if we are unselfish with the credit. If the suggestion proves successful and recognition comes from our superior, or from other quarters, we should make sure that proper credit is given— in public, if possible.

THE PRINCIPLE OF COMMUNICATION

The more a person knows about a matter, the more interest and concern he will develop. When a manager makes an obvious effort to keep his people informed, he is telling them, 'I think you are important. I want to be sure you know what is going on.' If he withholds information, he makes it quite clear that he feels it is of little importance whether or not his people know what is occurring.

PRINCIPLE OF
COMMUNICATION

*Motivation to accomplish results
tends to increase as people are informed
about matters affecting those results*

This is well illustrated in the case of a large machinery manufacturer. One plant had an acute cost problem—its manufacturing costs were so high that the product was rapidly being priced out of its markets. The plant manager appointed a study team of department heads to investigate the problem. They found that the cost accounting system was technically excellent, but did not give foremen information or understanding about their costs. Foremen initiated their own budgets but, it turned out, they did this mechanically. They did not really understand why their variances occurred. More than this, they received budget reports three weeks after the fact, which meant that, in many cases, they could not take corrective action until it was too late.

Following the recommendations of his study team, the plant manager corrected this by modifying the budgets so they could be quickly and easily understood by the foremen. He had his controller set up a system for daily reporting of costs so the foreman was informed of his variances almost as soon as they occurred. Foremen were then given intensive training to ensure that they understood the plant cost structure and the budget system. The budget efficiencies of each department were regularly communicated to all supervisors and a contest was introduced to award recognition to the best performers. As a result of this attention to communication, the plant was able to save 25 per cent of its total controllable cost budget.

Communication helps make work purposeful. It gives meaning to the job. If we know what the goals are and what progress is being made towards them, we feel that we are a vital part of the team.

THE PRINCIPLE OF RECOGNITION

People will consistently work hard if they get continuing recognition and satisfaction from their efforts. When we give credit to a person who has earned it, we are making clear that we consider him an important and worth-while member of the team. The boss in particular can enhance this feeling of satisfaction through his appreciation of the good work done. Recognition must be sincere. We know when we have done a good job. The smooth sound of flattery fools most of us for only a short time.

PRINCIPLE OF
RECOGNITION

Motivation to accomplish results tends to increase as people are given recognition for their contribution to those results

An interesting example of the application of this principle is the case of an electronics company which manufactures consumer products and which upgrades sales results by providing for continuing recognition of sales accomplishment. For instance, it runs a yearly contest for wholesale distributor salesmen, offering a graduated series of prizes so that salesmen get increased reward and recognition by making from 100 per cent of quota to as high as 300 per cent or more. Among the prizes the salesman can earn is an easily identified ring with a diamond of from one-quarter to one carat, to mark different levels of achievement. The entire distributor sales team must make at least 100 per cent of quota before any member becomes eligible for prizes. This approach provides for both individual and team recognition in achieving top sales.

THE PRINCIPLE OF DELEGATED AUTHORITY

When we tell people, 'Here is a job to do, you can make your own decisions on how you think it should be done', we make it plain by our actions that we feel they are capable and important individuals. If, on the other hand, we require our people to run to us for every small decision, it is clear that we look on them as we would children who cannot be trusted.

PRINCIPLE OF DELEGATED AUTHORITY	*Motivation to accomplish results tends to increase as people are given authority to make decisions affecting those results*

The best managers delegate as much authority as possible and avoid close or detailed supervision. The pattern of delegation spreads from top to bottom of the organization. The climate established at the top tends to filter quickly to lower levels.

Giving people authority to make their own decisions gives them a vested interest in the results they accomplish. There is no greater energizing force than to put a manager in charge of a segment of the business, give him authority to make the decisions that spell success or failure, and to reward him for his achievement.

As a case example, in a plant of an electric utility company, a group of thirty-seven men was used to stock coal. A normal stocking rate was fifty-five wagons a shift. In an emergency, it became necessary to stockpile an extra supply of coal. Instead of ordering the men to fill the new demand, the supervisor used the principle of delegated authority. He explained the problem and pointed out why it was vitally important to build up the stockpile as quickly as possible. The group was delegated authority to set its own objectives. The men decided that they could stock sixty wagons each shift. Furthermore, they agreed to postpone their holidays during the three-month period it would take to get the job done. In carrying out their own recommendations, they worked willingly seven days a week, plus overtime, and equalled or exceeded the objective they had set for themselves on each shift.

The best approach for the manager in using these principles is to understand each of his people and to work with the separate individuals on their own terms. Followers, as well as leaders, have characteristic modes of action. As the principle of human reaction establishes, people who act consistently in the centric mode react best to the rational centric mode and can be moved progressively towards mutual radic action. However, since they will return to the spontaneous centric mode for each new situation, the manager must be prepared to recycle his approach to fit the need. If a person maintains a centric pattern, this is neither good nor bad; it is a fact the manager must work with if he is to succeed in his task of motivating others. When he finds individuals who maintain a radic mode of action, the manager must shift into the rational centric to establish the premises for the basic relationship and to determine his own best posture; however, he can move quickly to the rational radic mode and maintain it with minimal effort and maximum satisfaction.

To work effectively in the omnimode, the manager should master several basic techniques, which are developed with each individual and tailored to his special needs. These techniques begin with acquiring a real understanding of each person, both as an individual and as a member of the group.

UNDERSTANDING PEOPLE

A manager can best help his subordinates get the satisfaction they want from their jobs if he knows their special needs. While everybody has similar basic drives and urges, each person tends to react in terms of his own experience and personality. Perhaps one person secures his feeling of recognition and importance from money, another from status, a third, from new challenges and experiences. If we want to know people, it is necessary to develop a personal relationship that encourages confidence on both sides. This should be informal, but not so personal that we lose objectivity. It is a good rule for the manager to avoid becoming emotionally involved in the personal problems of his subordinates. This is certain to lessen his effectiveness.

A manager can learn about his subordinates through observation and study. If he asks questions during appraisal interviews, as well as in counselling and working with his people, he will find out what they want from their jobs, what their goals are, and something about their homes and families. This will give him an insight into the mainsprings of their motivations and help him become a more effective motivator.

All this requires careful handling. Most of the information we secure is highly personal and, necessarily, subjective. We must keep in mind that people tend to present their own side of the story, and it is usually in their favour; often, too, they will tell us what they think we want to hear, not the literal facts. If we are not sure of the accuracy of our information, we may want to verify it from other sources. This requires tact and caution. Divulging a confidence will automatically block off the source of supply.

The basic drives and urges impel each person to be most concerned about his own objectives, his family, and possessions. As managers, we must be continually alert not to judge the person's special interests and drives, but, rather, to concern ourselves primarily with his work and behaviour.

ENCOURAGING A FEELING OF PROPRIETORSHIP

Our basic drives impel us to show most interest and concern in things that belong to us. If something is ours, we have full control of it. We can shape and build it as we think best. This is one reason why the independent businessman gets such satisfaction from running his own enterprise.

We can help people capture much of this feeling of proprietorship on the job by proper motivation. This can be accomplished by giving a person a chance to participate, keeping him informed about matters that concern him, letting him make most of his own decisions, and giving him an opportunity to develop the knowledge and skills he needs. All these factors are building blocks in helping him become an entrepreneur in managing his own business unit in his own interests and those of the company. Satisfaction derived from fulfilling his teleological drive and territorial and acquisitive urges is deep and enduring. The more a person feels he owns part of something, the harder he will work to make it succeed.

DEVELOPING TEAMWORK

People have deep cultural urges to work cooperatively and to share with others in the accomplishment of common objectives. They want to feel that they are part of the team, and to be accepted and liked by their fellows. The greater this team feeling, the more strongly they will feel impelled to work hard and productively to achieve the goals of the group. Some managers are accepted as members of their groups and get their results by working with the team. Others remain in the centric mode, giving directions and commands from outside the team. In the long term, we know that the team effort gets the best results.

How can the manager encourage the radic approach? One method is to create as many opportunities as possible for members of the team to work together and with him. The creation of task forces for special projects, delegation of specific tasks to small work groups, and committee participation are effective ways of providing closer working relationships.

The manager himself should work closely with individual members of his team as often as he can. Use of a line assistant may be a handicap because it tends to screen the boss from personal contact. Frequent discussion on the job, counselling and coaching to improve skills, and other job related activities also help develop this team feeling.

As cohesiveness develops, deep-seated cultural urges impel the members to support one another and to work for the objectives they accept. This can become a disadvantage unless the manager can work as part of the team, rather than outside it. It may also be a handicap if it sets one group against another. Strong inter-group teamwork is best developed by having different groups work together on joint projects and exchanging both members and leaders for specific assignments.

MOTIVATING DOWN, UP, AND ACROSS

We have no difficulty recognizing our accountability for motivating those who report to us. But, most often, we overlook our obligation to inspire and encourage our boss and the people at our own level.

Often, the boss needs to be motivated. He may fail to take certain steps or to perform work he should undertake on our behalf. When this is the case, the professional manager does not retire into his shell. By using the tools of participation and communication, he can awaken the boss' interest and energize him to take the necessary action.

Recognition can be practised upwards as well as downwards. When the boss does a good piece of work as it relates to our responsibilities, a sincere and honest compliment will help to motivate him to accomplish other good work on our behalf. Often enough, the boss is the one at the soup tureen. He ladles out recognition, but rarely receives it.

People at our own level, also, must be motivated. This is largely a matter of using the recognized principles of motivation. If, when people are asked to participate in solving a problem, for example, we give generous appreciation for their contribution, this will help motivate them to sustained efforts on our behalf.

As is true in other aspects of management, change is the only constant in motivation of people. In utilizing new findings in motivation and leadership, professional managers have discovered that change is best achieved by identification and agreement of objectives, rational analysis of the best alternatives available, and implementation in terms of the practical requirements of each situation. This view avoids doctrinaire commitment to any one approach, but uses elements of all methods which, on analysis, promise benefits commensurate with their human and financial costs.

The vital lesson to be learned is that, within an evolving organization, change can be accomplished in a logical, evolutionary manner by utilizing the best of the past and integrating this with new knowledge and techniques as quickly as they can be proved valid. Here, both behavioural scientists and professional managers are arriving at similar answers. Flexibility is mandatory, for, while there are principles to serve as guides, the methods used must be as varied and changeable as people themselves. If individuals are to have full and satisfying jobs with as much responsibility and authority as they can handle, a sound rational organization must be established which will clealy define the broad limits within which freedom can be exercised. Full and continuing delegation calls for control by exception and this is possible only if comprehensive planning is maintained. Within this framework, people respond eagerly to the opportunity to become part of a close-knit team, to establish challenging objectives for themselves, to control their own work, and to help others with their specialized skills.

To conclude, it becomes increasingly clear that theories of self-actualization and ideal leadership styles, if taken too literally, can mislead practising managers and lead to wasted effort and resources. Effective motivation does not follow from current fads or panaceas. Rather, it is the result of the practice of the complex and difficult work of management, using a variable style most responsive to the demands of the people and the situation.

SUMMARY

(a) Motivating is the dynamic activity in getting results through and with other people. Motivating is defined as the work a manager performs to inspire, encourage, and impel people to take required action. We can predict that people's needs will change and the effort necessary to motivate must change with them.

(b) The individual and the leadership of the organization both tend to act in the spontaneous centric mode. This gives rise to continuing conflict which can be resolved only by successful movement to the radic mode, and, eventually, to the omnimode. Study of history shows the fumbling and often unsuccessful attempts to accomplish this transition. F. W. Taylor advocated the change in mechanical and human terms, and developed useful methods. Leading companies, as well as theorists, made constructive contributions, including those of IBM, Armco Steel, and the Western Electric Company, together with Mary Parker Follett, Chester I. Barnard, and Elton Mayo.

(c) More recently, behavioural scientists have advanced theories of motivation which have been both helpful and misleading. Organismic theory and self-actualization are leading themes. They arise from the thinking of Rousseau, who believed that man was good and his bad institutions debased him, and the doctrine of the whole, as expressed in Gestalt and holistic theory. The concept of self-actualization comes from the work of Kurt Goldstein and Abraham Maslow. It evolved into the 'X-Y' theory of Douglas McGregor and later work by Chris Argyris, Frederick Herzberg, and others.

(d) Behavioural science theories that there is one ideal leadership style, that conventional organizations are obsolete and that participation and involvement are the best motivators for productivity, are now being seriously questioned. Researchers have made it clear that there is no ideal leadership style and that since motivational needs differ, the methods used must also be highly flexible.

(e) Several principles can be distilled from the great mass of work that has been done on motivation. These include the principles

184

of participation, communication, recognition, and delegated authority.

(f) In motivating others, the important considerations for a manager are to understand the people with whom he works, to encourage a feeling of proprietorship, to develop teamwork, and to motivate up, down and across the organization.

11.　BUILDING A STRONG TEAM

'Nothing that is worth knowing can be taught,' said Oscar Wilde. His comment becomes meaningful if we recognize that all of us have innumerable abilities which need to be developed but which cannot be successfully imposed on us. From our analysis of the genetic drives and their influence on behaviour, we know that if the body possesses a capability, the teleological drive will impel its meaningful use, for purpose must be established for each structure that exists. If the drive is not satisfied, tension is created, which, in turn, will be converted into cultural drives or, if this is not possible, into aggressive or undesirable behaviour. Thus, if we are prevented from using our arms or legs, we struggle against the restriction; if our muscles are strong and active and we are made to move slowly and deliberately, we become tense and uncomfortable. This is true for all our capabilities, including many of which we are not consciously aware. If we have an inborn capability, the genes which structured it also monitor it, so that we are teleologically driven to formulate the purposes which will enable us to satisfy it. This application of the teleological drive is converted into many cultural urges; on the job, it is satisfied by the activity of development.

Developing people is the work a manager does to help people improve their knowledge, attitudes, and skills. The professional manager knows how to help his people develop so that they will increase their personal range of knowledge, make greater contributions to the successful operation of the enterprise, and, as a corollary, to their own personal welfare.

186

WHY DEVELOPMENT FAILS

Efforts to help managers develop their knowledge, attitudes, and skills often fail. There are many reasons. One is that success in management depends on the ability to deal effectively with fast-changing and usually ill-defined human and technical problems, and not on rote performance of prescribed skills. Most programmes fail to identify management and organization development needs accurately, and, as a consequence, cannot provide participating managers with the skills necessary to solve their real problems. The most prevalent reason for the lack of success of an enterprise's development programmes is its failure to think through the objectives and methods to which it can best commit itself. Instead, enterprises tend to rely on a miscellany of educational exposures which, it is hoped, will help managers improve their performance.

These efforts, too often, are based upon what happens to be the 'in' programme for the season, whether this be management by objectives, leadership styles, job enrichment, or sensitivity training. Much money and effort are invested. Often the entire management group, from chief executive to first-line supervisor, diligently complete the required sessions. Despite the faddish character of the programmes, they may be solid, carefully developed, and have significant potential. However, managers often simply do not practise the new approaches which they have been taught. This may be because the new methods, while sound, require more time and effort than operations-oriented managers are willing to invest. Resistance to change is a second factor. The new approach may be distinctly superior to what the company currently practises, but, almost always, greater time and effort are required to implement than to teach it. And once the programme gets beyond the scope of the management development staff, the organized effort to monitor application is not available, so the fruit fails at its budding.

A third, and not always obvious, reason that a management develop-ment effort fails is lack of an orderly, logical, formalized system of management into which it can fit. An engineer or doctor can quickly master and use new techniques because he can fit his new knowledge into an existing, rational framework of concepts, principles, and methods. Most important, he already has a vocabulary which precisely defines what he needs to know. New management approaches too frequently introduce new vocabulary featuring poorly defined and arbitrary substitutes for more commonly understood and accepted terms. This not only compounds the difficulty inherent in learning new habits, but also adds confusion in dealing with established methods.

Mastering the embryo profession of management is no different from mastering other more mature professions such as engineering, medicine, or law. A manager must acquire the basic knowledge of his profession. He can do this by laborious trial and error or through years of experience or he can learn most of the facts, principles, and vocabulary he needs through a sound educational programme. Since most managers have not learned to manage in their formalized education, much of this education must take place on a continuing basis within the company. In his education, the manager can proceed most effectively if the company has already established its concepts, principles, techniques, and vocabulary of management.

The most elementary principle of learning establishes that any new knowledge or skill must be reinforced by successful use until it becomes habitual. Very few companies require their managers to practise on the job what they have learned in the classroom or seminar. In fact, the eager enthusiast who returns with new ideas almost invariably finds he is talking a new language and is advocating methods which run contrary to long-entrenched practice. Development requires not only acquisition of new knowledge, but experience in use of new practical skills which can be gained only through practice on the job. It must also be supported and reinforced by other related activities, including carefully thought through objectives, sound organization, performance standards, and balanced compensation.

A sound organization must be established before people are developed. Managers should know what management work they are required to perform. Their responsibilities, authority, and accountability should be carefully defined. They should know to whom they report and who reports to them. They should be able to perform their work without duplicating or overlapping similar work done elsewhere. They should delegate effectively and have sound working relationships with their subordinates, superiors, and other groups in the company.

Performance standards are indispensable to sound development. People should know for themselves where they are strong or weak in their performance. They need yardsticks to measure their own performance. Their security drive gives rise to cultural urges which ask constantly 'How am I doing?' If they do not know to what extent they are accomplishing their objectives, or whether their work is satisfactory or unsatisfactory, these urges are unsatisfied and tension and dissatisfaction result. Given this information, people have one of the best incentives for strong self-development.

Balanced compensation is another basic requirement if development is to be successful. People want to feel that greater financial rewards await them if they upgrade their skills and abilities. This will satisfy their acquisitive urge, which, because it is open ended in most societies, has no innate controls as there are for hunger or sex. As a result, most people are not content with acquiring enough money to satisfy their material needs. They continually want more. This is particularly true of rewards for their skills. Increased technical requirements in a job should be recognized by increased financial rewards. A person should not feel that he has to get onto the managerial ladder to improve his financial standing. Management positions should embrace constantly increased management responsibilities, so that as an individual progresses up the ladder he will be paid for greater competence in his management work.

Developing managers should be held primarily accountable for management performance. They should be required to get their results primarily through the planning, organizing, leading, and controlling work that they do. If they are held accountable for these results, they will place greater stress on these management skills, leading naturally to improvement.

In developing managerial skills, an early requirement is a rational and orderly approach to the appraisal of performance. This is a primary responsibility of every manager, from top to bottom of the organization.

PERFORMANCE APPRAISAL

Performance appraisal is the work a manager performs to evaluate the performance and capabilities of himself and his people. A manager must carry out this responsibility himself; it cannot be easily delegated. Performance appraisal is of critical importance because it literally weighs a man and his future career in the balance. Because we cannot yet determine scientifically how well or poorly an individual is doing on the job, management appraisal in the final analysis becomes a matter of personal judgement. It makes great demands on objectivity and analytical capabilities; the way a manager appraises others is a good measure of the performance of the manager himself.

Managers often say, 'I appraise people all the time.' This is probably true. However, our security drives and cultural urges impel us so that

189

we want to know what the appraisal is, and if there are deficiencies, to correct them. Most managers have definite opinions as to the capabilities of each of their subordinates. Unfortunately, these evaluations are not always well based and are not often communicated. There is a human tendency to allow personal emotions to dominate good judgement. Often, we base our overall impression of an individual on one outstanding trait. For example, if he is a hard and conscientious worker and we like him for it, we may not only rate him high on this trait, but also on everything else. On the other hand, if a man once made a bad mistake or turned in a poor job, we may let this colour our subsequent judgements of him and thereafter he is consigned to the 'poor performance' category.

FACTORS IN SOUND APPRAISAL

A number of questions generally arise when appraising performance, While, as yet, we have few principles to guide us, there are some basic considerations that should be kept in mind.

Personality or Performance Appraisals? We often find our thinking at cross purposes as we try to decide whether we are determining what kind of man a person is or what kind of job he is performing. The answer depends on the purpose of our appraisal. If we are concerned with helping a person to improve his knowledge, attitudes, and skills to help advance his personal objectives and those of the company as a whole, our primary consideration should be to appraise the person in terms of his work and results. An appraisal of his personality should be made only as it relates to his ability to do his work.

Appraisal Forms. The yardstick used in the appraisal of a manager is his ability to manage, his ability to perform the management work of planning, organizing, leading, and controlling, plus whatever technical work is assigned to his position. The results of such work should be the basis for determining how well he is doing his management job. Appraisal forms vary widely, but should include a measurement of the methods used and the results accomplished in performance of both management and technical work. The most successful approach is to have the manager develop his objectives, programme, schedule, and budget and to appraise his performance in terms of this plan.

Individual contributors, who are not managers, should be appraised in terms of their primary technical responsibilities. Their appraisal forms should concentrate largely on technical work and results as measured against objectives, programmes, schedules, budgets, and standards.

Frequently, the appraisal process compares one individual with another. However, it is difficult, and often unfair, to compare the performance of different individuals unless they are doing the same work under the same conditions.

Consistent Appraisals. It is difficult to secure consistent evaluations. Some managers appraise on the high side, some on the low. Others distribute their appraisals in a fairly even pattern. No matter how sincere the appraiser, his evaluation may be influenced by personal factors, prejudices, or preferences of which he may be quite unconscious. Judgement is also relative. An outstanding man will look better in a mediocre group than in an outstanding group.

Group appraisals minimize these inconsistencies by bringing together appraisers who evaluate the individual from different viewpoints. This gives greater balance and objectivity. If a staff management development group maintains a continuing review of all appraisals, it will also help identify and compensate for inconsistencies.

Finding Time. The manager must set aside several hours for each appraisal. He cannot expect to do a fair and comprehensive job with less. This time will be augmented by notes he will keep each day of outstanding performance, or deficiencies which have been demonstrated by his people. The individual manager must often carve this time from his already busy day. But he must do so if he is to do a good job. It takes time to establish rating patterns so that the tendencies of individual raters can be noted and corrected and to secure common understanding of how to rate consistently. For the working manager, it will require one to three years of study and practice to develop sound appraisal skills.

Using Appraisals. The appraisals, in and of themselves, are a source of information. However, to get the greatest returns on the investment of time, they should be used in as many ways as possible. They can be used to plan career paths. Armed with a meaningful series of appraisals, the manager can best counsel an individual on his career opportunities and what he must do to qualify for them. The manager can use the appraisal data to prepare replacement tables for his own department by determining which positions each of his people is qualified to fill, how long it will take them to prepare for those positions, and what specific training they require, He can identify the people in his group and other groups of the company who can be expected to fill each position as it becomes vacant. He should have at least two people in mind for each position. If the candidates are in his own department, the manager can work with them to help them develop the necessary skills; if they are in other departments, he can coordinate his thinking with that of the accountable manager.

HOW TO APPRAISE CURRENT PERFORMANCE

There are many different ways of appraising performance. The technique outlined below summarizes successful experience in a variety of organizations.

(a) *Developing the Appraisal Plan.* The manager should think through what he wants to accomplish with appraisals. Is it to encourage efficient performance, to help people use their abilities to the full, to screen out poor performers and help place them where they can be better used? Or is it a combination of these? The manager must establish standards that will provide evidence of successful accomplishment of the objective; he should make these measurable. He then develops the programme steps, schedule, and budget. He prepares procedures to cover approaches that must be standardized, such as preparation of career path plans, management inventories, and counselling sessions.

(b) *Developing Appraisal Forms.* If the manager is to do a consistent job of appraisal and counselling, he will need standard forms to help provide uniformity to his approach, a basis for permanent records, and a means of communication. Appraisal forms are usually developed by the organization development or the training department. The manager should check with the appropriate department to be sure he thoroughly understands their use and his specific responsibilities.

If a manager is developing his own forms, there is no better basis for appraisal than to assess actual performance against understood and accepted plans, for the individual's plan sets forth the results he has committed himself to accomplish, the steps he will take, the time limits, and the resources to be used. The appraisal form should include four sections.

Section 1: Summary of overall performance for the year, compared with plan.

Section 2: The career path plan: what avenues of progression are open and what must the individual do to qualify for them?

Section 3: Review of personal characteristics that affect performance and promotability.

192

Section 4: The personal improvement plan: what objectives, programme, and schedule will the individual follow to improve his own performance?

(c) *Considering Self-Appraisal.* Self-appraisal requires the individual to evaluate his own performance, most often by using a copy of the standard appraisal form. If the individual participates in a logical planning and control system, he will already have reported and evaluated his own performance in his regular monthly or quarterly operating report and his self-appraisal will really be a review and summary of this. This has many advantages. The subordinate is required to think through his own performance in terms of the standards by which he will be measured. This encourages self-examination, which helps satisfy his teleological and security drives and may lead him to critical conclusions about the kind of job he is doing. In practice, the subordinate will appraise himself lower than would his manager. Because of this, self-appraisal can serve as an effective starting point for later counselling.

The self-appraisal should not be used by itself to evaluate a subordinate's performance. It is entirely too subjective and leaves room for too many abuses. However, the self-appraisal is an excellent adjunct to any other method of appraisal adopted.

(d) *Getting Help in Appraisals.* The manager can make the appraisal himself by reviewing the man's performance, making an independent decision on the overall rating and entering the final statement on the appraisal form. This, of course, would be subject to review by his own superior. This method is fast and direct. Presumably, the manager knows most about the person being appraised. However, this method can lead to distortion because of personal considerations, or because the manager may see a particular team-member through uniformly bright or gloomy spectacles. This is the 'halo effect'. A better approach is to ask two or more individuals on the same, or a higher level to undertake a joint discussion and analysis of the individual being appraised. The accountable manager will still make the final decision. The group will only advise and counsel with him; it will not make decisions. This method helps the manager to arrive at a logical and equitable composite appraisal.

If a specialist from the organization development department is available, he might act as an independent observer. He can help reconcile differences of opinion and will contribute his knowledge of rating tendencies and approaches used in other groups. He does not participate as an active member of the appraisal process. This helps bring one consistent viewpoint to a large cross-section of appraisals and will give more uniformity to the appraisal.

(e) *Evaluating Potential.* Evaluation of potential for advancement should be a part of the overall appraisal process. However, the appraisal or potential should be kept separate from the appraisal of performance, even if completed during the same group session. When both are to be discussed at the same session, the appraisal of performance should be finished first, followed by the appraisal of potential.

Past performance is the best predictor of future growth. If the individual has developed and improved consistently in the past, he will probably continue to do so in the future, for successful performance brings rewards that reinforce the pattern. If he has reached a plateau and is no longer growing and improving his capabilities, most likely his performance will stay on the same plane unless a new and potent moving force can be introduced, for he has probably developed cultural urges that compensate for his lack of progress on the job.

Simply indicating that a person is a 'poor' or an 'outstanding' candidate for promotion is not enough. Promotable to what? If the manager identifies the individual's probable ability to fill specific positions, the appraisal will be much more useful. Furthermore, if the manager has a position in mind for the individual, an estimate can be made as to how long it will take him to prepare for the position and what training he requires to fill it satisfactorily.

Psychological tests, if properly used by competent professionals, can be helpful in determining potential. Aptitude, interest and personality tests may identify characteristics and abilities which have not been demonstrated in day to day performance. Psychological tests should be used only as one tool in the appraisal process; they should not be relied on completely, nor should the manager use them as a crutch. Nothing can supplement his first-hand knowledge of the individual and his personal judgement as to the individual's capabilities for advancement.

(f) *Summarizing the Findings.* The conclusions made during and after the appraisal should be summarized in writing to maintain accurate records and to serve as a basis for counselling and subsequent appraisals. The summary of the conclusions should be positive; yet, the manager should specify how well or poorly the work was done. He should give facts and figures, keeping in mind that he will need to justify his statement to the man he has appraised. The manager should comment only on those personality characteristics which need attention if the work is to be improved.

The following is an example of a poor appraisal summary: 'John Lean has failed to reach his objective of improving sales volume. His sales call frequency is poor. He shows little interest in his work and often fails to attend sales meetings. John has little potential for promotion.'

A much more useful appraisal summary follows this pattern: 'John Lean set an objective of increasing his key accounts from 20 to 26 and improving sales volume from $30 000 to $34 000. He secured two new accounts, $33\frac{1}{3}$ per cent of his objective, and increased sales to $30 500, $12\frac{1}{2}$ per cent of his objective. The sales force averages are 75 per cent and 50 per cent. He ranks twelfth among fifteen sales engineers. He can improve by identifying potentially profitable customers (his last customer analysis is three years old) and increasing his call frequency. At present, about 80 per cent of his calls are on six customers who give him only 15 per cent of his volume. John showed real initiative and did a splendid job in the computer sales contest two years ago and has demonstrated excellent ability. He attended only two of the past eight sales meetings and we should discuss the reasons for his absences so he can get back on top, where he belongs. Although John's sales performance has slipped, he has shown that he has the ability to qualify for senior sales engineer. To qualify, he should meet his plan for at least two years and rank among the top four salesmen, which he has done now for nine months.

(g) *Keeping Records of Appraisals*. The manager should maintain a copy of all performance appraisals in the individual's personnel folder. He may also want to prepare a graphic summary of overall status by preparing colour-coded organization charts. The rectangles on these charts

Name:	Age:	Date:
Promotable to:		Date Ready:
		Training Needs:
Replacement:		Date Ready:
		Training Needs:
Replacement:		Date Ready:
		Training Needs:

Fig. 11.1 Coded chart rectangle. Information pertinent to performance, promotability, and training needs can be shown for each position.

are prepared in enlarged form, with a condensed statement of the pertinent information. An outline which might be used in recording the promotability ladder is shown in Fig. 11.1.

Each rectangle is often colour coded with transparent marking ink, using a colour code based on traffic light patterns, with green representing outstanding, yellow, satisfactory, and red, poor. The left half of the rectangle is coloured to indicate performance, the right half to show promotability. Thus, a rectangle with green in the left half and yellow in the right would indicate that the individual has outstanding current performance and satisfactory promotability. The code for posting training needs is keyed to the developmental opportunities that are available, for example:

A   Needs more experience in present position.
B   Rotate to other function on same level.
C   Understudy another job preparatory to promotion.
D   Secure more supervisory experience.
E   Complete specified in-company educational courses.
F   Complete specified outside educational courses.

Thorough performance appraisal is useful to the manager in several ways, many of which have been discussed above. Perhaps the most productive use, and the use which benefits those who have been appraised, is the communication of appraisal results through a performance counselling session.

PERFORMANCE COUNSELLING

Performance counselling is the work a manager does to discuss performance and capabilities with each of his people. Counselling, as is true of other management skills, goes through predictable evolutionary stages. It begins in the centric mode and, with knowledge and application, matures into the radic approach. In the spontaneous centric mode, it will amount to occasional informal discussions, an infrequent compliment and real attention only when things go wrong. The better method is to learn to counsel in the radic mode, so that discussion of overall performance will be a carefully planned part of management responsibility. Counselling skill is not only the basis for sound motivation, but also facilitates communication and is an indispensable part of personnel development.

COUNSELLING IN THE CENTRIC MODE

The natural and intuitive approach for the manager in counselling is to give first priority to his own interests and concerns. When he uses this counselling style, he does very little listening. Usually, he outlines his subordinate's deficiencies as he sees them and then states precisely defined improvements.

The centric approach is generally used by managers who are not sure of themselves or who have not developed the skills necessary to counsel effectively. The manager's security urges force him to monopolize the conversation so that he can protect himself and his territory by ensuring that his subordinate will not bring up embarrassing or contradictory points. *He usually fails to realize that this one-sided conversation blocks constructive discussion and develops little real motivation to improve on the part of the subordinate.*

The centric approach to counselling puts the subordinate on the defensive. Calling him to account with little opportunity to defend himself engenders anxiety and frustration. The subordinate's security urges will force him to respond in the centric mode to protect his territory and, as stated in the principle of human reaction, the centric reaction will be increased. *Probably, he will leave the counselling session feeling resentment, rather than satisfaction and heightened loyalty to his boss.*

COUNSELLING IN THE RADIC MODE

Using the radic mode to counsel, the manager gives as much concern to what team-members want to get from the interview as he does to his own interest. By putting his subordinate first, he lays the groundwork for getting most out of it for himself. When he uses the radic mode, the manager's objective is to help the individual make the best use of his abilities.

The manager helps assess his subordinate's performance and encourages him to develop his own programme for self-improvement. This requires skill and demands a certain degree of humility. The manager must assume that the contributor knows best what he wants to do and that he can find his own answers if given the necessary encouragement and support.

The radic method of counselling is most effective. It affirms the individual's importance and encourages him to evaluate his own strengths and weaknesses. Since he reaches his own conclusions and decides for himself what he will do, he will undertake the necessary action with vigour and enthusiasm. He has made an investment in his territory and will use it to his best advantage.

While counselling is a continuing day to day process, the formalized counselling session that follows performance appraisal is most important. Although this is a structured interview, the following methods will also prove effective in other, routine situations in which talking to people occurs.

PLANNING THE COUNSELLING SESSION

The manager must decide in advance precisely how he will conduct the session. He needs to think through what he will say and what conclusions he will try to reach. It may help to outline his approach. *He must keep in mind the purpose of the session—to help the individual to improve himself.* The manager must make sure he has the important facts of his subordinate's past experience, education, work history, and other related data. He should review the notes of the last counselling session, particularly the individual's personal improvement plan. The manager should study carefully the last appraisal and related notes concerning his performance since then. It is necessary to establish the individual's strong and weak points; at the same time, the manager must review his own deficiencies which may have contributed to less than perfect performance on the subordinate's part.

The manager should anticipate, if he can, the individual's reaction to the points which will be brought out. Even though the manager is acting in the radic mode, the team-member may not understand this and may respond in the centric mode. The manager should prepare himself for such a reaction with alternate discussion points. He must establish the conclusions he will try to reach and the constructive suggestions he will offer. To make sure he covers the ground in the time he will have available, the manager should prepare a tentative programme and schedule to help guide the discussion.

The session should be conducted in a quiet, relaxed atmosphere, not in the hurly-burly of operations. The manager should arrange beforehand for a suitable place. His office may be acceptable if he can avoid telephone calls and block out visitors for the period of the interview. Otherwise, he may want to meet in a conference room or library, at a club or hotel, or even to arrange a quiet visit during the evening or weekend.

The manager should notify the person he will counsel at least one day in advance. He should make sure the time he has arranged is convenient for the individual. In most circumstances, it is best not to arrange the meeting more than one week in advance. Too much time may build up unnecessary tension.

A friendly relationship should exist before the manager undertakes the counselling session. He should make sure the individual understands that he is considered an important member of the team. The manager's approach will vary with his own personality and that of the team-member

Questions about family, work, and hobbies may help break the ice. The manager may want to mention problems or matters of mutual interest. The manager should show realistically and sincerely that he appreciates the individual's past performance; it is important to mention outstanding improvements that he has made since the last counselling session. This phase should not be prolonged, but the manager must make sure he has established rapport before continuing.

The manager should briefly review the purpose of the interview with the individual to make sure that both are on common ground. He should emphasize that the appraisal and counselling are designed to help the team-member improve and develop his own skills. The manager should point out the benefits of doing a better job, and of preparing for future advancement. He must make it clear that he wants to help the sub-ordinate make the best use of his abilities, and that the manager doesn't want him to miss future opportunities because of performance that is not up to standard, but which could be improved. It is important here to give the individual an opportunity to discuss his own hopes and ambitions.

Various approaches can be used to discuss performance. The best will depend on the relationship the manager has developed, his personality, and the characteristics of the person he is counselling. The manager should try to develop a method with which he can be comfortable and which he can use without strain. He may follow the general outline of the appraisal form in his discussion, or he may want to develop his own guide.

A good way to establish a sound base for the counselling discussion is to ask the individual to appraise his own performance. If he has already appraised himself, the manager can now ask him to review his appraisal.

The manager should adopt a positive tone when counselling. This is no time for reprimand or rebuke. If this should be necessary, it should be done at another time. *The object is to counsel for improvement, not punishment.* The manager should adopt the attitude that both he and his sub-ordinate are striving to help the team-member turn in a better performance, to his own net advantage.

The manager should make his theme, 'listen more and say less'. He should ask questions to get information and to encourage the other person to talk freely. His job is to see that the important areas for discussion are covered and that the individual has an opportunity to analyse his own performance and to develop his onw programme for improvement. Criticism should be avoided; as the principle of human reaction establishes, this inevitably creates resistance. The manager should discuss the facts of the individual's performance, the available alternatives, and the benefits to be gained from improvement. One common counselling failure is that the participants have a pleasant discussion, but reach no positive conclusions. To minimize this possibility, the manager must focus on those areas of performance that require major attention. The manager should encourage his team-member to analyse the reasons why he is not up to standard. These are the areas for improvement on which he should concentrate to upgrade his overall performance.

The manager may now prefer to close the first phase of the counselling session and arrange for a second session at a later date. If he does, this will be a good opportunity for the individual to give further thought to the matter, and to decide what he can do to improve his performance in each area that was discussed. If a second session is impracticable, the counselling should continue, covering the following points.

Possible means of improvement should be discussed. The manager's purpose is to help the individual examine different ways in which he can improve his performance. To do this, the manager should isolate each improvement area in turn. He should ask for the individual's suggestions and contribute his own. As many alternatives as possible should be proposed and examined. For each improvement area, the manager should help the team-member to decide which alternative he will act on. The manager must remember that the individual's teleological drives impel him to accomplish his objectives, not the manager's. This is why it is most important that he decides for himself what he will do. The manager must make no promises to encourage him. Generally, it is a mistake to link the improvement discussion with promises of a specific promotion 'if he improves'.

There should be agreement on a personal improvement plan which the team-member will follow to overcome deficiencies and strengthen performance. He should prepare a programme and schedule which spell out the specific activities he will undertake to improve. The manager should ask him to write this out, specifying what he will do and when he will do it. The manager should receive a copy of this plan and tell his team-member he will follow it up with him by on the job discussions and coaching. The discussion should then end on a positive and friendly note.

Many managers let counselling drop after the session is completed. However, a formal discussion once or twice a year cannot be expected to do the job. The manager must follow through to ensure that his investment in time and effort is amply repaid in the improved performance of his team-member.

It is important not to trust everything to memory; the manager should write down important points of the discussion. He should attach these to the personal improvement plan that the individual has prepared. Both should be filed for future reference. They will be invaluable to the manager as he works with his team-member on the various aspects of his personal improvement plan.

The manager can maximize the value of his counselling session by evaluating his own performance at the session. He should carefully review his approach, the results he accomplished, and the problems and difficulties that came up. He should outline the specific steps he will follow to improve his own counselling skills and to overcome the deficiencies he has identified in himself. Consistent self-evaluation is one of the best ways to improve and refine counselling ability. The manager should follow up with his subordinate on his personal improvement activities. As the manager continues to counsel and coach, he must be patient and understanding. He must not expect changes overnight. Improvement comes in small instalments.

DEVELOPMENTAL PROGRAMMES

Managers develop themselves; however, formalized training and developmental opportunities can help them improve their knowledge, attitudes, and skills. *Developmental programmes are the formalized action steps a manager takes to accomplish his developmental objectives.* In our survey of developmental programmes, we shall identify each as it relates to the objectives of acquiring knowledge, changing attitudes, and improving skills.

IMPORTANCE OF EXAMPLE

The most important developmental influence is the example of a good boss. People tend to manage as they are managed. The manager who plans, organizes, leads, and controls as part of his normal, day to day job will find that team-members tend to emulate him. If he concentrates on the operative aspects of his job and holds his management subordinates accountable for personal accomplishment of technical work, he will discover that this also becomes their emphasis.

Most managers find that team-members also tend to emulate them in their approach to people. If the manager's approach is self-centred, with most of his concern for his own interests, his people will reciprocate, both towards him and to others on the team. If the manager adopts and advocates a radic approach and habitually asks, 'What's best for the department as a whole?' he will find that this approach begins to gain currency and eventually will become the accepted standard.

COACHING PROGRAMMES

Coaching is the personal activity of the manager to instruct and develop employees on the job. Coaching involves creating opportunities on the job to help an individual improve his strong points and overcome weaknesses. This requires that the manager observes his team-member on the job and points out methods and opportunities for improvement.

Coaching requires that the manager creates developmental opportunities. He may assign the individual to new and different tasks or he may give him a special problem to work out on his own initiative. The vital requirement in coaching is that the manager personally observes and follows up the assignment so that he can instruct team-members. This necessitates a great deal of time and attention. However, it is one of the most important responsibilities of a manager, and will result in improved performance more quickly than any other method.

JOB ROTATION

Job rotation is the movement of a person from one position to another on the same organizational level for purposes of development. This rotation should never become a game of musical chairs with people moving about at random. Each rotational move should be planned on an individual basis. The purpose should be to increase the knowledge and experience of the individual in line with enterprise needs and improve the overall efficiency of the enterprise.

Rotation from one function to another at the first level of supervision is particularly important, but also most difficult, because first-level supervisors are called on to perform the largest proportion of technical work. If the manager who is being rotated has been doing a good deal of the work for his subordinates, his rotation may mean the loss of a key technician. If the replacement does not have an equivalent technical skill, effectiveness may suffer.

However, if supervisors are in the habit of doing the team-members' work for them, it is well to note what is taking place and to insist on more effective delegation as a prerequisite to job rotation.

Building from Bottom Levels. Job rotation should begin at lower supervisory levels. This has several advantages. For one, it ensures that managers will receive functional experience in lower-level positions, which have greatest functional content. This minimizes the need to demote higher-level managers temporarily to lower-level positions so that they can get functional experience. A person who has once had this experience retains it, no matter how high on the management ladder he climbs. He will always be able to bring this technical insight to the management decisions he will make. Rotation at lower levels is also less expensive. Salaries are lower. The potential loss due to temporary inefficiency is more restricted, and the impact of learners' mistakes is localized.

Eliciting Suggestions of Subordinates. The suggestions of team-members should be given every consideration in job rotation. The best approach here is to involve individuals directly in planning rotation possibilities, both inside and outside the department. If they are to participate intelligently, employees will have to understand the purpose and method of rotation. As they contribute their suggestions, they will develop a proprietary interest in the undertaking. This will help to forestall and overcome possible feelings of anxiety and frustration and will encourage enthusiastic participation.

COMMITTEE PARTICIPATION

Membership of a committee can be a useful development activity. However, the manager should be made a working member, with full participation in committee assignments and discussions. Simply to observe the committee deliberations is rarely worth while.

As a participant in committee affairs, the manager can often secure better insight and understanding of the different viewpoints represented. He can see better where his own unit fits into the total scheme and the importance of his contribution for overall success.

FORMALIZED EDUCATIONAL PROGRAMMES

These are the best means of acquiring new knowledge, reviewing new developments, and learning about innovatory thinking and practice in other organizations. Seminars, offered on a scheduled basis by consultants, universities, and associations, can be a valuable means of presenting new findings in management and technical functions and giving participants an opportunity to review and discuss their implications with others of similar experience and interests. Seminars usually require from one to five days and may be offered at a public location, attended by representatives from many enterprises, or conducted in-house, limited to selected people from the host enterprise. Public seminars offer the advantage of cross-fertilization: many different viewpoints are represented and helpful ideas often result from discussion and participation. In-house seminars permit more sharply focused subject matter and can be addressed to actual operating problems.

Advanced management courses, ranging from two or three weeks to a year, or more, are also offered by universities, consultants, management associations, and other groups. These may be attended as residential courses, taught by a regular faculty, as evening or extension courses, or in a scheduled series of three to twelve one-week sessions. These courses permit more extensive study and analysis and are more nearly equivalent to a regular university programme. Where the shorter seminar is valuable for survey and overview purposes, the advanced management course usually results in detailed understanding of the subject being taught.

Self-study courses are available for both home study and on the job use. They include the standard correspondence course, in which the manager completes a series of work and study assignments monitored by one or more faculty members whom he knows only by correspondence. Also available are courses based on tape cassettes, programmed instruction manuals and case- and workbooks.

The manager will derive greatest benefit from formalized eduational programmes when he can relate them to an overall objective and programme and make them part of his continuing education. If he is pursuing his own self-education, he should first determine his objectives. Is he interested in systematically developing mastery of the work of management? Does he want to become more proficient in one management function or activity? Is his primary interest a functional area such as electronic data processing, marketing, or accounting? Or is he mostly concerned with developing skills in interpersonal relationships, interviewing, or computer programming? The manager cannot accomplish all of these at once or through any one course. He must clearly state his specific objective and standards, then search out all the available offerings in his field of interest. He should secure a copy of the curriculum or a detailed statement of the programme offered. It is beneficial to ask for names of previous participants in the programme. The manager should contact them, outlining his objectives and asking for frank comments. He will generally get them. When he enrolls, he should commit himself to the time he will need to do a good job. If he registers for a seminar or advanced management course, he will generally receive pre-programme readings or other preparatory material. He should complete this carefully, for he will be at a disadvantage if he is not prepared when he begins the session. During the course, he should become acquainted with as many people as he can with similar problems. He will find that continuing these contacts after the course can be both valuable and stimulating. Finally, he must commit himself to take specific action on his job as a result of the course. He should develop a programme for his own performance, discuss it with his superior and subordinates as soon as he returns, then put it into effect.

If a manager is approving the attendance of others at formalized educational courses, he should always satisfy himself that the participant knows why he is attending, that he is prepared to invest the necessary time and is required both to report on his experience and to undertake a definite follow-up programme when he returns to his job.

In-House Programmes. Formalized educational programmes can be prepared by the organization's own organization development or training staff. They may be available from outside consultants or educational groups. In contrast to those open to the public, in-house programmes can be tailored more specifically to the needs of the company, incorporating cases and assignments related to the current situations, and can contribute to the solution of operating problems.

In-house programmes often fail because they are put together from a miscellaneous collection of information gathered from books, reports, and articles and do not represent a logical, integrated addition to knowledge. The better approach is to establish clear educational objectives for the subject area, establish standards for both acquisition of new knowledge and development of skills, and develop the material within this framework. The course should be pre-tested several times to ensure it is capable of meeting the established objectives and standards.

In-house programmes are best taught by selected members of the organization who are specially trained for the assignment. They will usually require about ten days for this training and should plan to devote four to six hours to preparation for each hour of class time. The 'how to teach' sessions can be conducted by the management or organizational development staff. Since the instructors selected and trained in this fashion gain more themselves than anybody else, this is one of the best means of developing and improving personal skills. The management or organizational development or training staff is equipped to plan, conduct, and monitor in-house programmes and can usually work most effectively with outside educational institutions and consultants in planning, evaluating, and administering the selected programmes.

Increasingly, in-house educational programmes are being used to initiate and develop companywide systems of management. When this is the objective, a primary requirement is that the top executive group both adopts and practises the management concepts, principles, techniques, and vocabulary that are being taught for use throughout the organization. Under the best circumstances, a large investment in time and money will be required to implement a systematic, orderly, and logical approach to managing the business as a whole. The effort is foredoomed to partial or complete failure unless it has the active support and example of each manager, from the top down. Since directors are becoming increasingly aware of the critical importance of professional management to long-term success and profitability, periodic review and recommendation by the board is highly desirable.

Job Enrichment, Job Enlargement, and Team-Building Programmes. These are general programmes designed primarily to change attitudes and improve interpersonal skills. The specifics, and particularly the terminology, used in the programmes vary, depending on the originator or sponsor, but the basics are essentially the same. The objective is to improve management attitudes and performance. This is accomplished primarily by increasing delegated responsibility and authority, giving each individual greater opportunity to plan and control his own work, and greatly intensifying the tempo of communication, participation, and involvement in decision making.

A basic premise is that both managers and individual contributors can best study, analyse, and improve their own jobs and performance. Each manager is helped to assume responsibility for his own group. Frequently, he is taught skills of discussion leadership and group problem analysis, so that he can involve his own people with maximum effectiveness. Work simplification and methods improvement techniques are also used. An early move is for each group to study its own jobs and recommend steps for assignment of increased responsibility

206

and authority. At the operator level this is most feasible in non-union companies. Job enrichment programmes have more force if an incentive or profit-sharing programme is in effect which promises individual returns when an individual or group successfully handles more responsibility.

In job enrichment and team building, each person is given maximum opportunity to develop his own objectives, programme, and schedule. The reporting system is tuned to his special requirements so that he learns quickly and precisely how he is doing in terms of his understood and accepted standards. He is kept fully informed of overall progress and results through group meetings, bulletins and reports and, frequently, special video tape or telephone links. Questionnaires are used to elicit his opinions on current happenings, proposed plans, and new developments. He is kept constantly informed of survey results. The net effect is to make each individual feel that he is a fully functioning part of the organization and that he has a real financial, as well as emotional, ownership in the results.

SUMMARY

(a) A manager should help his team-members develop their knowledge, attitudes, and skills. This development is supported by objectives, sound organization, performance standards, and balanced compensation. Developing subordinates involves performance appraisal, performance counselling, and developmental programmes.

(b) The manager uses performance appraisal to evaluate his own performance and capabilities and those of his staff. The personality of an individual must be separated from his performance to establish a sound appraisal. There is no standard form for such an appraisal, although one built around accomplishment of objectives, programmes, schedules, and budgets is recommended. Comparison of individuals is difficult and often inaccurate for the purpose of a performance appraisal. Group appraisals of individuals minimize inconsistencies. The time must be found for performing appraisals of every member of the group. To be effective, the information in the appraisals must be put to use. Self-appraisal is an effective supplementary method of performance appraisal, although the manager should be aware that a subordinate will often tend to grade himself down. The advice of other managers, and especially that of the manager's own superior, will be valuable in preparing an appraisal. In preparing the appraisal, the potential of the subordinate should be stressed and a summary of the appraisal conclusions should be prepared, both as a record and for performance counselling.

(c) A performance counselling session is conducted by the manager for each member of his group. During the session, both performance and capabilities are discussed. The centric mode is ineffective when counselling because it puts the subordinate on the defensive and creates resentment and frustration. The use of the radic mode involves planning the counselling session, anticipating reactions, conducting the session in a friendly, relaxed atmosphere, and using a positive approach to the business at hand. Criticism is out of place in the counselling session and listening is more important than talking. Areas of improvement should be stressed with alternate plans of action. Follow-up sessions are advisable to review progress on the personal improvement programme developed for the subordinate during the counselling session.

(d) Developmental programmes provide opportunities for each individual to improve his personal skills. Most important is the example of the superior, for he will set the pattern which others will emulate. Coaching programmes enable the manager to work personally with his subordinates and instruct and counsel them in their work. Job rotation provides varied experience in different jobs which a person holds progressively, following a plan designed to improve his personal abilities. Committee participation provides useful exposure to a wide range of problems. Formalized educational programmes are the best means of acquiring new knowledge, and help in changing attitudes and improving skills. Seminars and advanced management courses are most valuable, if part of an educational plan and not attended haphazardly. Self-study courses are flexible and can be paced to suit individual needs. In-house programmes have special advantages in that they can be closely tailored to specific needs; however, they are expensive to develop and must be pre-tested. Job enrichment and enlargement and team-building programmes can be used to help people accept more responsibility and authority, do a more effective job of planning and controlling, and improve personal and group relationships.

12. CONTROLLING FOR RESULTS

A plan establishes a course of action which a manager is committed to follow in the future. While it is important to know where he wants to go, the ability to stay on the predetermined course is equally vital. *Management controlling is the work a manager does to assess and regulate work in progress and to assess results secured.*

We often think of controls as an inquest into the past, but with modern tools of information handling, control has become a dynamic and fast-changing function, fully capable of moving with the parade of events.

IMPORTANCE OF CONTROL

Control relates directly to our basic drives, for it is a cultural means of achieving security. Controls safeguard the work we do, and its results, and protect our material and emotional investment. If we have a clear objective in mind and work hard to accomplish it, the natural apprehension we feel, that we may not achieve what we want, stimulates the added effort we need to ensure success. Cultural derivatives of the security drive extend to many aspects of control, ranging from the intensified cohesiveness of a group of people which feels threatened to the need of individuals for limits within which to work.

The ability to collect, analyse, store and report information is the key to fast, precise and flexible controls. Computerized information handling and retrieval have enabled us to make important breakthroughs. One

209

development is our ability to exercise control over work as it is being done without waiting for the results to be completed. The more closely work in process can be monitored and results compared with the plan, the more quickly information can be provided and the necessary changes accomplished.

When we develop controls that enable us to regulate work in progress, we can bring deficient action back to the desired plan and, in the process, learn enough to move to a higher level of accomplishment. In modern usage, management controls can be compared with the mechanism used by the aircraft pilot to enable him to carry out his flight plan. The pilot receives information from his instruments which tell him whether or not he is on course. He has rudder, ailerons, and flaps to bring his plane back if it is deflected. In the process of correction, he may find out enough about local turbulence or air conditions to plan and seek another altitude or direction and thus proceed more efficiently towards his objective.

Controls are an important adjunct to delegation. The manager can get others to do work for him and can permit decisions to be made in his name only to the extent he can ensure that the work is done properly and the decisions are made within established limits. Thus, the better the controls, the greater the potential for delegation.

Controls provide limits which establish the area of personal responsibility and accountability we must have if we are to satisfy our territorial needs. They provide the feedback on performance that is basic to a feeling of security and confidence in the work we do. Controls also satisfy our security needs by limiting the aggressiveness of others to their own areas so they do not usurp authority and responsibility which we feel we should be exercising.

CLASSIFICATION OF CONTROL

Controlling is divided into four activities.

Developing performance standards is the work a manager performs to specify criteria by which work and results can be measured and evaluated. A performance standard can be anything used to differentiate between good work and poor work. It is evidence of acceptable performance.

Measuring performance is the work a manager performs to record and report the work being done and the results secured. Measurement is the communication medium for keeping managers informed of performance against standard.

210

Evaluating performance is the work a manager performs to analyse and interpret performance and results. Evaluation requires comparison of actual performance and results with the standard, and identification of deficiencies.

Correcting performance is the work a manager performs to rectify and improve the work being done and the results secured. Corrective action closes the planning and control gap and leads to improved plans and a higher level of performance.

Performance of the control activities is coordinated by inputs and outputs of information from the management information system. The MIS provides the data used for performance standards, records and reports, both progress and results, circulates data necessary for evaluation and provides the basis for performance correction. Although most of this may be automated, the performance evaluation activity requires continuing managerial attention.

EVOLUTION OF CONTROL

The controlling process goes through predictable stages. First is the spontaneous centric in which the manager controls largely to further his own interests and objectives, often at the expense of those of the group as a whole. During this stage, the manager expects others to do their work his way and to meet the level of performance which he sets. Since the natural leader is usually expert in the work of the people he supervises, his standards are high and demanding. During this early stage of centric control, the manager spends a great deal of time inspecting and observing everything that is done. Evaluation is largely the comparison of work and results with the manager's personal standards. Performance correcting centres on the manager trying to get people to change to more nearly approximate his personal preferences.

Spontaneous centric controls make the leader the focus of power. Both praise and correction stem from him. When things go wrong, his reprimands and instructions run through the layers of organization, setting up whirlpools of activity at each level, until the word finally reaches the level where corrective action can be taken.

Spontaneous centric control can be highly effective. If the manager is a good performer, he requires that others follow his established and proven pattern. Since he is constantly observing, he acts on mistakes promptly. While this may engender resentment, and even frustration, it does have the salutary effect of keeping people on their toes. However, spontaneous centric control limits the scope of the manager to personal observation and appraisal. It discourages initiative and independent action because people begin to feel that the boss is always peering over their shoulders. Eventually, some managers reach a transition stage. They find that they cannot keep up with everything themselves and either learn to change from personal to management control, or momentum declines, growth is discouraged, and the best people leave.

When a manager moves to rational radic control, he establishes performance standards based on his plans; such standards are objective, impartial and based on the results to be accomplished, not on special characteristics of personality. At this stage, the manager is not concerned with reports of routine or minor deficiencies, but directs his control efforts largely to problem areas outside the command of his subordinates.

Rational radic control frees a manager from the need to remain cognizant of detail. It gives him a tool for analysing results so that he can anticipate and correct variances before they occur. Furthermore, it encourages his people to use their imagination and resourcefulness in developing their own ways of doing their work and in making their own decisions. At this stage, the manager has learned to develop concern for the needs of those he controls, as well as to satisfy himself. He gives others an opportunity to set their own standards, within limits. He develops reports and other control techniques which enable individuals to identify and correct their own mistakes before they are called to account.

The evolution from spontaneous to rational modes can be expedited if the manager studies and applies the principles and techniques of control. The mark of true professional competence is the ability to use the omnimode, to know when to maintain close personal scrutiny and when to control by exception.

PRINCIPLES OF CONTROLLING

We have identified several principles which can be of value in understanding control systems and establishing effective control.

THE PRINCIPLE OF THE CRITICAL FEW

Everything is not of the same importance; always, a few things will have the greatest impact on the results to be secured. The key to effective control is to put the major effort behind the few important things and not to waste time on routine and detail.

PRINCIPLE OF	*In any given group of occurrences,*
THE CRITICAL FEW	*a small number of causes will tend to*
	give rise to the largest proportion
	of results

In exercising control, we can safely assume that this relatively small number of causative factors will be of greatest importance in securing the results we want; therefore, we should identify the critical factors that can be expected to give rise to most of the consequences.

In any group, for example, we can expect a few people to produce the most work, while another relatively small number will account for most of the errors. In sales, we can anticipate that a few customers will account for most of the profitable volume. In controlling quality, a small percentage of defects will cause the bulk of the waste. If we investigate safety factors, we find that a small number of employees and locations accounts for the largest number of accidents. If we are concerned with credit losses, a relatively small number of customers will account for the greater part of the bad debts. If we are concerned with inventories, we know that relatively few items in the total inventory will give most of the surpluses.

A good case in point occurred in an aluminium company, which analysed supplier invoices and found that 92 per cent of the cheques written at headquarters were under $1000, and accounted for less than 5 per cent of the cash which the company paid out. Using the principle of the critical few, the corporation now permits vendors to write their own cheques for amounts up to $1000. The savings in accounting, postage, and time amount to $200 000 a year. Many other companies have followed this lead with great success.

In another case, a Melbourne supply company wanted to improve results from its sales effort. Analysing its sales, the company found that 10 per cent of its customers provided 80 per cent of its business. Instead of diffusing its sales effort over the total customer group, the company had its salesmen identify the accounts with greatest potential. Objectives, programmes, and schedules were set to concentrate attention on these, and sales per call and total volume increased steadily.

The principle of the critical few is valuable in control because it enables us to focus the greater part of our energy and resources on the few variables that yield the greatest results.

THE PRINCIPLE OF POINT OF CONTROL

Control is much like a pyramid, with the greatest number of control

213

opportunities occurring at the base. First-line managers who supervise direct operations, such as manufacturing and sales, secure most of the direct results, spend most of the money, and manage most of the people. Since most of the action takes place at that level, the greatest potential for control also exists there.

PRINCIPLE OF POINT OF CONTROL

The greatest potential for control exists at the point where action takes place

The people doing the work have most acute and persistent concern for its accomplishment. The principle of point of control recognizes this and indicates that decentralized control will be most effective, provided, of course, that it is integrated with the overall controls necessary to maintain unification and coordination of effort.

In many cases, control information and action are initiated at higher levels in the organization, rather than at the point where action takes place; the total control effort is thus slowed down. This principle establishes that control should centre on the person accountable for carrying the work through to completion. He should have the most information about the work that is being done and the results that are secured, and should be the first to receive it.

Application of this principle is illustrated by the case of a diversified manufacturing company with headquarters in Liverpool. Reports of factory variances were sent directly to the managing director, who had his staff analyse and return them through channels to the factory managers. This caused continuing explanation and rationalization through eight levels of organization. A new managing director had his staff work with department and factory managers to establish objectives, programmes, schedules, and budgets at the first-line supervisory level and provided supervisors with reports of performance. Reports decreased; there was less need for coordination; and operating control was more effective than it ever had been in the past.

THE PRINCIPLE OF SELF-CONTROL

When we check other people and tell them how to correct their work, they resent our suggestions and will act on them with little enthusiasm. However, if people have the tools to check themselves and can correct their own mistakes, they will find much greater satisfaction in doing a good job.

214

PRINCIPLE OF SELF-CONTROL

Self-control tends to be the most effective control

As an example, a Johannesburg plastics manufacturer received a large contract for overseas shipment that necessitated a three-shift operation. Materials handling equipment always seemed to be in short supply on the night shift. The superintendent was called continually from sleep at his home to help locate the necessary equipment. Finally, he had each foreman programme and schedule the materials handling equipment he would need for his shift. He reconciled these with the foremen and held them accountable. The first time he was awakened, he demanded that the foreman refer to the schedule and follow it. He repeated this three times. Thereafter, he slept without interruption.

Self-controls are effective only if the person doing the work participates in establishing the plans and standards for which he will be held accountable. Each person who controls his own operation should receive the reports he needs to evaluate his own performance and to take the corrective action necessary. Variances should always be reported to the superior, or to a third party, for proper checks and balances.

DEVELOPING PERFORMANCE STANDARDS

Managers often avoid setting standards because they are not sure of the difference between excellence and mediocrity in the work they do. It is the rare manager, indeed, who can state the difference between good organization and poor, between outstanding and inadequate communication, or between superior and mediocre training of people. This inability to establish criteria of excellence may stem from lack of experience; most often, it marks a failure on the part of his superior, who may not know how himself, or, if he does, has not effectively communicated the knowledge to the manager.

Standards are avoided, also, because managers are afraid that their own deficiencies will be revealed. This fear is natural until the manager realizes that it is far better for him to have a positive guide to improvement, rather than to be judged without recourse.

Standards are often arbitrary and unrealistic. They may have been established to satisfy the centric needs of one person or one group. When a level of performance is required which is patently beyond the scope of the situation, the standards fall into disrepute. In effect, bad standards drive out the good.

215

BASING STANDARDS ON GUIDING PLANS

Every good plan can serve as the basis for a good standard. The plan establishes what the action is to be and is used in a second role to measure action and results, when it becomes a performance standard.

After an objective is stated, standards can be developed by determining what will constitute acceptable evidence that the desired results have been achieved. Programmes, schedules, and budgets can serve as performance standards.

KEEPING STANDARDS REALISTIC

Standards serve as incentives to improvement only if they are realistic and attainable; setting standards too high discourages achievement; setting them too low encourages slack effort.

The best method for establishing realistic standards is to analyse and appraise past performance and to determine, on the basis of what has already been achieved, what reasonable improvement can be expected and the extra effort and resources necessary to attain it.

SECURING UNDERSTANDING AND ACCEPTANCE

Performance standards will be virtually useless in practice unless they are understood and accepted by the people who are accountable. Acceptance is best secured through participation. If people help develop the standards by which their performance is to be measured, they will understand the basis for the standards and will accept them most readily. This follows from our natural spontaneous centric reaction and our innate tendency to be most interested in, and work hardest for, our own objectives and territory. Communication is an important factor. People should be kept informed of problems and changes and their suggestions should be encouraged.

KEEPING STANDARDS FLEXIBLE

Once standards are set, there is a tendency to regard them as fixed and changeless monuments to achievement; however, they should be as flexible as the plans on which they are based and should be revised as frequently. This flexibility, however, should not allow standards to be changed at whim; once established and agreed to, they should be altered only if there is sound reason.

Flexibility is eminently feasible with the computer. With fast and accurate information processing, real-time control can become a reality, but this calls for careful study and revision of standards both to reflect unexpected problems and to provide for new levels of achievement not anticipated in the original plan.

MEASURING PERFORMANCE

A report is a verbal or written statement of progress and results. The recording of information and the preparation and use of reports is a basic responsibility of every manager. Informal, spontaneous reporting goes on continually which keeps the manager apprised of work under his direct supervision; however, he must also initiate and use reports which provide intelligence to others in the system and which keep his people informed. Distinction between system reports and individual reports helps to clarify this.

System reports are the organizationwide flow of information which provides each manager with information he requires to fulfil his accountability for part of the current operation. These reports should be keyed to critical objectives, since these represent the results desired in the critical performance areas. The information reported should measure the degree to which outstanding performance is demonstrated, both in meeting critical objectives and the specific objectives, programmes, schedules, and budgets derived from them.

The general tendency is to report too much information to too many people. As a general rule, each manager needs the information necessary to assess and regulate the work and results for which he is accountable. The frequency and detail of system reports will vary with the organizational level. The first-level supervisor receives the most frequent and detailed reports. He will receive daily or weekly reports on such items as labour costs, controllable overheads, materials, and supplies. At higher levels, these will be consolidated, with reports primarily of exceptions.

Individual reports are the reports the manager initiates and puts forward to his immediate superior for personal review and discussion. Some of the information from the individual report becomes an input to the reporting system; its chief value, however, lies in its use for counselling by the superior at periodic intervals. The individual report is most easily rendered on the same form as the plan itself. Such a report is illustrated in the example below, which shows an individual's current progress for the specific objective 'Coordination of specifications' (discussed in chapter 6).

Programme steps	Account-ability	Schedule (completion dates)	Budget ($ or mandays)
1. LIST REQUIREMENTS. Sales manager to prepare written list of industry and customer requirements.	JBP	15/5	2 man days
(Electric motor data available in 30 days due to survey delay.)		(20/5)	(3 man days)
2. PREPARE SPECIFICATIONS. Sales manager to prepare written list of specifications from requirements, including details of function, accuracy, capacity, reliability, flexibility, and cost. (O.K. RTM to procedurize.)	JBP	1/8	1/2 man day
3. RECONCILE WITH SALES. Engineering manager to prepare written report to sales manager after analysing specifications. In this, he either approves the written list of specifications by signature or recommends alternatives for presentation to customer. (O.K.)	ROL	1/9	1 man day

ADOPTING A STEWARDSHIP CONCEPT OF REPORTING

Stewardship reporting measures an individual as manager of his own business. It holds him to account for the cost of the people, materials, tools, and facilities entrusted to his care. This kind of reporting is not based exclusively on accounting precepts, but on concepts of management accountability, so that each manager is given a clear picture of the money value of his operation and the results that he is getting.

Stewardship accounting is possible only if a manager is delegated authority over money spent in his department, or on behalf of his department; otherwise, he cannot be held to an obligation for the expenditure. It therefore follows that a stewardship report should focus on controllable items of expense. While expense for which the manager has little or no control should be reported, these items should be identified as such.

REPORTING PROMPTLY

In a fast-moving and competitive industry, an outdated report leaves management in the stadium instead of in the ball game. The quality and speed of reporting largely depend on the soundness of the basic planning. The more complete and accurate the plans, the easier it is to report progress and variances and exceptions as they occur. Reporting is sometimes hampered by a desire to give managers a completely documented and detailed statement of results. A manager does not need this to control, for a control report is not a budget and should not attempt to recapitulate budget data. What the manager needs is an analysis of the items for which he is accountable, with the variances and exceptions highlighted so that he can focus his attention immediately on areas that require action.

MAKING REPORTS UNDERSTANDABLE

Reports should be presented in language that is understandable to the people for whom they are intended. Often, accounting and financial terminology are used which has only a vague familiarity to the manager using the report. The cryptic nature of computer print-outs often complicates the problem. Managers should be trained to understand both the terminology and the significance of the information reported to them.

EVALUATING PERFORMANCE

Once the data are in and the manager has a basis for comparison, he must analyse and interpret progress and results. Evaluation requires a comparison of the actual performance with the standard and an identification and explanation of deficiencies.

There are two types of deficiencies. *Variances are deficiencies which fall within the allowable limits of tolerance.* Variances are within the command of the accountable manager and can be corrected by him. *Exceptions are deficiencies which fall outside the limits of allowable tolerance and must be given consideration by somebody other than the accountable manager.* Exceptions generally involve two or more departments, or are of such magnitude as to have impact on overall results.

As a general rule, exceptions should be reported to a staff agency outside the manager's chain of command, as well as to his own superior. If exceptions are reported only within the chain of command, the report should go at least two levels above the accountable manager to get the required objectivity and perspective.

In analysing deficiencies, it is important to determine the allowable limits of tolerance. In most operations, we do not expect results to

219

coincide with the plan to the last penny or the last centimetre. Most often, we consider results satisfactory if they come within reasonable distance of the plan. The permissible range of tolerances should be established beforehand, so that there is understanding and acceptance before reporting begins. In a new operation, it may be necesary to accumulate historical evidence of results to assess the potential degree of accomplishment.

In most cases, it is desirable to hold the manager accountable for all deviations from standard and to require him to make corrections for his variances which fall within the limits of tolerance. If this is not done, the tolerance becomes the standard.

THE EVALUATION DISCUSSION

Too often, evaluation does not include meaningful discussion of results by the individual and his superior. Formal performance reviews, which provide for discussion of results over a six-month or annual period, are valuable summaries; however, they should be supported by more frequent evaluation discussions, as often as weekly and at least once each month. These focus on current progress and results, are usually brief, and are quite informal.

The manager should hold the evaluation discussion where there is a minimum of interruption and distraction. The accountable person should review his progress against plan, explaining exceptions and variances in detail. Problems should be identified and explored. The significant elements of the plan for the next period are then developed and the important elements discussed.

CORRECTING PERFORMANCE

Control is effective when it motivates managers to take prompt, decisive steps to correct matters that are out of phase. Performance correction includes both current deficiencies and those long-term ones for which action can be initiated with a reasonable probability of success.

If the manager is to initiate performance correction, he must know what work he is expected to do and what authority he has to take corrective action. He must also have command over his own performance. If he cannot make the changes necessary without constantly checking with his superiors, he cannot be expected to carry out performance correction in a timely and efficient manner.

The two types of performance correction are management action and operating action. *Operating action is a short-term, emergency type of corrective action which is necessary when variances occur in the routine operation; management action is the development of new or improved plans, organization, or controls, usually long term in nature.* For example, perhaps deliveries are falling behind. To correct the lag, another man is put on the job. This operating action is taken on short notice. It corrects the immediate situation by treating the symptoms, but there is every possibility that the underlying cause remains.

If operating action is to be truly effective, it should be supported by the necessary management action. This means that a manager should analyse the basic causes of variances and determine the need for changing and improving his plans, organization, leading, and controls. In the case of slow delivery, for example, he may discover that his schedules are too tight. A readjustment may make the extra man unnecessary. Perhaps the organization of the work is at fault, in which case a rearrangement may improve the flow and help him get more work done in less time.

HOW TO CONTROL AGAINST PLAN

In applying these control fundamentals, there are several points that require attention.

REQUIRE REGULAR REPORTS

The manager should receive periodic reports which keep him informed of the status of the work and the results that have been achieved. He can ask for special reports when required, but these should be few in number.

USE A STANDARDIZED REPORT FORM

For ease of reading and analysis, a standardized report form should be used by each person in your team. Since standardized forms become outdated, the manager should review every report form at least once annually, asking himself and the members of his group such questions as: (a) What is the objective of this report? (b) Is it still necessary? (c) Can it be combined with another report? (d) What will happen if it is eliminated? (e) How can it be made shorter, more understandable, more useful?

SUMMARY

(a) Controlling work and results is a necessary part of management. It is most effective when applied to work in progress. Controls satisfy the territorial and security drives.

(b) Controls evolve predictably from centric to radic. Spontaneous centric control is initially effective and centres power on the manager. Later, when the group becomes larger or the quantity of information expands, the manager is no longer able to remain in control of all necessary information. Then, he must begin to develop radic controls which take into consideration the needs of others. Eventually, the omnimode is used by the manager who has become a true management professional.

(c) Certain principles aid the control process. (i) The principle of the critical few states that in any given group of occurrences, a small number of causes will tend to give rise to the largest proportion of results. (ii) The principle of point of control states that the greatest potential for control exists at the point where action takes place. (iii) The principle of self-control states that self-control tends to be the most effective control.

(d) Control may be classified into four activities: developing performance standards, measuring performance, evaluating performance, and correcting performance.

(e) Performance standards should be based on the plan for action. They can be part of the objectives, especially specific objectives. The standards should be realistic and have the understanding and acceptance of the members of the group. If standards are inflexible, the group will not be able to meet the objectives of the plan. Standards should not, however, be changed at whim.

(f) Measuring performance keeps a manager abreast of what has happened and why it happened. It also helps him build on the past for the future. The manager should be accountable for the reporting of performance as promptly and clearly as possible.

(g) Evaluating performance compares the actual performance with the standard, and identifies and explains deficiencies. Variances are within the command of the accountable manager, but exceptions require that others be alerted or involved.

(h) Correcting performance requires the manager to overcome variances and exceptions. He may take either operating or management action. Operating action is short-range, often emergency action and management action is long-range, planned action.

(i) Regular reports during scheduled periods provide necessary controls against the manager's plans. A standardized report form may help the reporting process, although the form should be regularly revised.

REFERENCES

1. Washburn, S. L., 'Speculations on the Interrelations of the History of Tools and Biological Evolution', in *The Evolution of Man's Capacity for Culture* (arr. by J. N. Spuhler), Wayne State University Press, Detroit, 1959, p. 31. Used by permission.
2. *Process* is defined as a series of actions leading to an end. The term implies progressive motion towards some objective.
3. *Behaviour* means a particular pattern of action.
4. *Work* is defined as the application of energy necessary to carry out purposeful action.
5. Konrad Lorenz presents a persuasive argument for aggression as a drive in itself, rather than a cultural urge, in *On Aggression* (translator, Majorie Kerr Wilson), Harcourt, Brace & World, Inc., New York, 1966.
6. Robert Ardrey presents a provocative and debated concept of territoriality in *The Territorial Imperative: A Personal Inquiry into the Animal Origins of Property and Nations* Atheneum, New York, 1966.
7. An interesting collection of articles which reveals much about territorial and aggressive impulses:
   Montague, M. F. Ashley (editor), *Man and Aggression* Oxford University Press, New York, 1968.
8. Allen, Louis A., *Management and Organization* McGraw-Hill Book Company, Inc., New York, 1958.

9. The pioneering classification was that by Henri Fayol. See his *General and Industrial Management* (translator, Constance Storrs), Sir Isaac Pitman & Sons, Ltd., London, 1949.

   Another classification will be found in the *Common Body of Knowledge Required by Professional Management Consultants* Association of Consulting Management Engineers, Inc., New York, 1957.

   A diagrammatic representation appears in R. Alec Mackenzie's 'The Management Process in 3-D', *Harvard Business Review* November–December, 1969.

10. The author appreciates the collaboration of Joseph Mohan, Armco Steel Corporation, in helping develop the leading function concept during 1959–60.

11. M. Scott Myers has written: 'The functions of management are commonly defined in business school terminology as planning, organizing, leading and controlling. . . .' (*Every Employee a Manager: More Meaningful Work Through Job Enrichment* McGraw-Hill Book Company, Inc., New York, 1970, p. 63. Used by permission.)

12. Lewin, Kurt, *Field Theory in Social Science: Selected Theoretical Papers* (editor, Dorwin Cartwright), Harper & Row, New York, 1951, pp. 188–199, 275–289. Used by permission.

13. Fayol, op. cit., pp. 26, 37. Used by permission.

14. Taylor, Frederick Winslow, *The Principles of Scientific Management* Harper & Brothers, New York, 1942, pp. 5, 10–69. Used by permission.

15. ibid., p. 9.

16. ibid., pp. 31, 33–34.

17. Belden, Thomas Graham, and Belden, Marva Robins, *The Lengthening Shadow: The Life of Thomas J. Watson* Little, Brown & Company, Boston, 1962, p. 146. Used by permission.

18. *Armco Policies* Armco Steel Corporation, Middletown, Ohio, 12 December, 1919.

19. Metcalf, Henry C., and Urwick, L. (editor), *Dynamic Administration: The Collected Papers of Mary Parker Follett* Harper & Row, New York, 1940.

20. Barnard, Chester I., *The Functions of the Executive* Harvard University Press, Cambridge, 1938, pp. 274, 279. Used by permission.

21. Bennis, Warren G., *Changing Organizations* McGraw-Hill Book Company, Inc., New York, 1966, p. 181. Used by permission.

225

22. Weber, Max, *The Theory of Social and Economic Organization* (translators, A. M. Henderson and Talcott Parsons; editor, Talcott Parsons), The Free Press, New York, 1964.

——, *From Max Weber: Essays in Sociology* (translator, H. H. Gerth; editor, C. Wright Mills), Oxford University Press, New York, 1958.

23. For a concise statement of organismic theory, see: Hall, Calvin S., and Lindzey, Gardner, *Theories of Personality* John Wiley & Sons, Inc., New York, 1957, pp. 296–335.

24. Goldstein, Kurt, *The Organism: A Holistic Approach to Biology* American Book Company, New York, 1939.

25. Summarized by Hall and Lindzey (op. cit.), p. 327. Used by permission. For a statement of A. H. Maslow's concepts, see his *Motivation and Personality* Harper & Brothers, New York, 1954.

26. Kast, Fremont E., and Rosenzweig, James E., *Organization and Management, A Systems Approach* McGraw-Hill Book Company, Inc., New York, 1970, pp. 89–90. Used by permission.

27. McGregor, Douglas, *Leadership and Motivation* MIT Press, Cambridge, 1966, pp. 6–7. Used by permission.

28. Herzberg, Frederick, *Work and the Nature of Man* The World Publishing Company, New York, 1966, p. 42. Used by permission.

29. Argyris, Chris, *Integrating the Individual and the Organization* John Wiley & Sons, Inc., New York, 1964, pp. 38–39.

30. Bennis, Warren G., op. cit., pp. 3–4.

31. Weick, Karl E., *The Social Psychology of Organizing* Addison-Wesley Publishing Company, Inc., Reading, Massachusetts, 1969, p. 20. Used by permission.

32. Lowin, Aaron, and Craig, James R., 'The Influence of Level of Performance on Managerial Style: An Experimental Object-Lesson in the Ambiguity of Correlational Data', *Organizational Behaviour and Human Performance* 3, 1968.

33. Carey, Alex, 'The Hawthorne Studies: A Radical Criticism', *American Sociological Review* June 1967, pp. 406, 407, 416. Used by permission.

34. Lee, James A., 'Behavioural Theory vs. Reality', *Harvard Business Review*, March–April, 1971, p. 28. Used by permission.

35. Powell, Reed M., and Schlacter, John L., 'Participative Management: A Panacea?' *Academy of Management Journal* 14, 2, 1971, pp. 165–173. Used by permission.

36. Stogdill, Ralph M., 'Individual Behaviour Group Achievement—A Behavioural Model of Organization', paper presented at the annual

meeting of the American Psychological Association, Washington, D.C., 3 September 1969. Used by permission.

37. Lee, James A., op. cit., p. 28.
38. Marrow, Alfred J., David G. Bowen, and Seashore, Stanley E., *Management by Participation* Harper & Row, New York, 1967, p. ix. Used by permission.
39. Lippert, Frederick G., 'Toward Flexibility in Application of Behavioural Science Research', *Academy of Management Journal* **14,** 2, 1971, pp. 165–173. Used by permission.
40. Lowin, Aaron, 'Participative Decision Making: A Model, Literature Critique and Prescriptions for Research', *Organizational Behaviour and Human Performance* 3, 1968, p. 97. Used by permission.
41. Beckhard, Richard, *Organization Development: Strategies and Models* Addison-Wesley Publishing Company, Inc., Reading, Massachusetts, 1969, pp. 14–21. Used by permission.
42. Schein, Edgar H., and Bennis, Warren G., *Personal and Group Change Through Group Methods: The Laboratory Approach* John Wiley & Sons, Inc., New York, 1965, p. 204. Used by permission.
43. 'Sensitivity Training', *Journal American Medical Association* 27 September, 1971, **217,** 13, p. 1853. Used by permission.
44. Kappel, Frederick R., *Business Purpose and Performance* Duell, Sloan and Pearce, New York, 1964, pp. 237–238. Used by permission.
45. McGregor, Douglas, *Antioch Notes* Antioch College, Yellow Springs, Ohio, **31,** 9, 1964. Used by permission.

INDEX